D0542516

GE.

This book is to be returned on or before
the last date stamped below.

		1 7 DEC 2004 LK
13. JUN GE	30 SEP 00 GE	
28. SEP GE	28 MAR 01 GE	0 5 SEP 2005 EW
06. MAR GE	MAY 01	
		1 7 OCT 2005 EW
27. MAR GE	15 JUN 01 GE	
	23 FEB 02 GE	1 0 NOV 2005 EW
17. APR GE		3 0 NOV 2005 EW
08. MAY GE		
06. DEC GE	11 JUL 03 IK	
7 MAR 00 GE	14 OCT 03 IK	2 3 DEC 2005 EW
	9 DEC 03 IK	2 6 APR 2006 EW
18 MAR 00	13 APR 04 LK	- 2 JUN 2006 EW
13 APR 00 GE	26 APR 04 LK	1 4 OCT 2006 EW
25 JUL 00 GE		6 DEC 2006 EW
13 SEP 00 GE		
	06. DEC GE	21. JAN GE

940.544 98

SEARBY, JOHN
THE BOMBER BATTLE FOR BERLIN

DUMFRIES AND GALLOWAY
REGIONAL LIBRARY SERVICE
Catherine Street, Dumfries. Tel. Dfs 53820

THE BOMBER BATTLE FOR BERLIN

THE
BOMBER BATTLE
FOR BERLIN

Air Commodore John Searby
DSO, DFC

	Dumfries and Galloway	
HJ	Class.	940·5AA
	0 0 2 7 1 4	

Airlife
England

Copyright © The executors of the late John Searby, 1991

First published in the UK in 1991 by
Airlife Publishing Ltd.

British Library Cataloguing in Publication Data
Searby, John
    The bomber battle for Berlin.
    1. World War 2. Air operations. Berlin 2. Great Britain.
    Royal Air Force. Bomber Command
    I.   Title
    940.544941
    ISBN 1 85310 128 1

All rights reserved. No part of this book may be reproduced or transmitted in any form
or by any means, electronic or mechanical including photocopying,
recording or by any information storage and retrieval system, without permission
from the Publisher in writing.

Printed by Butler and Tanner Ltd., Frome.

Airlife Publishing Ltd.

101 Longden Road, Shrewsbury, England.

Contents

Foreword

by Marshal of the Royal Air Force
Sir Michael Beetham GCB, CBE, DFC, AFC, DL

The Bomber Offensive against Germany in the Second World War was unique in that it was the first time such a method of waging war, independent of action on land or at sea, had ever been attempted. Furthermore it became of crucial importance after the fall of France and the evacuation from Dunkirk in 1940 because it was then the only way that Germany could be directly attacked until the Allied Forces were assembled in sufficient strength to launch Operation Overlord, the invasion of Europe, four years later.

Much controversy has surrounded the Bomber Offensive both over the targets selected for attack and whether on its own, given more resources, it could have forced the surrender of Germany. What is much more evident is that without the Offensive and its contribution to achieving air superiority, Operation Overlord could not have been mounted at all.

The Offensive lasted throughout the full five and three quarter years of the war. In its early days it was fairly ineffective but there was a learning process to go through and the resources were woefully inadequate for the job. However, by 1942, when Sir Arthur Harris took over as Commander in Chief, the resources were becoming available and, under his dynamic leadership, the effectiveness of the Offensive was steadily transformed to make what was a major contribution to final victory.

Forced to operate at night because of the strength of the enemy defences, the area bombing of industrial cities became the major and indeed only practical target objective until 1944 by which time better navigation and bombing aids had been developed and precision targets could be successfully attacked.

The sustained campaign against cities was an epic struggle with its successes and failures but all the time immense pressure was being exerted on the German people and the German economy and, never knowing where the next attack would fall, the Germans had to devote enormous resources to air defence. The toughest of all the cities to attack and also the most important psychologically was undoubtedly Berlin. Spasmodic attacks were made early in the war but in the winter of 1943/44 the city was subjected to a concentrated series of heavy attacks stretching over five months.

The Battle for Berlin is a story that needs telling and Air

Commodore John Searby has done this for us in a most authoritative way. His background for the task is ideal not only having extensive operational experience at squadron level rising to be a Squadron Commander in the Pathfinder Force and a Master Bomber, but also serving on the Planning staff at Command and Group level. He sets the raids on Berlin in the context of the overall Offensive and brings to life the atmosphere at squadron level where the courage, determination and morale of the crews never faltered in spite of the heavy losses.

The story will certainly appeal to anyone who took part in the Bomber Offensive and will bring back memories to those in particular who took part in any of the raids on the Big City. It will also appeal, I believe, to a much wider audience for whom the author has given just the right amount of background to make the story interesting. I hope you will enjoy reading it as much as I have done.

Introduction

Berlin was the ultimate goal. There were more profitable targets but none carried the prestige which set the German capital apart. During the four years before the Battle for Berlin proper commenced many attempts had been made to inflict on the enemy a degree of damage equal to that sustained by London during the Blitz of 1940 but no concentrated attack, such as that which finished Hamburg, had been achieved. Remote, cloud covered and heavily defended as the city was, the Whitleys and Wellingtons of an earlier day possessed little more than the basic aids to get them within striking distance. Manned by some of the most determined and experienced crews and battling through adverse weather, rarely did they get a glimpse of what appeared to be their objective — only to lose it again as they turned to commence the bombing run up to the target. We had neither the aircraft nor the equipment equal to the task and four years were to go by until we were ready. In the autumn of 1943 with a thousand four engined heavy bombers, fitted with the latest radar both for navigation and bombing, Sir Arthur Harris believed he could destroy Berlin.

Unlike Munich, Stuttgart or any similar objective there was no easy approach to the German capital. In past years range considerations dictated the direct route out and back, though the Wellingtons on one disastrous occasion had flown the long trek via Denmark and the lower Baltic with barely enough petrol to make it back home — and not all were fortunate; but the Lancasters and Halifaxes possessed ample range permitting greater tactical freedom. Whatever the route, a Berlin sortie represented a long cold ride through six hundred and fifty miles or more of defended territory scanned by powerful search radars backed by an ever increasing force of twin and single engined night fighters — a force which was to prove a decisive factor in the long drawn out struggle.

As the crews entered the briefing room their first thought was for the wall map behind the dais and one heard the whispered words . . . the 'Big City', as they studied the tapes and arrows indicating the route to be followed, and the clearly marked enemy defences — flak and searchlight belts. Once they knew the target they adopted the customary nonchalant attitude as if it made little odds, but there was always a sinister touch about the enemy's capital. Berlin was for real.

When the Battle began in late 1943 there were few of the pioneers left — the men who had flogged the old bombers to war had departed and a high proportion had been killed in action. The tough Short Service Officers and the stalwarts of the Royal Air Force Volunteer Reserve were thinly spread as Flight Commanders throughout the rapidly growing number of four-engined Squadrons which now stood ready to transport four times the weight in explosives and incendiaries carried by the 'Wimpys' of yesteryear. The sleek Lancasters and Halifaxes, stuffed with radar aids, employing new techniques involving precise timing, concentration and height bands, and backed by a taut system of maintenance, enjoyed a fresh confidence in the long arm of Bomber Command whilst a flood of freshly trained crews — the best from the Empire Air Training Scheme which nourished the many Bomber Groups — had filled the gaps created by the massive battles over the Ruhr and Hamburg. Young, enthusiastic and immensely proud of the role and responsibilities in Squadrons whose battle honours included every target in Germany and Occupied Europe, they listened keenly to every word of advice from those who had travelled the road — from hard-bitten Flight Commanders and sometimes casual, faintly cynical two-tour men who had survived the previous encounters. In the Pathfinder Force there were, in theory, no tyros. All were supposed to be battle hardened, specially selected officers and NCOs whose qualities fitted them for the important task of marking the targets for others to bomb. But this was not always so; we received 'pressed men' from other Groups and some very young indeed — volunteers in name only, but rapidly assimilating the spirit and high sense of duty which motivated Bennett's Pathfinder Group from first to last. I interviewed all new crews to No 83 Squadron, and made them welcome, but there were surprises from time to time . . .

'Why did you volunteer for Pathfinder work?'

The captain, a young Pilot Officer, answered for his crew, 'We didn't Sir; we were told to pack our bags and get down here as soon as possible.'

'Do you know the terms of service in the Pathfinder Force — sixty sorties straight through?' (The tour of duty in the Main Force was only thirty.)

'Yes we do know that Sir — but it's OK now that we've got here.' As a crew they had around ten sorties to date; which meant — if all went well — they would require to fly a further fifty with the Pathfinders. They seemed undaunted by the prospect.

Following the successful operations centering on the Ruhr and Hamburg it seemed that one more supreme effort would put paid to a target which had eluded us for so long. Sir Arthur Harris, Commander-in-Chief, Bomber Command, was dedicated to the belief that the war might be brought to a close by a massive onslaught from the air — and he postulated a situation which, given a sufficient number of Lancasters backed up by an accelerated production drive, would result in 'a state of devastation in which surrender is inevitable'. He had implicit faith in the aircraft and by November 1943 he was ready to wipe out Berlin. He would have liked the Americans to join hands with Bomber Command in this all-out effort.

'We can wreck Berlin from end to end if the Americans will come in on it. It will cost us 400–500 aircraft. It will cost Germany the war.'

This prophecy was not borne out, neither in results nor in the number of casualties: the campaign lost Bomber Command 1,047 aircraft, each carrying seven or eight officers and NCOs and in the event was an all Bomber Command show: the American 8th Army Air Force was in no wise fit for such a long penetration into German territory — that would not happen until the following March when they would enjoy the protection of the Mustangs with their extended range. By then Berlin was no longer important in the scale of events, neither was Bomber Command in a position to sustain the casualties stemming from the ferocity of the German night fighter defences.

In his belief that the war might be brought to an end by a crescendo of heavy bomber attacks, Sir Arthur's case was strengthened by the sequence of highly effective attacks which took place during the months preceding the opening of the Battle of Berlin. Over the Ruhr operations had been conducted with an accuracy hitherto undreamed of, thanks to 'Oboe', the ground operated radar which performed to an accuracy of three hundred yards at a range of two hundred and fifty miles from the transmitter — a phenomenal leap forward in the difficult struggle to achieve precise marking of a target. Contrary to earlier expectations it had a long life and the enemy never succeeded in jamming the transmissions: it was to move on to the Continent after the invasion and continue to serve the Allied effort. At Hamburg the case was different since this city and port lay beyond the reach of the instrument. But there was another aid — an airborne device which presented a picture on the cathode ray tube in the navigator's compartment, called the H2S. This instrument was most effective where contrast obtained, as in the reflections returned by areas of land and water: in other circumstances it relied on prominent buildings such as in built-up areas, on lakes and rivers, and much depended upon the skill of the operator. At Hamburg the conditions were ideal and it was here that it was brought into play with excellent results; but after Hamburg there was nothing comparable to bring to bear on the spreading city of Berlin. In the PFF concentrated training of operators was devoted to studying the likely picture this city would present on the radar scope, in an attempt to get the most from the equipment, and there were some operators whose skill exceeded the rest. They did in fact obtain some useful results when the battle commenced but on the whole the mish-mash of ground returns enabled the navigator to deduce very little and we were thrown back on the basic disciplines, bringing in the radar whenever possible in conditions likely to produce reliable results such as crossing a coastline or identifying a lake on route. Over Berlin itself we got little help. Weather too, was a factor — and a big one — in the conduct of an operation so far into Germany; forecasting was the best possible and no effort was spared — even the dispatch of a fast Mosquito to report on weather in the area on a given day — but it was no simple matter and all too often the bombers arrived to find thick cloud gathered over the city. Then there were the defences . . .

The enemy had ample time in which to make ready to defend his capital city. Surprise was virtually impossible to achieve and recourse was made to diversion attacks by Mosquitos of the PFF Light Night Striking Force — a flexible force of the greatest importance and whose record in keeping the sirens going in Berlin is an outstanding feature of the Battle. Air Vice-Marshal Bennett used them frequently and with considerable effect: their flying qualities, high speed and ability to attack at thirty thousand feet rendered them secure from all but the luckiest hit by flak or, very rarely, from interception by the enemy fighters. In the diversion role they were exploited to the full and thereby reduced casualties among the 'heavies' by drawing the Berlin defenders away from the main objective. Even so, the enemy retained an advantage stemming from a complete surveillance of all approaches to Berlin and by the time the bombers were nearing the city his fighters were airborne and in action. A fleet of Lancasters and Halifaxes numbering seven or eight hundred aircraft is not readily concealed and as the Battle progressed more and more bombers were attacked on the route to the target and whilst over the city itself; along the way back to the coast the interceptions multiplied and losses mounted. A heavily laden bomber flying at around two hundred miles per hour had little scope for effective evasive action against fighter attack — and this was especially true of the Halifax and Stirling whose performance did not match that of the Lancaster at height. Once attacked the crew stuck it out grimly and depended on the alert gunners to drive off the fighter, but the .303 turret machine guns were no match for 20-millimetre cannon in the nose of the German fighter, which could stand off at a range beyond the effective use of the bomber armament. After bombing the situation improved measurably but the return home was in nearly every instance made in the teeth of a headwind which pulled back the groundspeed and gave an important advantage to the defenders. A tired crew became vulnerable and there was no second chance offered: constant vigilance was needed and the gunners of Bomber Command — so often taken for granted — wrought mightily to save the aircraft. In biting cold with no opportunity to leave the turrets over a seven or eight hour stretch they were the eyes of the lumbering bomber and we owed them much. The six hundred or so miles back to the English coast was a ding-dong struggle for survival and as the tempo increased during the early months of the New Year the Battle became a long drawn out agony — and the last of its kind. The German Night Fighter Force was at the very peak of its strength and efficiency, battle-tried and very experienced; our casualties were heavy. The sprawling conurbation which represented Berlin often defied the heroic efforts of the Pathfinders to mark clearly the objective whilst the massed heavy gun batteries and hundreds of searchlights produced a nightmare unequalled in the experience of the veterans — and they were few indeed.

We did not fail for lack of trying. The dire period from January to March 1944 tried the heart and sinews of every bomber crew which staggered home — and many did not make it. The writing was on the wall, and something more was needed if victory was to be won. But there was nothing left in the kitty. History provides parallel situations of greater magnitude — the Nivelle offensive and Passchendaele come to mind — yet neither was backed by a sequence of successful operations such as we had conducted over the Ruhr and Hamburg and which gave grounds for believing we should attempt the final stroke. In modern parlance 'we had everything going for us', but it was not to be. The Battle was halted; it was proving too costly and the Command was needed for the support of the D-Day operations a bare three months ahead. Such action was timely: the battering we received over the North German Plain cost us more than a thousand aircraft and between seven and eight thousand lives. Berlin wasn't worth it.

The onus of fighting the battle fell on the Squadron Commanders of that day. Visits by Air Marshals were one thing but the blood and muck of the successive onslaughts were sorted out in the Squadron Commander's office. Few of the troubles and anxieties inherent in the exercise of command at Squadron level ever got further than the office door: it was a matter of pride and the good name of the unit. Two operations are examined in these pages; one which took place very early in the war and one during the precise period in which the all-out battle raged. Each commands interest and illustrates the problems and the courage of Harris's men who were no better and no worse than those who fought the war in other spheres — by land or by sea.

Chapter 1
The Background — Bomber Command Organisation and Control

By the autumn of 1943 Bomber Command, under the direction of a resolute Commander-in-Chief, was an expanding Force capable of inflicting massive destruction on the enemy's homeland. The range, bomb capacity and flexibility of the new bombers had forced the enemy into a defensive posture compelling him to divert a significant slice of his total resources to the protection of his cities: the vast numbers of men and women directed into the various aspects of a nationwide network to combat the effects of the bomber offensive impacted heavily on his front line strength. Apart from the essential warning systems and the active fighter defences, plus a million and a quarter men to man the anti-aircraft guns and searchlights placed around the cities, manpower was swallowed up in the fire and ambulance services, the cleaning up after attack, the rebuilding of factories and housing for the homeless, the repairs to port facilities and transportation — all of which represented a constant flow of personnel who might otherwise have been engaged in producing armaments or filling the gaps in the front line. The enormous effort needed to transfer some part of his industry to remoter areas, such as the Black Forest, where it was relatively safe from air attack, may not be discounted and there are many examples of a similar nature. Thus, quite apart from the specific damage done to war production, the steady threat imposed by a powerful bomber force across the North Sea hived off two million men in uniform and many thousands of civilians on a permanent stand-by, awaiting the all-too-frequent scream of the air raid sirens.

The six front line Bomber Groups, each commanded by an Air Vice-Marshal, mustered a total of around eight hundred four-engined aircraft: the Lancaster force had increased to five hundred aircraft and the Halifaxes to three hundred whilst the Mosquito element totalled some fifty aircraft. In November a further Group was created for a specialist role in the field of radio countermeasures. Sir Arthur Harris's plea for accelerated production of the Lancaster had been answered and a steady increase in the numbers of this formidable bomber became apparent as the months passed. Ultimately this total would exceed one thousand aircraft. When we consider the losses, or wastage as it was termed, during the Battle when the Command turned over its strength we may gauge the effort mounted by the men and women in the aircraft factories who toiled mightily to achieve what at one time would have been reckoned an impossible task. It was not a matter of building another five or six hundred Lancasters — that presented no great problem — but one of maintaining the front line strength at the established figure. Thus, losses in combat, aircraft which struggled home to effect a crash landing at base and were declared beyond economical repair, wastage in the training units, replacements for aircraft withdrawn for important modifications — all needed to be offset by a steady flow off the production lines and represented additions to the initial build-up. A bad night for a squadron might leave a gap of four or five aircraft and crews in the battle order; replacements were required without loss of time if the unit was to be kept up to strength and it was not unusual for the new aircraft to arrive the following afternoon. Such action stemmed from superb organisation at all levels and we were seldom let down by the Maintenance Units.

The Pathfinder Force, which had begun life as a small Group only, increased greatly in size throughout 1943 and formed the spearhead in attacks against heavily defended targets. This was its role; independent operations by No 5 Group under command of Air Vice-Marshal Cochrane achieved marked success against selected targets, commencing with the famous attack on the Möhne Dam in May of that year, and there were to be similar feats of outstanding airmanship in the future, but the slogging match was for the crews of the PFF who marked the Ruhr, Hamburg and, in fact, every major target in Germany. There were the 'Marthas' and under the direction of Air Vice-Marshal Bennett, himself an experienced operational Captain; they bore the brunt of the target marking. The policy of the Commander-in-Chief centred on the area attack as opposed to precision bombing and he was well served by the crews of No 8 (Pathfinder) Group. It should be stated that No 5 Group took part in all heavy attacks alongside the other Main Force Squadrons, but in the matter of precision marking, using their own technique, they enjoyed the fullest support from the C-in-C.

The Mosquito force, part of Bennett's command, assumed greater importance as the months passed. No 109 Sqdn commanded by Group Captain Harry Bufton pioneered the development and ultimate use of the precise 'Oboe' radar equipment responsible for the destruction of Krupps and similar Ruhr targets, whilst further Squadrons of these aircraft were created and committed to the nightly assault of Berlin. The Light Night Striking Force, as Bennett called it, harried the wretched inhabitants of that city with monotonous regularity: their high speed and ability to carry a four thousand pound bomb, which they off-loaded from a height of around thirty thousand feet, presented the enemy with a well-nigh insoluble problem and the contribution of these speedy little bombers to the Battle of Berlin was considerable. Alas, their numbers were small: everybody wanted them — notably Fighter Command although some saw service with Coastal — and it was not until the war was nearly over that Bomber Command possessed two hundred Mosquitos. At the time of the Battle some fifty aircraft were under Bennett's control: a larger force of a hundred or more might well have saved us the kind of casualties visited upon the 'heavies'.

This is problematical, but the fact was that the Germans could not catch them and their casualties were slight, whereas the toll of the four-engined heavies mounted steadily.

Before we leave the subject of aircraft some explanation of the equipment carried may be useful to the reader. The 'black boxes' — a common term for the electronic aids — increased both in number and importance as time went by, whilst the appearance of a perspex housing for the radar scanner situated beneath the belly of the bomber indicated the progress made in solving the problem of 'seeing in the dark'. However, these refinements came late in the day though without them we could have done little better than in the early days of the bomber offensive. The story of bomber navigation had not been a happy one up to mid-1942 and it may assist the reader if we trace the developments over the first three years of war. Bomber Command stood or fell by the skill of its navigators: this is not always appreciated but it remains an indisputable fact. Working under the worst possible conditions — cramped for space under poor lighting conditions, subject to cold, a high noise level and the vibration of the aircraft, attempting to take sextant observations with heavily gloved hands and computing the observed altitude of the star or planet against a background of constant apprehension, while half listening to what the Captain was saying to other crew members since it might be important or vital to their well-being — this was the lot of the navigator, and too often we took him for granted.

Bomber Command began the war with no aids to navigation other than ded. reckoning (DR): solving the simple triangle of velocities combining Course and Airspeed, Wind Vector and Track and Groundspeed. The use of the Mark IX Bubble Sextant was not universal though by dint of pushing hundreds of young officers and NCOs through a four-week course at the School of Air Navigation a rule-of-thumb method was taught. This required no mathematical knowledge of spherical trigonometry — one followed a strict sequence using the information given in the Nautical Almanac and the Latitude tables and the result was a position line: two such lines fixed the aircraft's position and three produced the 'cocked hat' with the aircraft in the centre. The effort involved in obtaining a two-star fix was considerable — the aircraft must be held on a steady course and over enemy territory this was not a popular exercise. One stood in the hatch 'goofing' the star through the eyepiece and endeavouring to maintain a steady bubble — an error of one minute of arc was equivalent to a mile on the ground! Then followed the plotting with the table shaking madly and if one ran into trouble from below the effort was largely wasted: the pilot would take evasive action and the navigator would sit tight and hope for the best.

The standard method of navigating required a course to be worked out from base to the first turning point using the forecast wind speed and direction. Usually we made a check at the coast by identifying a particular landmark and this gave a means of computing the wind at the height flown: from then on the new wind was used for the next leg and one hoped to get another pinpoint on the enemy coast, but weather was always a factor to be reckoned with and cloud frequently obscured all below us. No further check could be made until a new pinpoint was obtained and we ran on DR until this happened, the error, if any, multiplying all the time. On occasions we were miles off track and map reading over enemy territory on a dark night was not easy. There was no bomb aimer lying in the nose at that stage of the war and the navigator, armed with a map, left his table to peer down into the blackness below. He might be lucky — spotting a lake or river — more often he saw nothing which would help him and the aircraft droned on, the pilot chivvying his navigator about getting them lost and so forth. The sudden arrival of a few bursting shells would indicate a built-up area below, perhaps, and by a little conjuring the navigator might deduce something from the novelties thrown up by the opposition. 'Bombed on ETA' was often recorded by the interrogating officer on the return of the aircraft, which meant the crew had seen nothing but by keeping the air-plot going and making use of the forecast winds for the area they contrived to get somewhere in the vicinity of the target. The loop aerial helped on occasions but was not very reliable and it was possible to obtain a 'Butser fix' at quite long ranges. The latter was generally a last resort and depending on conditions could vary between thirty and fifty miles in accuracy when reception was poor, and at best put one five to ten miles from the true position. Nevertheless, it was the final answer in emergency and brought many a bomber home to this country. These were early days and the first step forward was taken with the introduction of the Astrograph, a device which projected star curves onto the chart table and required the navigator to precompute beforehand the time he would take his sextant observation: it was not popular and disappeared eventually. The Pole Star was a good standby since a line of position might be readily obtained — providing always one had a clear sky overhead. But none of these methods could equal the securing of a good pinpoint by the human eye. With a full moon to assist, and by careful observation, canals, rivers and rail tracks might be identified: an experienced crew confident of their approximate position were often successful.

The first real breakthrough came with the introduction of 'Gee', and from first to last it proved the most reliable of all aids continuing in use throughout the remaining years of the war and saving many a crew from disaster. Inevitably, it was jammed by the enemy and therefore its use over Germany was limited, but nearer home it offered a safe passage back to base regardless of weather since the bomber could 'home' on the transmissions with perfect confidence. On the outward journeys we could fix position accurately as far as the Dutch coast and over France at greater ranges: the method was simple and a skilled operator needed no more than a minute to obtain his position. As the Force expanded the problems associated with the return of up to a thousand aircraft were greatly simplified by the fitting of 'Gee', especially in winter when visibility and low cloud bedevilled the landing process whilst the hazards of a 'ditching' off the East Coast were, to a certain extent, reduced if the operator in the aircraft could get off smartly the precise point of striking the water.

When first introduced and before the enemy commenced jamming, it was hoped to use the equipment for precision bombing as far as the Ruhr but accuracy at such a range was less than satisfactory and it remained a prime aid to the navigator over an area up to a hundred miles from the English coast.

'Oboe', which appeared at the end of 1942, was the most precise of all aids to marking the target, though limited in range to around two hundred and seventy miles when the air component of the system — the Mosquito — flew at twenty-eight thousand feet. The higher the aircraft the longer the range but for all practical purposes this figure, which took in the Ruhr, was about the limit. It was not an easy technique and the greatest accuracy in flying was demanded of the Mosquito crews of No 109 Sqdn. The range limitation ruled out use of this equipment for attacking Berlin but it should be noted that 'Oboe' was largely responsible for the destruction of Krupps and other major Ruhr industries. Whilst it was technically possible to extend the range by use of repeater aircraft this was not done since it was believed that the latest in the succession of radar aids to bombing and navigation — the airborne H2S — would take over the role for targets at extended ranges. This equipment represented a very big step forward and there were great expectations aroused as to its performance. The fact that it was self-contained within the bomber, independent of ground control, meant that the range was limitless.

In effect H2S took a radar picture of the ground below and ahead of the aircraft; the pulsed transmissions from the rotating scanner situated beneath the belly of the bomber were reflected back by ground features to form a display on the cathode ray tube in front of the navigator who related this to his latest position. Where contrast was sharp, as between land and water, an excellent picture was often obtained: rivers and canals would show up and lakes were easily defined, but a built-up area would require very careful interpretation. The greater the experience of the operator the better the results obtained: in most instances he was equipped with a radar map showing the outlines he could expect to see on the tube though much depended upon conditions; the reflections sent back by buildings varied considerably, being affected by the angle at which the aircraft was approaching the city. In the case of Berlin good results were difficult to obtain: the tube would reveal a whole mass of reflections and the Spree, a small river only, was barely discernible: similarly the many small lakes were swamped by the clutter of bright reflections. Following on Hamburg where the H2S had performed excellently, Berlin was a profound disappointment and we were virtually thrown back on to methods of the not too distant past. Eventually, improved versions of the equipment produced better definition.

The fact that German night fighters were equipped with a homing device which detected the H2S transmissions introduced a fresh problem since it was then a relatively simple matter to pick up the bomber stream. 'Naxos', as it was known, became operational at the time of the Battle and later in the year it gave rise to anxiety, imposing restrictions on the use of H2S, and there is no doubt concerning the part it played in the German defence of their capital city. Nevertheless H2S was a boon to the navigator as an aid to conducting his aircraft to and from the target and was widely used in the Pathfinder Force as a standby when visual marking was not possible: many targets were identified and marked after flares had been dropped solely by the use of the equipment. A combination of H2S and visual marking was standard practice by the autumn of 1943.

Reference had already been made to the reliance placed on the tail and mid-upper gunners of the bomber: theirs was an unenviable task at best. The introduction of backward looking radars under the control of the wireless operator gave early warning of impending attack. 'Monica' and 'Fishpond', fitted at the beginning of 1943 to all heavy aircraft, in no wise relieved the gunners of the necessity for constant watch and ward, but they did serve to alert them whilst the enemy fighter was out of visual range, thus decreasing the possibility of a surprise attack. By virtue of their constant struggle to knock down the invading bomber the Luftwaffe pilots gained enormously in experience; the priority allotted to fighter defence secured for them the latest and best in armament and search radars; replacement crews were immediately available to offset losses, and in addition to the flow of young men from the training units, seasoned pilots were transferred from the declining bomber force. In view of this increased threat from the German Night Fighter Force any device which would help to relieve the strain on the gunners was doubly welcome and these radars proved their worth.

The multiplicity of electronic aids carried in the aircraft, coupled with such instruments as air and ground position indicators and a distant-reading compass located in the tail with repeaters set on the flight deck, resulted in a massive maintenance programme both for daily servicing and for periodic inspection. This was but one aspect of the effort needed to keep the bombers in the air; the customary fitters, riggers, armament personnel, safety workers and instrument specialists were joined by an army of radar and radio mechanics who swarmed over the aircraft doing their daily serviceability checks. The swelling numbers of sophisticated and highly sensitive items of equipment carried in the bombers demanded more and more from the ground staffs, whilst dependence upon the 'black boxes' increased steadily. Fortunately, the basic navigation and communication equipment seldom failed: the Distant Reading Compass with its master unit in the tail end, the 'Gee' box and the vital crew communication system proved rugged and utterly dependable throughout.

Bomber Command was essentially a night raiding force. This policy had been forced upon us early in the conflict when the cherished belief that bombers in formation by day could rely on mutual defence from their turret guns had been exploded: the attacks on German warships in the Heligoland Bight during December of 1939 had resulted in heavy losses and with a few notable exceptions such as the Augsburg raid and Le Creusot (discounting the Light Bomber operations by No 2 Group with fighter cover) we remained committed to the night offensive. Fighter Command possessed an abundance of short range fighters but very few twin-engined squadrons fit to escort the 'heavies' by day. After D-Day when air superiority had been established over the fighting fronts we did enjoy air cover but in the main our war was fought in the dark. In terms of defensive armament we lacked the ability to knock down an enemy fighter standing off at six hundred yards and firing his 20mm cannon: the .303 turret guns in the Lancasters and Halifaxes were good for short range work and were a deterrent to a fighter making a close attack, but that was all. The penalty for carrying heavier weapons of the .5 calibre was a reduction in bomb load. In an attempt to reduce casualties among the bombers, Beaufighters, and later Mosquitos, mingled with the stream, but this was not strictly an escort role: their special equipment (Serrate) enabled them to pick up enemy fighters and follow them. This proved successful and there were notable scorers such as Wing Commander Bob Braham who commanded No 141 (Fighter) Squadron, but the overall effect on the casualty rate among the bombers was small. The build up of the German Night Fighter Force towards the end of 1943 and the losses sustained as the Battle progressed were a source of constant anxiety and there remained but one course open to us, namely that of breaking down the enemy system of control by using to the utmost the radio countermeasures devised by the scientists and developed by Air Vice-Marshal Addison in command of No 100 Group — a force created specifically for this purpose.

The 'jamming' of radio signals was a ding-dong battle between ourselves and the enemy. From the very outset it engaged the attention of the signals specialists: and as the war progressed it attained an elegance and degree of refinement beyond the comprehension of the uninitiated. Countermeasures swung back and forth: for each new device an antidote was sought though the life cycle of some of the elaborate measures taken to confound the enemy were of short duration. The dropping of metallised strips during the Battle of Hamburg in July 1943 was a most effective method of jamming the enemy radar and produced chaos: the German controllers were foiled in their attempts to distinguish individual aircraft among the clutter on the cathode ray tube. Success was immediate and total but the technique became less and less effective as wave-lengths were changed. Likewise the very early form of countering the German RT transmissions to their night fighters (known as 'Tinsel') produced results but was eventually overcome by the enemy. In the Wellington and Whitley era crews had great faith in the dropping of empty beer bottles which it was believed reacted upon the searchlight and ground flak batteries and I recall the loading of a crate of these items in the tail of a 'Wimpey' flown by a Canadian crew: their faith in the method was unshaken and the rear gunner described to me the subsequent wavering of the searchlight beam as the bottle dived to earth. This was a 'countermeasure' though it may have had a purely psychological value since the truth of the claim has never been substantiated.

Throughout the spring and summer of 1943 the awareness of the enemy was borne in upon the bomber crews. In June and July we were greatly surprised when German fighters intercepted us over the North Sea. In the evening, with Lancasters seen against the sunset in the west, they made head-on attacks — not all that successful but evidence of their being prepared and anxious to engage us before we got as far as their own coast. Such engagements were of short duration — the enemy pilots trusted to their being able to get in perhaps a single burst at the oncoming bomber — but it happened: the power and accuracy of their early warning Freyas situated on the Dutch and German coast was such we were blips on the tube soon after take-off from base, giving them ample time to get airborne and meet us head on. In the afterglow of the setting sun I saw them sweep past and disappear — a 'once only' chance of knocking us down over the sea but they obviously deemed it worthwhile. I think this latest tactic did much to put into operation the countermeasure known as

'Mandrel' from which we drew great benefit as the year rolled on. Equipped with powerful transmitters tuned to the German wavelengths a fleet of four engined aircraft patrolled the North Sea at a set distance from the enemy coast jamming the Freyas which looked towards England, coarsening the tuning and spreading the beam, so that identification of a single bomber was difficult if not impossible. This important step in the countermeasure war was logical and effective and as long as we could detect quickly any change in the German transmissions it worked well. Coupled with 'Tinsel' it saved many crews, though 'Tinsel' still left something to be desired and a more effective jammer to counter the VHF radio telephone control of German fighters was evolved. This equipment was eventually carried in aircraft of 100 Group and worked in conjunction with 'Mandrel': the effect was one of causing the enemy to abandon the simple 'box' system whereby a single fighter was directed to any bomber entering a particular area and led to placing of all available fighters under one controller who concentrated them on the bomber stream wherever it might be passing to the great advantage of the defence. Unwittingly we had caused the enemy to adopt a system which had dire results for Bomber Command, and after the turn of the year the problem increased in magnitude; the casualties began to mount and fresh measures were necessary. Since the whole of the available fighter force lay under the direction of a single German controller the electronic attack was taken to the 'running commentary' which guided the fighters and the enemy responded by using different channels and switching his frequencies. Thus the countermeasure war swung back and forth. One result of this change of policy on the part of the Germans was that of splitting our forces and laying on 'spoof' attacks to confuse the opposition and there were many successes achieved thereby. The operations of Air Vice-Marshal Bennett's Mosquito force contributed notably to the 'spoof' plans, as at Peenemunde, where No 139 Sqdn succeeded in drawing away a high percentage of the opposing fighters to Berlin leaving the main target clear during the first half of the attack.

At Squadron level we knew little of the foregoing though we were always briefed on the activities of the 'spoofers'; the intricate moves in the countermeasure business remained a close secret. We knew the location of the 'Mandrel' screen as it was termed but the rest remained wrapped in silence: but it was a comfort to know that unseen and unheard by us forces were at work on our behalf to dupe the opposition.

The professionalism which marked the planning and execution of attacks by the growing bomber force was reflected in the Staffs at both Command and Group level. The interval between the Berlin fiasco of 7 November 1941, when staff work was criticised following the losses sustained on that night, and the dispatch of up to eight hundred four engined aircraft two years later to that same city, was marked by changes other than those brought about by improvements in aircraft and methods. Sir Arthur Harris has been termed ruthless in his direction of the bomber offensive and unco-operative in the loaning of his Squadrons for work which, in his opinion, represented a deviation from the main aim; and this is correct. Almost from the day he assumed command a new sense of urgency and resolution swept through the Groups and Squadrons: he could not suffer fools and officers who fell short of his standards received short shrift. Conversely those who took decisions, based on experience and a belief that such a course was in the best interests of the men who flew the bombers, were backed up with the full authority of the Commander-in-Chief. I recall an instance where the Duty Group Captain cancelled a full-scale operation minutes before take-off: no more senior officer was available for consultation and the onus was on him. The C-in-C who normally kept in touch with the Command Operations Room was away that night and the weather was closing in: fog at the bases was forecast for the return, although at an earlier Met. Conference it was not thought likely to warrant a cancellation. Thus, the Duty Group Captain, in the absence of an officer of Air Rank, cancelled the attack by several hundred bombers. Next morning we stood around the desk in the Ops Room waiting for the Commander-in-Chief to start his daily conference and a certain nervousness was apparent. Sir Arthur walked into the Ops Room and asked his usual question as to how things had gone the previous night. There was a pause; neither the Deputy nor the Senior Air Staff Officer nor the Air Commodore Ops ventured a word — and, finally, the Group Captain responsible spoke up.

'I cancelled the operation just before take-off Sir.' There was a silence — then the C-in-C asked the reason. He hated anything of this nature, but he was quite calm.

'Risk of thick fog on the return Sir.' Sir Arthur pondered this — looked at the Met. Officer who nodded his confirmation. And the moment passed. It was unheard of for a mere Group Captain to take such action but he was supported. A less determined man might have taken a chance — but not this one. The prospect of hundreds of bombers milling round the country endeavouring to find a clear airfield was grim: tired crews boring their way through the swirling mists of East Anglia in the dark were in greater danger than over enemy territory.

Sir Robert Saundby, Deputy Commander-in-Chief, controlled the Air Staff and all day-to-day decisions were usually taken by him. A most experienced officer, he was approachable and exceedingly shrewd in his judgements. Few would question that statement. He bore the brunt of the daily round and once the C-in-C had selected the target for the night he oversaw the planning of routes, the mode of attack, the diversionary raids and the wave timing. In this he delegated much of the detail to the Senior Air Staff Officer but he was always on hand to discuss and settle the many problems which attended the organising and dispatch of the bomber force. The Senior Meteorological Officer was present at the nine o'clock conference in the Operations Room when Sir Arthur chose the target for the night: such choice stemmed from a combination of priority and forecast weather conditions in the area. Quite often it was no easy choice — the weather might be marginal, cloud over the target — or bad icing conditions — but it was necessary to balance this against weather conditions for the return. It could be good for bombing over Germany but totally unsuitable for landing the Force back at base. Diversions to other airfields in Scotland or the West Country meant the scattering of the Force with subsequent delay in getting them back to their home airfields . . . and in the worst case a high accident risk when attempting to land in bad conditions. Always, one had to watch the weather hour by hour and at midday a second Met. Conference was held in the Deputy's office. Meanwhile planning was in progress down below in the Operations Room below ground from which the various Bomber Groups were alerted and ordered to produce a given number for the night: the early telephoned messages (spoken over a secure line) were confirmed by teleprinter. The Command Operation Order known as Form 'A' was usually received by the Group Headquarters well before noon. This form contained all essential information but a more detailed instruction (Form 'B') went out from Group to Stations.

With the formation of the Pathfinder Force under command of Air Vice-Marshal Bennett another stage was introduced into the planning. A 'hook-up', meaning a telephone conference between the Command Ops Staff and the Pathfinder Headquarters discussed the method of marking the target and any diversionary forces designed to mislead the enemy. 'H' hour and wave timings for the different Groups and other important aspects. The Ops Room staff listened in on the many telephones available in order to keep themselves abreast of the planning. It would be their responsibility to tie up the loose ends once final agreement had been reached and to pass information to other interested parties. For instance, Fighter Command must be informed of the routing and timing of the bomber force both on the outward and return journey: Coastal Command controlling the Air Sea Rescue organisation, with its fast launches: the Royal Navy convoying ships off the East and South Coasts must know the route out and in otherwise they would fire first and ask questions afterwards! The Army operating gun and searchlight defences could be very helpful quite apart from their active role in loosing off at strange aircraft: the use of the searchlights in assisting a limping bomber and warning it away from balloon barrages was not unknown. These and many others had to be in the know. The machine worked smoothly and to a regular sequence.

At Group level the planning was conducted on a more personal note: the Air Officer Commanding knew all his Squadron Commanders and the orders stemming from Command Headquarters were translated into people and aircraft. The Group, in the best conditions, was a family and on the big board in the Operations Room Captains were listed by name alongside their aircraft. It was customary for a conference, similar to that conducted at Command, to take place between the Group and Stations where tactics were discussed and precise height bands allotted to Squadrons attacking the target. Similarly, a rendezvous point on the coast would be agreed in an attempt to concentrate the Group aircraft and improve the wave pattern. Weather, enemy defences, bomb and fuel loads, special signals instructions and possible diversion airfields in the event of the weather turning sour at the bases: these were some of the points raised.

The huge bomb capacity of the Lancaster lent itself to a wide variation in the type of load carried. After 1942 the common load for a Ruhr sortie was one four thousand pound bomb plus twelve small bomb containers each loaded with ninety four pound incendiaries. The 'cookie' — a widely used expression indentifying the four thousand pounder — could be either Medium or High capacity depending on the target. The former had better penetrating qualities with a lower charge/weight ratio than the latter, which was thin skinned and produced enormous blast effect on landing. Neither bomb possessed good ballistic qualities but the overall effect was satisfactory and the high capacity bomb was favoured for destroying factories. A combination of these weapons and the showering incendiaries was very effective since the bomb blast scattered the burning magnesium over a wide area. Four and eight thousand pound 'cookies' were frequently loaded into the bomb bays of the Lancaster and for the special high precision attacks on pin-point targets the twelve thousand pound 'Tallboy' — superbly engineered and finished to ensure well-nigh perfect ballistic qualities — could be carried in specially modified aircraft. On certain targets we carried the one thousand pound medium capacity bomb — a most effective weapon for nearly all requirements and I recall dropping five of these bombs on the Genoa docks with what appeared to be satisfactory results. It had good penetration qualities — there were no 'duds' and at Montchanin, the great power-switching station near Le Creusot we off-loaded another five with delayed fuses which dug well in and exploded twelve hours later.

The tiny four-pound incendiary packed ninety per aluminium container was responsible for much of the damage done to the enemy's cities and it was never improved on throughout the war.

Attempts were made to group or 'cluster' these weapons in order to give them better ballistic qualities but in the main they were showered down along with the high explosive. The scatter was formidable and not infrequently they fell on aircraft flying below: this was a hazard we had to accept. Later types of incendiary designed to be aimed more specifically at a target proved inferior — the thirty pound phosphorous and 'J' bombs — and despite the obvious disadvantages of the smaller weapon it was never displaced. The laborious business of packing hundreds of containers was time-consuming and as the Battle speeded up an enormous volume of these little bombs were needed, but the armament staffs toiled mightily and never failed to produce the goods.

The Battle of Berlin commenced in November 1943; that is the official date, and it continued until March of the following year. However, this was not an unbroken onslaught against the German capital: such a course was impossible since we were at the mercy of the weather and there were other demands on the bomber force. Between the beginning of November and the end of the year the Command operated on no less than forty occasions including sixteen heavy attacks on targets such as Dusseldorf, Modane, Ludwigshaven, Frankfurt, Stuttgart, Leipzig and eight heavy raids on Berlin. At this time of the year with the customary fog and bad weather over the bases this was no mean achievement: the small attacks comprising twenty-four in all were made by Mosquitos of the Light Night Striking Force which kept the sirens going all over Germany until the weather improved sufficiently to get the larger forces into the air. This was but the overture: the Battle was renewed with increasing ferocity in January and the last full scale attack took place on the night of 24 March — a night of disaster which resulted in the scattering of the Force and the loss of seventy-two aircraft: a missing rate of over 9 per cent . . . to be followed a few days later by the hell of Nuremburg which cost us ninety-five bombers: a loss, so heavy, as to endanger the future prospect of sustained and massive long-range operations, at least in the absence of radical remedial action.

Chapter 2
The Early Attacks on Berlin

At the height of the Luftwaffe onslaught on Britain, in the summer of 1940, Mr Churchill had not lost sight of offensive action against Germany proper. In a Minute to the War Cabinet he said this:

'The Navy can lose us the War but only the Air Force can win it; the Fighters are our salvation but the Bombers alone can provide the means of victory.'

As early as July, with the Germans occupying great areas of France and our Army powerless after being clawed off the Dunkirk beaches, he found time to address the Chief of the Air Staff in these words:

'In case there is an attack on the centre of Government in London, it seems very important to return the compliment the next day upon Berlin. I understand you will have by the end of this month a respectable party of Stirlings ready. Perhaps the nights are not yet long enough. Pray let me know.'

The likelihood of invasion occupied the minds of most of us: defence of this Island was of paramount importance yet the Prime Minister could look further ahead; he wanted offensive action and the means lay within his reach. To those who questioned the wisdom of stirring up the hornets' nest the justification lay in the freeing of our fighter airfields from daily attacks by an enemy operating from across the Channel: bomber raids on the German homeland meant the deployment of defending fighters — a diversion of some part of the enemy strength. Thus, while others were wringing their hands (and a few were willing to seek terms from the enemy) Churchill wanted Berlin bombed immediately the enemy showed himself over London . . . and, following the dispatch of some eighty bombers, air raid sirens were heard by astonished Berliners for the first time.

That the enemy should increase his attacks upon our capital city in consequence was inevitable, but the Royal Air Force fighter airfields on which our salvation depended became no longer a prime target for the Luftwaffe, leaving the Spitfires and Hurricanes free to destroy the German bombers. Air superiority was secured and the promised invasion was never launched.

The fall of France in May of 1940 cost us dear and not the least of the problems stemming from that defeat was the loss of the advanced airfields and bases which had bulked large in the Western Air Plans prepared before the War. At one stroke, the bomber element of the

Royal Air Force lost the use of facilities lying within easy range of the more important German targets: for the future the launching and recovery of both bombers and fighters would take place in this country: the 'half-way house' in Northern France had disappeared adding hundreds of miles to a bomber sortie with the attendant fuel problems to which we may add the imprecise forecasting of weather over the North Sea leg — imprecise because we had few means of obtaining the pressures and temperatures essential to the Met. Officers' task. Similarly, the warning period for the Germans increased greatly as they developed equipment capable of picking up at long range the approaching force of bombers. Against this kind of background the Whitleys, Wellingtons and Hampden aircraft of 1940 and 1941 performed their tasks: sorties were long and flown in all kinds of weather — ice, thunderstorms and snow were common enough in Winter whilst a marked strengthening of the north-west winds might put a question mark over the petrol remaining in the tanks.

During the period known as 'the phoney war' a great deal of time and effort had been expended in the distribution of leaflets over Germany and as far east as Warsaw on occasions. This exercise in psychological warfare was a complete waste of time and looking back one wonders just what we had hoped to achieve beyond providing the enemy with a quantity of waste paper for domestic use. The crews of that era hated the 'bumph raids' — the long flights across Europe often undertaken in weather which called for the utmost in pressing on with what they believed to be the most unrewarding of all war missions — where there was no end-result in terms of damaging the enemy war effort. Yet, whilst the Germans ridiculed our efforts there was a 'spin-off': crews gained experience in navigating by night at a time when such experience was sorely needed. This is the most one may say of the Nickel operations, to use the code-name then in vogue.

On the night following the first enemy bombing of London on 24 August 1940 a force of eighty-one Whitleys, Wellingtons and Hampdens set out for Berlin, to the great satisfaction of the Prime Minister. An eye for an eye and a tooth for a tooth — with the ancient city of London in flames behind him he looked eastward for the salve to assuage the pain and misery of its citizens. As the reports from the dispatching airfields were passed to his War Room he studied the great map of Europe; he was at one with the bomber crews setting course from the Yorkshire, Lincolnshire and Norfolk coasts and as the night drew on he made frequent requests for news of progress. There were no Stirlings flying that night and these, the first of the true 'heavies', would not be in action until the turn of the year.

On this first attack crews encountered a problem which was, with rare exceptions, to bedevil successive attacks on that city — a situation which was virtually impossible to forecast in the absence of vital meteorological data: thick layers of cloud with few gaps obscured the target. Some fifty crews claimed to have reached the area and of these twenty-nine reported favourable results, glimpsing the city briefly and releasing their bomb loads on what they believed to be the chosen objective. Twenty-one aircraft returned to England with their loads tucked up in the bomb bays — unwilling to let them go since they were uncertain of what lay below. Others jettisoned over the North Sea on the return journey. Eighteen bombed alternative targets in North Germany whilst seven returned early to base with technical defects. Five aircraft failed to return including three which 'ditched' in the sea and whose crews were rescued subsequently. As to the results of this operation, reports were received via secret sources confirming damage and fires in various parts of Berlin. It was not a bad beginning, the ice had been broken, and the morale effect was considerable. The following account by a young New Zealander, a navigator who achieved a distinguished record as a Pathfinder later in the war, recaptures something of the spirit of the pioneers:

'When our Squadron Commander announced the destination at briefing it caused no more than normal apprehension — rather a feeling of excitement . . . an eagerness at having the opportunity of hitting at the heart of Germany — in the face of bombastic boastings by Hitler and Goering. At this early stage of the war our main fears during operational flying concerned poor navigation due to lack of aids and sudden deterioration of the weather. We relied on a carefully prepared flight plan plus map reading. Even astro-navigation had yet to be included in the training curriculum and the sparse radio aids were confined to getting us home. It was possible to raise a QDM (magnetic course home to base) and with greater effort now and again a 'fix' — usually second class. We took off and crossed the Dutch coast on time which indicated the forecast Met. winds were reasonably accurate and on ETA we were in an area of much hostile activity. Timings varied, aircraft were loosely spread. The sky was clear on this occasion — I convinced myself I could identify the Siemens-Schukert works with the aid of the target map — started the bombing run and released our load; the rear gunner announced he could see the explosions but as to the success of the operation we had no means of telling save that of waiting for the Intelligence report published some months later. There were no fighters seen but flak was heavy. A strong head wind caused some anxiety on the return and there were frequent examinations of the petrol gauges but we got back to Honington safely — with seventy gallons remaining — not much in the way of a margin for coping with an emergency. Since the weather and particularly the winds at height were much as forecast this was taken as confirmation that we had bombed the designated target! My total flying time was 117 hours by day and 39 by night including my training in New Zealand.

The very next day we had a visit from the Commander-in-Chief [Air Marshal Sir Richard Peirse]. I was somewhat unique in the sense that I was the first commissioned Navigator to be posted to the Squadron and therefore I was included in the group of Officers assembled to meet the great man. The conversation went something like this, as my Commanding Officer introduced me,

Wing Commander: "This is Pilot Officer Hall, Sir."
AOC-in-C: "Ah, when did you last operate, Hall?"
Myself (rather eagerly): "Last night Sir."
AOC-in-C: "Good, good. Where did you go?" (I think, "Doesn't he know? He sent me there.")
Myself: "Berlin, Sir."
AOC-in-C: "Good. What did you think of it?"
Myself (realising this was no time to say that I had been frightened stiff): "Very interesting, Sir."
AOC-in-C: "Good, good, and how many trips have you done?"
Myself (proudly): "Three, Sir."
AOC-in-C turns on his heel to the Squadron Commander and says crisply, "And now I'd like to talk to someone with experience." '

The author of this little anecdote — Group Captain 'Sammy' Hall OBE, DFC — returned to the German capital in 1943, which he marked for others to bomb, but he never forgot the early attempts when each sortie was as much an adventure as an operation of war. Widely known for his expertise and good humour he survived a full Pathfinder tour in addition to his earlier Wellington experiences.

The creation of a powerful bomber force capable of striking repeated severe blows over a wide area of Germany and Occupied Europe proved a long and protracted exercise: three years were to elapse before it evolved as the result of many trials — and many errors.

In the first instance we had no experience of such a weapon: unlike our sister Services it was not a matter of carrying on where we had left off in 1918. The Navy went to war from the first day possessing vast experience of the task it would undertake whilst the British Army could draw on the lessons of a hundred campaigns; not least of which had been learned in the titanic struggles of the First World War. The Independent Air Force formed by Lord Trenchard in early 1918 —

representing the very first notion of the long range strategic offensive — had never gone into battle. The remnants of that ambitious plan, the huge Handley Page V1500s, had mouldered on the airfields from which the force would have been launched; to disappear completely in the feverish scramble to crush the infant Royal Air Force in the years following — another kind of battle fought in the corridors of Whitehall against Admirals and Generals who resented an independent third Service. That they were defeated is past history: the towering figure of Lord Trenchard stood between the preservation of a force which had proved itself in the recent conflict and the absorption of its Squadrons by the older Services. Had it been otherwise the strategic bombing offensive which harassed the enemy unceasingly for more than four long years might well not have taken place.

In the interval between August 1940 and November 1941 Bomber Command attacked Berlin on more than fifty occasions: forces were small and results difficult to assess. Day photographic cover of Berlin lay in the future — a technique which would ultimately reach perfection at the hands of the Spitfire and Mosquito pilots of the Photographic Reconnaissance Unit (PRU) who flew over hostile territory in daylight, relying on height and speed to escape interception by the enemy — and a certain amount of reliance was placed in the reports of agents dispatched through neutral countries. It was about this time that the shadowy figure of the 'Swedish businessman passing through Berlin' made his appearance, bringing valuable information when there was little else to back up the reports of the operational crews.

Occasionally Intelligence Officers permitted their imagination full play — and who could expect otherwise when the Captains of that day were convinced as to what was seen in the bombsight lens? One can't argue with a man who has just returned from doing the job. Thus, steadily, by various means and over the following months a reputation for pulling off a difficult long range operation with uncanny accuracy grew up around the bomber Groups. So much so that one Air Marshal expressed the belief that it mattered not whether there was a moon to aid the navigators; as long as the visibility remained clear even small targets such as oil installations could be found and attacked.

The great sprawl of Berlin offered many pin-point objectives and in the first volume of the Strategic Air Offensive the historians quote verbatim a section of the report on the Berlin operation of 7 October 1940: they state that such reports 'were typical of those made throughout the year making a complete nonsense of the doubts and anxieties which had been expressed from time to time about night bombing'. Included in this particular Night Raid Report is a long list of selected aiming points such as the Chancery, the War Office,

Electricity Works, Coal Gas Works, Marshalling Yards and Chemical Works implying a cautious selection of objective and meticulously accurate bombing — all in darkness with the various targets set amid a vast conurbation. Similarly, the reports seldom record 'any difficulty in reaching and locating the target, whether it be an oil plant, a marshalling yard, an aircraft factory or an individual building in the city'. Thus, it is not remarkable that the Air Marshals of that era derived great comfort from studying the Intelligence Summaries which came after each raid. Their crews disappeared into the night intent on using their best endeavours to carry out the instructions given at the briefing session: there was no helpful 'Gee' at that time for this type of radar aid was still under development — no Air Position Indicator or Air Mileage Unit — whilst the later refinements such as 'Oboe', 'Monica' and 'Fishpond' were little more than pipe dreams. The navigator was equipped with nothing more than his chart table, dividers, a course-and-distance calculator and the necessary maps of Germany. The Mk IX bubble sextant and astrograph had appeared on a few squadrons but failed to inspire any real degree of confidence; the instrument was unhandy and the operation cumbersome. Few captains welcomed a longish period of straight-and-level flying over hostile country whilst the navigator took a run of sights. The assistance given by the WT operator in terms of fixing position was slight: at long ranges the Butser Fixing Station situated in the Portsmouth area was notoriously chancy and subject to the vagaries of atmospherics, whilst the loop aerial was of little use over Germany.

In the autumn of 1941, after a spell of Atlantic ferrying duties, I returned to Bomber Command to find the bubble had burst: the fat was in the fire and the kind of complacency which had existed over the past year in respect of the accuracy of our bombing had disappeared almost overnight. The painstaking efforts of a professional civil servant had proved beyond a shadow of doubt that we were not only failing to hit the target but we were missing it by miles.* As for the precise bombing of Berlin that too was a 'busted flush' and the Navigation Staff at Command Headquarters was engaged in a painful exercise: back-plotting hundreds of navigators' charts relating to various raids on Germany. Mr Butt, and that was his name, had started something and at that time no one could guess the outcome: his careful examination of many night photographs — taken with the very few cameras then in use, to the tune of some six hundred exposures — had presented the Air Staff with the unpleasant truth. The remedy was one of fitting every aircraft with such a camera. Thus, in the light of a magnesium flash bomb dropped with the high explosive and the camera shutters timed to open during the bombing run, ground detail would be recorded for the experts to analyse.

* Butt Report 18.8.41

Since I had experience of long range navigation I was ordered to take part in this dreadful 'chore' though the slogging through chart after chart with parallel ruler, compass rose and dividers sharpened up my plotting technique. On the North Atlantic I had flown as a pilot sitting up front with a small chart of the great circle track on my knees, taking sextant shots through the perspex windscreen — not the best of positions but better than nothing: twenty or thirty miles off track in mid-Atlantic meant little and there was always the chance of correcting position with a subsequent fix. Again, after a fair amount of experience, the seat of one's pants helped enormously — one got a feeling for both weather and position whilst the star shots were taken at leisure with no kind of interruption: so that a moderate 'cocked hat', from two major stars coupled with a Polaris sight, often resulted. After that one hoped for good clear weather to make the landfall and map-read one's way back to Prestwick. I had little faith in the wartime radio aids around 1941 and cannot recall a single occasion when they operated in my favour. All of which sounds or rather reads very well — but I assure the reader it bore little relation to the task of navigating a bomber over Germany. That was a far more difficult undertaking and my sympathies lay with that band of stalwarts — the bomber navigators on whose skill the success or failure of the mission depended. At the time of my return to the war they were in the dog-house over a situation quite beyond their powers to remedy.

We did not know it then but 'Gee' was just around the corner — the first and always the most reliable of the new aids under current development. Even so, the range of 'Gee' was limited to a few hundred miles but a combination of both Gee, Astro and Ded. Reckoning represented an enormous step forward. In the event Astro was to fall by the wayside — the time consumed and the unhandiness of the method ruled it out for all but the keenest operators. After the stint at the charts it was decided I should fly with a Squadron on a few occasions to gain more insight into the problems of the navigator and after a short burst at Honington with No 9 Sqdn — and an almost perfect flight to Bremen and back with the Flight Commander of 'B' Flight, Squadron Leader Charles Innes, where I messed up a Pole Star shot and brought us over the guns around Rotterdam, I set out for Pocklington to join No 405 Squadron. The flight in the Wellington with Innes was my first experience of night operations over Germany: he was as cool as a cucumber and as we ran up to the Bremen docks amid a perfect hell of bursting shells he suggested I might like to take up position in the perspex Astro hatch and study the 'fall of shot'. I did so and was very frightened at what I saw going on outside the aircraft — so much so that I retired from my position of vantage and sat on the main spar to recover my nerve. The noise of the bursts was terrible — great claps of thunder and so near that I marvelled we were not hit. It was on the return journey that I assisted the navigator with nigh disastrous results! After that my cover was 'blown' although everyone was very kind about it. All my previous experience was as nothing — it was a different world — and I learned the hard way.

My short attachment to 405 — a Canadian Squadron — is memorable: not only for the Berlin operation of 7/8 November 1941 but for their attitude to the business of bombing the enemy and the genuine warmth of my welcome. Whereas I had experienced some difficulty in fitting into the programme at Honington — and this stemmed entirely from a reluctance to remove a crew member in order to accommodate a stranger, which was well understood — they were anxious to press on with their own problems of crew training and a visiting fireman was no help — a reverse situation was encountered at Pocklington. The Canadian attitude was one of 'if the man is daft enough to risk his neck let him have a go — and the best of luck'. They did more than that and allowed me to take a crew to bomb the Channel Ports but not before I demonstrated my sincerity in a 'second dicky' trip to Hamburg in a Mark II Wellington captained by a New Zealand Sergeant named Williams. An attractive personality, he was the very stuff of which bomber captains were made — determined to force his way through regardless of weather and enemy opposition to drop the three thousand pound load of high explosive on the docks which lined the River Elbe. The weather deteriorated as we neared Heligoland and we altered course for a point to the south-east of Hamburg prior to making our final approach to the target. In thick cloud and heavy rain we sought blindly for a reference point, dropping to four thousand feet over the German coast and encountering a curtain of light flak fire from the defences. The stuff whizzed past the Wellington — red and green blobs of incendiary shells, close and nasty, any one of which might have done for us all, but Williams was going to have his pinpoint and eventually the navigator, lying prone in the nose, declared he was satisfied and up went the nose in a steady climb back to bombing height. At ten thousand feet we were in thick cloud again — the captain flying very accurately on his instruments as if engaged on a training exercise.

We must have flown into a huge cu-nim because the next few minutes brought nightmarish conditions with lightning flashes, torrential rain and upcurrents of great strength which tossed the Wellington around the sky in the most sick making fashion — but Sgt Williams stuck doggedly to his instrument panel, reassuring the crew from time to time and expressing the belief we should come out of it very soon. We did so, to be grasped by a forest of white beams and engaged by heavy flak accurate for height and close at times — too close for my peace of mind and all of which, according to our stout captain, confirmed our nearness to the target. More heavy cloud and the navigator piped up to say we were only a matter of two or three minutes away from the dropping point and he was ready to go back into the nose and do the business (no bomb aimer was carried at this time and the navigator did everything). To my dismay, Sgt Williams cut into the navigator's announcement and said he would not drop on this run unless they had the docks in the bombsight: he would do another run losing a couple of thousand feet in the hope of seeing the ground! Silence in the aircraft — from the crew, that is — and a sheet of cloud hid us from the searchlights — a blessed relief. Then he was addressing me — would I kindly go to the rear of the aircraft and operate the hand pump which replenished the oil tanks in the engine nacelles?

'Just a few strokes, Sir, we have to do this from time to time (apologetically).'

Of what kind of metal was this youngster made?

At eight thousand feet we began a second run towards the area where we expected the docks to lie and the ground gunners redoubled their efforts; both heavy and light flak streamed up from below and again we drove into a cloud layer with a few gaps.

'Can you see the docks Freddie?' from the Captain.

'I can see the river — can't we get the hell out of this . . . OK keep her straight — we're heading directly towards them . . . left a bit . . . steady, steady . . . *bombs gone.*'

And that part of the business was over. I felt the vibration from beneath as the thousand pounder and the four five hundred pound bombs left the racks. Then we were in thick cloud and the nose was pulled up sharply as the shells burst around us . . . up, up until the Wimpy was standing on its tail . . . the stick went forward and Williams put her in a steep dive turning out toward the coast but holding the nose down until she commenced shaking violently and I wondered if the airframe would hold out much longer. We lost the flak for a brief spell but they picked us up once more as we neared the estuary of the Elbe where Williams put up another acrobatic feat — then silence as we flew out over the North Sea. What a display of guts from that young New Zealander, was the thought in my mind. There was no other aircraft in the vicinity — we had the whole of the Hamburg defences to ourselves to the best of my belief and it was a very dicey affair from first to last. We landed back at Pocklington and I thanked the young captain for the ride.

'Sorry about the rough stuff,' he grinned, but these Wimpys can take it — I'd rather fly one of these old crates than anything else.' A few days later, on 7 November, Berlin was laid on.

Bomber Groups Nos 3 and 4 were the chief exponents of the long range Berlin attacks, though the Hampden Squadrons of 5 Group had borne their share of the early raids. These aircraft were gradually withdrawn in view of their limited range and to meet the accelerating demands for more and more sea mines to be laid in the estuaries and approaches leading to the German naval ports — an exercise they performed with marked effect and to the complete satisfaction of the Royal Navy who provided a special staff at HQ Bomber Command to co-ordinate the work of the two Services.

The Whitleys of No 4 Group — a slow, tough and very reliable bomber — had pioneered the early attacks and acquired valuable experience: their navigation was superior for that era though always faced with the old, old problem of striking the target once having found it. Air Vice-Marshal Coningham, who commanded the Group for the first phase of the offensive, frequently dilated on the difficulties of locating and bombing the objective whilst bequeathing to posterity a single phrase summing up our frustrations as 'a never ending struggle to circumvent the law that we cannot see in the dark'. Nevertheless, the Air Marshals see-sawed as to what might be achieved in varying conditions of weather and visibility: some believed their crews to be capable of achieving the nigh-impossible — and I refer to the attack on the German oil plants — a single installation set in the Ruhr and other complexes which had to be literally 'winkled out' — in circumstances and with equipment which ruled out such precise bombing. This writer believes that a great deal of time lost in conferring and writing letters might have been saved if Air Marshals had on occasions gone out to see for themselves, but there is little or nothing in the many comments, remarks, letters and pronouncements to suggest that they went into the air: a single sortie might have produced startling results. All possessed distinguished records stemming from the first conflict, but the fact remains that opinions and decisions based on personal experience are worth a mass of reports on paper. Thus, from first to last, with notable exceptions such as Sir Basil Embry and Bennett, our Air Marshals in Bomber Command were not permitted to see at first hand the trials and tribulations of their crews. It has been argued, with some reason, that such a policy was dangerous, and highly secret information would have been at risk in the event of capture by the enemy.

In the weeks preceding my visit to Pocklington, Berlin had been attacked on a number of occasions. A handful of the four engined Halifax bombers had joined the huge Stirlings of No 3 Group whilst the Avro Manchester completed the trio of 'heavies'. I visited Linton-on-Ouse together with the No 4 Group Navigation Officer, a persevering Canadian Squadron Leader, named Willis, whose enthusiasm for this super aircraft led him to exclaim, 'Now, at last we have an aircraft for the navigator — and not for just the pilot'.

He took me though the fuselage to the well-designed navigator's compartment which represented a great advance in room and comfort and suggested we did a trip together — Berlin perhaps just for the pleasure! He was a pleasant man, striving to improve the lot of his navigators and I met him years afterwards in Montreal when we talked about those days. He wore his right arm in a leather supporting glove, having walked into a prop prior to take-off on a bombing mission — which was the end of his flying career.

We returned to Heslington Hall at York where No 4 Group HQ was located and there I was introduced to the AOC — Air Vice-Marshal Sir Roderick Carr — and one of the truly great Bomber 'Barons'. He was a man in the Trenchard tradition, I thought, easy to talk to, good at listening and eager to discover any fresh ideas or methods for improving the lot of his squadrons. Like his opposite number in No 3 Group, Sir John Baldwin, he knew almost everyone by name in his front line squadrons — was a frequent visitor to the airfields and was liked for himself. Over lunch he plied me with questions about the promised new devices and was generous in his interest in my previous occupation — in short he was one of those people who can instil confidence in his subordinates and draw the best from them. It came as no surprise to me when after the war I read Don Bennett's book 'Pathfinder', and learned that of all the 'Barons' Roddie Carr was the one who gave the Pathfinder Force unstinting support. If the PFF was created to lead and mark then he was all for it.

That same evening I met another officer who was to leave his mark on the Command — Squadron Leader John Fauquier — a tough Canadian who was to survive many operations of war including duty with the Pathfinder Force and command of No 617 — the famous Dams Squadron. He was a tremendous factor for morale, an outstanding leader and a powerful personality. As Flight Commander of 'B' Flight 405 he flew on the Berlin operation of 7 November and we shall meet him again in this narrative.

Pocklington was not a comfortable billet and in the bleak days of early November we shivered in the hutted accommodation common to many wartime airfields. No 405 was for the most part an all-Canadian Squadron but there were a few officers and NCOs on the aircrew roster who hailed from other countries such as my New Zealand pilot on the Hamburg operation. The easy relationship between officers, NCOs and airmen I found misleading for when, as they put it, 'the chips were down' they lacked nothing in zeal and enthusiasm. But it was a dreary camp and the Officers' Mess was short on warmth and comfort; I slept in a wooden hut where the draughts from the cracks between floor and wall caused my jacket, which hung on a peg, to swing gently to and fro until I plugged the gaps with newspaper. Accustomed to a dry cold the bitter winds of that first week in November tried the Canadians sorely and relief was found in bottle form — the party spirit was well to the fore and everyone joined in. A long way from home and stuck in a situation over which they had no control they accepted the weather, the wooden huts and the war with a cheerfulness which did them credit!

Berlin had been under attack several times during the previous weeks: the operation of 8/9 September was the biggest up to that time when 129 aircraft were detailed; and for once the skies over the German capital were free from cloud. The Intelligence summary stated that 'bursts were seen close to all the aiming points and large fires were started at the Alexanderplatz, the Frederickstrasse Station, Koepenick, Zehlendorf, Charlottenburg, Tempelhof airfield etc, etc. Impressive bursts of four thousand pound bombs were observed at Koepenick and close to the Alexanderplatz'.

A total of 300 aircraft were dispatched that night including the Berlin force from which twenty failed to return, one crashed into the sea, two crashed on landing and one blew up on take-off. On 21 September seventy-seven bombers set out for Berlin whilst another sixty-eight were detailed to attack Frankfurt and Ostend. A recall signal was dispatched to the Berlin and Frankfurt echelons and the report for that night reveals that not all aircraft received the message. Nineteen bombers attacked Berlin and the overall casualties are listed as three Wellingtons and one Whitley missing and a further sixteen crashed on return, including two in the North Sea and one in the Humber. From all of this we may deduce that weather was the governing factor in nearly every instance and the forecast for the second operation was a bit near the bone. A recall was a most infuriating intervention — one beat it back to base after jettisoning the bomb load (some didn't at this stage of the war) gnawing one's knuckles and hoping like hell to make it before the fog closed over the runway!

In late 1941 Bomber Command disposed of some forty-seven front line units with a further three squadrons in the process of rearming. The Wellingtons, Whitleys and Hampdens were still the backbone of the striking force, though three squadrons of Halifaxes and an equal number of Stirlings and Manchesters had appeared in Nos 3 and 5 Groups. The Lancaster was to succeed the Manchester in mid 1942 and there were some hair raising stories concerning the latter when I joined 5 Group the following autumn: the Vulture engines were apt to fail in flight with burned ignition leads and cracked bearing webs. It was a colossal engine for its day; the huge airscrew and massive cruciform cylinder blocks inspired awe — but it was a failure. The loss of one engine set the crew a problem since the Manchester was only just capable of maintaining itself in the air under these conditions and one of the leading lights in No 5 Group — Squadron Leader Herring (Kipper to his friends) — did in fact pull it off on returning from the 'Big City'; everything which was not bolted to the airframe was flung out, including the machine guns — and the Elsan to lighten the aircraft as they crossed the North Sea at a few hundred feet above the waves with the crew at ditching stations.

After the weather flak was the principal hazard in 1941. The defensive belt of guns and searchlights set up a year earlier was a notable feature: extending from Denmark through Holland and Belgium and as far south as Paris it was intended to shield the German Reich from attacking bombers. Served by numerous radar installations which scanned the approaches, the night fighter airfields received ample warning of the impending attack, whilst the ground gunners made ready to track and shoot down individual raiders. The effect was one of deploying much of the available defensive effort in an area of 'passing trade' as opposed to concentrating around the vulnerable cities — a policy which was changed as the bomber offensive gained momentum. Nevertheless it represented a challenge which could not be avoided and the solitary Whitley or Wellington was seen by the scanners, identified and followed into the 'box' where the local controller directed the waiting fighter pilot. Later, when we concentrated our bomber streams and adopted the 'wave' technique this system could not keep pace and a looser form of defence made possible by the increasing numbers of night fighters using advanced radar equipment took over.

As I sat in the briefing room at Pocklington in early November I listened to the Intelligence Officer armed with the latest information on the gun and searchlight zones. It was all matter of fact and nobody batted an eyelid. The ten crews of 405 Squadron sat passively accepting a repeat of that which they already knew. On the big wall map of Europe the green tapes crossing the North Sea to Denmark and on to eastern Germany, where the huge splodge of hatched green and red areas surrounded the target, drew their attention — and it seemed a very long way to travel. There were no questions — it was old stuff, anyway — and we passed on to the Met. briefing. Outside it was a bitterly cold day with the sun occasionally breaking through yet there was no hint of bad weather so that when the Meteorological Officer hung up his chart showing a cross section of what was expected I received a jolt — just one thing caught my eye — the pillar-like cu-nim clouds standing in regular formation over the sea route to Jutland.

Forecast temperatures were low and there was evidence of frontal activity off the Danish Coast. All in all I thought it likely to be a rough night. The convection clouds were not expected to rise much above ten thousand feet and there was risk of ice in such clouds. Over Germany heavy cloud could be expected with occasional breaks: this cloud could extend to ten thousand feet. Bomb loads for the Wellington IIs of 405 Squadron were 1 x 1,000, 4 x 500, 1 x 250 and two small bomb containers each holding ninety of the little incendiary bombs: no bad effort considering the distance to the target. The route

to the target lay directly east from the Yorkshire coast to Denmark —
for all No 4 Group aircraft whilst Nos 1 and 3 Groups flew almost
directly east from the Wash and Norfolk coast to the 'Big City'
following what was to become a well-worn track skirting the major
cities of Osnabruck, Hannover and Magdeburg.

The Command Battle Order for the night of 7/8 November
included 169 aircraft whose crews were briefed to attack Berlin:

No 1 Bomber Group	22 Wellingtons
No 3 Bomber Group	69 Wellingtons
	17 Stirlings
No 4 Group Bomber	42 Whitleys
	10 Wellingtons
	9 Halifaxes

This was the biggest force sent to Berlin up to that time but by no
means the full extent of Bomber Command's effort on that night. A
further 200 Hampdens, Manchesters, Halifaxes and Wellingtons were
dispatched to Cologne, Essen, Mannheim and smaller targets including the Channel Ports. Whilst weather forecasts spoke of cloud over
the Ruhr the more severe weather lay to the north and especially in
the area of the Bight and northern Germany generally. For the return
conditions were expected to be good with clear visibility at the bases.

The routes selected for the different Groups are evidence of careful
planning though night fighter activity at this time was slight and few
successful interceptions were staged by the enemy. Heavily engaged
on the Eastern Front he had moved many units from the West in
support of his drive across the Steppes to Moscow.

Our own Intelligence appreciation of Luftwaffe deployment on the
Western Front in late 1941 records 300 single engine and 230 twin
engine fighters at readiness. Whilst these are significant figures we
should bear in mind the enormous stretch of territory, extending
from Norway to the Biscay ports, together with heavy commitments
in North Africa and the Mediterranean theatre, which drew on GAF
strength in the West. At this time the expectation of a breakthrough
in the Russian campaign demanded priority in the supply of both
aircraft and pilots all of which affected the fighting efficiency of the
home-based units and in many instances their combat experience was
minimal. Thus, once through the defensive belt running roughly
parallel to the enemy coast fighter interception was sporadic and only
on rare occasions effective. The real hazards in 1941 were the
weather and the flak batteries, both heavy and light, coupled with
searchlight activity: the threat from night fighters, which reached
massive proportions at the time of the final onslaught on Berlin, lay
in the future when the expanding bomber force would compel the
enemy to attempt the destruction of the attackers along the approach

to his cities: a policy which, ultimately, would bear heavily on the course of the offensive as we shall see later in this narrative.

From a study of the take-off times for the three bomber Groups ordered to Berlin the eventual spread of aircraft on both the direct route and that via the Danish Islands is not remarkable. The Headquarters Staff in the Operations Room at Bomber Command had posed a double threat to Berlin with forces approaching from different directions which, in terms of night fighter interception, was sound enough but no attempt was made to concentrate aircraft either by route or in time. Small variations in routing for all Groups kept aircraft apart whilst the staggered take-off times produced a ragged concourse — and this may have been deliberate: setting up widely dispersed raiders guaranteed to fox the controllers responsible for directing any fighters available to intercept. At that stage in the bomber offensive the theory of 'concentration in space and time' had not been evolved but a highly significant letter from the Chief of the Air Staff, Sir Charles Portal, to the Commander-in-Chief Bomber Command was dispatched three weeks after this operation in reply to a letter from Sir Richard Peirse who had earlier dilated on the difficulties entailed in concentrating his Force. The CAS wrote:

'I have just been looking at your letter . . . in which you describe the difficulties of achieving concentration . . . A few weeks ago I met Staton who has views on this subject which appear to be very sound. I do not know whether you hold the same high opinion of him as a practical airman that I did but if you do you might care sometime to talk to him on the subject. We are sending an official reply to your letter asking you not to abandon the idea out of hand.'

The 'idea' to which Sir Charles Portal made reference would one day bulk large in the planning of all bomber operations. The officer named in his letter to Sir Richard Peirse was one of the best Squadron Commanders of his day and, later in the war, a byword for courage in standing up to his Japanese captors under conditions of extreme physical cruelty.

With a high percentage of the Command strength committed to battle on the night of 7 November, in forecast conditions which drew some harsh comment from the small number of Canadian officers and NCOs studying the chart produced by a nervous Meteorological Officer, the plan went forward and we trooped off to the Mess for the customary bacon and eggs — a luxury in those hard times. I sat down alongside my Canadian colleagues, since I was playing a minor role which would take me no further than Boulogne, and listened to views and opinions expressed without much in the way of restraint.

Only the previous night I had attended a party in the ante room to welcome two visiting Members of the Canadian Parliament — an occasion for everyone to speak up without fear or favour — and heard not a single voice raised in complaint. They were a cheerful lot — the Mess was cold — the weather bitter and Pocklington was dreary enough but they were not giving anything away. They drank until the early morning — furniture was broken and maybe a few bones — and there was a certain gloom over breakfast but that was life with 405 Squadron. I was accosted by an officer well over six feet tall who asked me if I was intending to fly with them: I answered 'yes' and he then asked me if he might try on my greatcoat in advance of my coming demise. He had left his somewhere in York and here was an opportunity to put things right: he didn't think I had the look of one who would need it much longer: casualties had not been light over the past weeks! Apart from this odd beginning we got along very well. But that was the previous night; a different mood prevailed at our pre-flight supper and there was no enthusiasm for the task ahead. The weather map had done the trick; those tall 'thunderheads' over the North Sea spoke a language well understood by all save the newest arrivals — and the latter were not represented in the tally of ten crews headed by John Fauquier in command of 'B' Flight. This was our first meeting and there would be others as the years passed, for he was an officer and commander of distinction with a reputation for bluntness: we were both Squadron Commanders in Bennett's Pathfinder Force and later John won further fame when he took over 617. With few breaks in his operational flying he passed from one post of responsibility to another but always close to the 'sharp end' surviving an almost endless stream of close-calls. His letter to me concerning the Berlin raid of 7 November is interesting:

'. . . at briefing where we were told our target was to be Berlin. When the Met. Man came along with his chart I immediately smelled a rat: he was nervous and seemed unable to make up his mind about the wind velocity for the return to base. Take-off was around 11 o'clock that night. All went well on the way out until we climbed out of the overcast which was solid all the rest of the way so that we had nothing but ded. reckoning and forecast winds to get us to the target. Finally, we reached the point where we thought, and hoped, Berlin lay beneath — dropped our bombs and turned for home. It wasn't long before I realised we were in trouble because the winds had increased greatly in strength and were almost dead ahead. Eventually, I lost height down to a few hundred feet — to avoid icing conditions and to save fuel since the head wind would be less strong.

I have seen the North Sea in many moods but never more

ferocious than that night. Huge waves of solid green water were lifted from the surface and carried hundreds of feet by the wind. After what seemed like hours in these appalling conditions I realised we were unlikely to make base. I had little or no fuel left and told the crew to take up ditching positions though our chances of pulling off a successful ditching in darkness amid that hell of strong winds and blown spray were practically nil. It was then I saw briefly one of those wonderful homing lights and made a bee-line straight for it, crossing the English Coast with all gauges knocking on zero. In a few moments we found what I thought was Driffield but it proved a non-operational airfield. I could just make out the runways — as it was early dawn — and slapped the wheels and flaps down whilst I still had power, only to find at a hundred feet the runway blocked with railroad iron to prevent the enemy making use of it. They had erected pylons of this stuff all down the runway but, of course, they forgot to put any kind of obstruction on the grass surfaces. I landed but swerved to port and damaged the starboard tail plane. All in all we were lucky and nobody was hurt, thank God. As soon as we climbed out of the aircraft we were surrounded by the Home Guard, who were most hostile in spite of our uniforms and the RAF roundels on the fuselage. They were going to lock us up! I asked repeatedly for the Colonel, or whoever was in charge, to make contact with Pocklington but he was still suspicious. He asked me when we had left England, and when I said, "eleven o'clock last night," he replied: "no aircraft can stay in the air that long."

Finally, everything was smoothed over and we were picked up and returned to Pocklington.'

Fauquier's luck held on this and other occasions but he was still a bit sour when I met him in the Mess the night following the Berlin raid, expressing himself forcefully on the subject of Air Staff planning at Headquarters Bomber Command. Although he makes no mention of it in his note to me his Wellington was heavily damaged by flak: the misery of that North Sea crossing with a seventy mile per hour headwind eating up the scant fuel reserve, and the expectation of a ditching in darkness and a wild sea, was shared by all save the Halifax crews who had no fuel worries and whose new four engined bombers carried them over the weather. What happened to the other nine Wellingtons? The weather encountered is summed up briefly as 'Bad; 10/10 cloud with few breaks' yet six crews battled their way to the target area and two caught a momentary glimpse of the city — 'Q' captained by Sgt Sutherland the 'G' captained by Sgt Suggitt: whilst others bombed on the estimated position. Sgt Hassan, flying Wellington 'D' dispatched a signal to base at 0223 'Operation completed' but of this gallant crew nothing more was heard and they may well have fallen victims to the fury of the North Sea, as did others when the petrol ran out. My pilot on the Hamburg sortie, Sgt Williams, abandoned his mission with zero oil pressure on one engine — but, typically, jettisoned his bomb load over what he believed to be Wilhelmshaven before staggering back to base on one engine. He told me a little of their experience, estimating the wind at height to be eighty mph with an outside temperature of −42C. Their slow crawl back to base with the Wellington capable of not much over a hundred and ten with one engine feathered and tending to overheat called for skill and determination but as he put it 'it was nothing to write home about — the alternative was a ducking.'

All in all No 405 Sqn had not done badly, but the Group as a whole took a beating from the impossible weather conditions obtaining over practically the whole route to the enemy capital. The old Whitleys — 'slow but sure' was their reputation — took between eight and eleven hours to fly this mission and crews suffered terribly from the bitter conditions; icing slowed progress for it built up in solid layers on the mainplanes and propellors, destroying the contour of leading edges on the wings and rendering the crew virtually blind as the opaque mass spread over the thick perspex windscreen. The extra drag imposed by the wing icing reduced lift and forward speed — a dangerous combination and only those who have experienced this phenomenon can appreciate the effects: the noise of ice flung by the propellors against the fuselage — a hammering which can penetrate the metallic skin — is unnerving and yet welcome for it better by far to be rid of it, though the process is frightening.

Studying the records of this night — getting on for forty years back — the evidence of tragedy piles up thick and fast among the Whitleys battling their way home to the Yorkshire airfields. Sgt Lloyd-Jones and his crew from No 78 Sqdn were fortunate in lobbing down at Coltishall with only two gallons remaining in the tanks (an incredible figure but this is what the Squadron diary records!) after throwing various items including the four Brownings from the rear turret into the sea.

The entry reads: 'owing to a misunderstanding the rear gunner jettisoned his four tail guns — aircraft landed . . . with only two gallons left.'

No need to apologise — the lives of Sgts Connolly, Wilson, Beaton and Cragg plus the captain outweigh four machine guns by quite a margin. Sgts Bell and Sargent with their crews did not make it — the last message from the first named stated 'task abandoned at 0225' which was the time they would be over Berlin or near it but could see nothing owing to the dense cloud. Pilot Officer Havelock of No 77 Sqdn reported 'severe icing from 2-10,000 ft, whilst Nos 51 and 102 Squadrons lost two aircraft each, of which one, Z6796 captained by Sergeant Matthews, called for a QDM at 0726 hrs — a highly significant timing. 'QDM', transmitted by the aircraft's wireless operator, means 'What is my magnetic course to steer to base airfield' and is acknowledged by the monitoring ground station which takes a bearing on the aircraft and responds with a reciprocal which, all other factors considered, will bring the bomber within reach of base.

At this stage of the bomber offensive we relied heavily on the QDMs particularly when the weather was bad and visibility reduced by low cloud and fog. Sgt Matthew's request for assistance was transmitted at a time when he must have been only a short distance from the Yorkshire coast, since other aircraft from his Squadron landed at 0700 and 0743 respectively — but he never made it and presumably fell into the sea with all tanks empty! Another Whitley from the same Squadron was 'fixed' by WT as being sixty miles north of the island of Borkum at 0642 that morning but never reached base. This position and time put him on track for England with another hour and a half to fly before crossing the coast — but nothing further was received and he too, was either short of fuel or had suffered flak damage, though the former cause is more likely since there is no mention of his reporting flak damage at the time his WT operator called for a fix. A similar fate befell P/O Tuckfield and P/O Brown of No 58 Squadron. Tuckfield's last known position is given as 54 17N 01 35E which put him some sixty miles due east of Scarborough heading directly for base, whilst in the case of Brown the Operations Record Book contains the entry 'believed landed in the sea'. There are other instances but the foregoing will suffice for No 4 Bomber Group which suffered heavy losses that night. The weather as described by the Halifax crews of No 76 Sqdn must have been appalling . . . 'as a result of the extreme cold Air Speed Indicators and Compasses were made unserviceable'.

I can recall no other instance of compasses freezing: the alcohol in the compass bowl being adjusted to withstand very low temperatures indeed. The powerful four-engined Halifaxes, not long in Squadron service, rode above the threatening cu-nims but out of the six aircraft detailed only two, Pilot Officer Calder and Sergeant Herbert reached the Berlin area; the remainder abandoning or seeking alternative targets. These two Halifax crews flew for eight hours that night whilst the humble Whitleys struggled on for eleven hours before reaching their home airfields! We now take a quick look at the other Groups — Nos 1 and 3 — to see how the Wellingtons and Stirlings fared on the more direct route across the North German Plain to the 'Big City'.

No 3 Bomber Group under the command of Sir John Baldwin, a highly respected Air Vice-Marshal with a reputation for speaking out, disposed of thirteen front line Squadrons though not all were at full strength. For the Berlin operation some sixty-nine Wellingtons and seventeen Stirlings were ordered into the attack, whilst a further forty-one aircraft were spread over the Ruhr area and Mannheim. The Berlin operation proved a failure and the officer who wrote up the Group Diary for that night makes no bones about saying so.

'. . . *Berlin*. This attack was not successful owing to 10/10ths cloud over the area. Quite a number bombed on the estimated position; others bombed alternative targets and a number joined in the rover's party around the Ruhr on the way back . . . one hundred and twenty seven aircraft took-off on this mainly unsuccessful expedition and twelve are missing. About 200 tons of bombs were dropped somewhere in Germany or Occupied France, however.'

A plain statement of fact with a cynical overtone: his reference to the 'rovers' party connotes a certain lack of precision in determining aiming points but this is understandable against a background of solid cumulus extending to great heights. Nevertheless the crews which failed to find Berlin made a creditable effort to bomb the Ruhr; carrying their loads back in the hope of finding useful breaks over the Ruhr which lay south of the return track; rather than wasting them indiscriminately somewhere in the Berlin area.

This particular 'historian' left out nothing essential to the record. He lists the missing crews giving the last known position or simply 'nothing heard after take-off': one entry catches the eye, '. . . Signal reads "Operation completed, am returning with undercarriage down",' this was sent from the Wellington flown by a Czech crew at 0100 to be followed two hours later by another crisp message — 'Landing in Sweden'.

Another entry concerns a crew of No 214 Sqdn, Captain P/O Ercolani, who were reported missing on 7 November but came ashore from their dinghy at Ventnor in the Isle of Wight after spending three long days at sea. Following the flak burst, beneath the aircraft their incendiary bombs caught fire and all effort to release the containers failed; thus for a short while with the bomb-bay alight they constituted a live target until pulling off a successful ditching close to the Dutch coast. The double hazard confronting the young captain was truly formidable: the necessity for getting his crippled aircraft on the water before the fire destroyed them and the task of bringing off a 'ditching' on a black night in a raging sea. Both tasks were accomplished to be followed by the agony of exposure to the elements as they drifted slowly towards the English coast, the frail rubber dinghy tossed sickeningly at the mercy of huge waves. Surely these were men of whom their Commander-in-Chief could be justly proud; and yet in bomber terms it was an incident calling for that same 'cold dour courage' found in every branch of the Armed Services of our Country when 'the chips are down'. They were fortunate for the sea claimed many that night. Of the eighty-six Wellingtons and Stirlings dispatched to Berlin Sir John Baldwin's Group lost nine aircraft, with further losses over Essen. In almost every case the returning crews reported impossible weather conditions: thick towering cumulus and temperatures low enough to freeze the alcohol in the compass bowls. The plight of the exposed tail gunners can be readily assessed; frostbite was a common experience.

No 1 Bomber Group contributed a relatively small number of Wellingtons for the Berlin attack — twenty-two set out for the 'Big City' and a further sixty were detailed to attack Mannheim and the Channel ports. Only nine crews of the Berlin party claimed to have bombed anywhere near that city and four failed to return — from the four Polish Squadrons operating under Air Vice-Marshal Oxland's command: three more Wellingtons were lost over Mannheim. The Group Diary records 'very adverse conditions' and attributes the losses to the very strong winds encountered. This statement clashes with the opening phrase in the section devoted to the Berlin and Mannheim attack. 'After five days inactivity owing to the poor weather, conditions tonight promised to be more favourable and Command ordered a maximum effort from Groups.' There could not have been a worse night for such an undertaking. A reference to 'excessive fuel consumption' reflects on the petrol margin, which, as mentioned earlier, bore heavily on the casualty rate and this is stressed in the phrase 'others that returned did so with only a short allowance of petrol left'. This matter of an adequate fuel margin comes under discussion in the subsequent correspondence between Sir Charles Portal, Chief of the Air Staff and Sir Richard Peirse, Commander-in-Chief, Bomber Command, as we shall see later in this narrative. No 300 (Polish) Squadron dispatched six aircraft to Berlin without result and these all returned to base, but of the four aircraft sent to Mannheim two were lost and the other two landed at Manston short of fuel. In no instance was the target identified due to weather conditions and four of their Wellingtons failed to reach the target area 'due to strong icing conditions'. A similar story obtains for almost every aircraft sent out by No 1 Bomber Group: bombs were released on ETA or, occasionally, after a fleeting glimpse of ground detail.

No 12 Sqdn, reckoned the best and most experienced in Air Vice-Marshal Oxland's Group, succeeded in getting only one aircraft to the target area, out of the five dispatched. Severe icing was encountered with a rapid build-up on wings and airscrews and the extra power demanded to keep the bombers flying drew heavily on the petrol reserves. This state of affairs coupled with the prospect of a strong headwind for the return compelled the remainder to turn back. Pilot Officer Heyworth, captain of a Wellington Mark II carrying eight five hundred pound bombs (no mean load for a Berlin sortie even in the best conditions) flew in cloud with tops at 19,000 ft: he experienced bad icing troubles and extreme cold: his colleague Pilot Officer Barnes with a battle-tried crew found his guns frozen up and ice so heavy on his bomber that to continue was impossible. The one man who got through, Pilot Officer P. J. Oleinek, was engaged by heavy flak fired through 10/10 cloud from which evidence he deducted they were in the vicinity of Berlin since it coincided with the navigation plot: he then flew around the area at 12,000 ft endeavouring to penetrate the thick cumulus shrouding the city — but all to no avail and he contented himself with dropping his bombs at intervals wherever the flak was most concentrated before turning for home. This aircraft flew for eight and a half hours before landing safely back on a Lincolnshire airfield.

And so ended a night of disaster. The final count revealed a total of thirty-seven aircraft missing out of the four hundred dispatched to Berlin and other targets. The 'Big City' claimed twenty-one from one hundred and sixty-nine which set out — and this, the biggest operation launched by Bomber Command to date achieved almost nothing, against which we may set many valuable lives. In those days a loss of this magnitude was a most serious and damaging prospect; the Command was still struggling and the loss of experienced crews, quite apart from the matter of the aircraft they flew, was a severe set-back: so much so that the attention of the Prime Minister was drawn to this debacle. He was not seeking a scapegoat — but in his customary penetrating and peremptory manner he wanted the facts. When he received the preliminary reports the Chief of the Air Staff was not satisfied. Sir Charles Portal — possibly the best Chief of Air Staff in our relatively short history — was unwilling to forward them to the Prime Minister since he disputed the arguments and explanations adduced by Sir Richard Peirse and the fat was in the fire.

Chapter 3
Questions at High Level

During my service in Bomber Command I have sometimes reflected on the reactions of our bomber crews to those occasions when the toll of lives has been heavy. Rarely did one hear any comment — the shocks were borne and accepted in the way one would expect — and the work of preparing aircraft and crews for the following night went forward: the gaps were filled to the best of our ability. This applied strictly to what might be termed 'fair fight' on the part of the opposition and the knowledge that we had been sent out in reasonable weather conditions so that the task was within our competence. After March 1942 when Sir Arthur Harris assumed command the confidence of the crews in the Command Staff was very real: we didn't see Harris but his personality overlaid everything we did. It is true that he inherited the benefits of scientific development and was provided with better aircraft — but none of these things could change the weather: that was a constant to be applied to every situation and his judgement was invariably sound. In company with hundreds of other men I have flown over Germany and Occupied Europe on some rough nights but always in the belief that we were not dispatched to Berlin or the Ruhr in haphazard manner: this belief was a powerful factor for morale, reinforced during the year I worked as a member of his Operational Staff. I saw his powerful fist slapped down on the synoptic weather chart on many occasions at the nine o'clock conference when Mr Spence, the Chief Met. Officer, produced the forecast. Both Mr Spence and his deputy Chris Drake carried a heavy responsibility; on the basis of their forecast the Commander-in-Chief having taken into account all relevant factors would make his decision. But it was not as simple as it may sound: Sir Arthur, on each and every occasion, accepted a dual responsibility — that of getting the Force to the target and, equally important, that of recovering up to a thousand aircraft on the return. There were some tense moments. Surrounding him stood his senior staff with his Deputy, Air Marshal Saundby, nearest: his long experience and wide knowledge of the task could never be discounted but Sir Arthur went it alone. Whatever discussion took place afterwards between C-in-C and Deputy C-in-C in the privacy of the former's office no man knew — and there must have been times when the latter's expertise came to the fore but at the initial planning conference as I have said Sir Arthur went it alone.

The quality of the HQ Staff could not have been so very different at the time the operation we are examining took place: and yet the Command was committed to battle in conditions totally unfit save for the few fringe targets such as the Channel Ports. At Station and Squadron level many had misgivings — and some of the Group Commanders expressed their concern — so why was no cancellation forthcoming? Why was this, the biggest bomber operation to date, sent off to struggle for up to eleven hours with towering cumulo-nimbus clouds, virtually unbroken cover over Berlin, severe icing conditons, a strong north-westerly gale for the return and insufficient fuel margins? No adequate explanation has been forthcoming but an examination of the correspondence subsequent to the disaster throws light on the attitude of mind then prevailing. We may commence with the covering letter to a preliminary report sent by Sir Richard Peirse (C-in-C Bomber Command) to the Chief of the Air Staff two days after the Berlin raid. From the opening sentence it is reasonable to conclude that Peirse had been invited to Chequers to explain his losses. That the Prime Minister was greatly exercised in his mind is plain from the letter he sent to the Secretary of State for Air immediately afterwards. First, Peirse's letter and preliminary report:

'I spent Saturday night at Chequers and discussed the subject of our Friday night's losses at some length with the PM. As usual he took the line that we must avoid these casualties which we could not afford; and as usual I took the line that if one operated at all one was bound every now and again to get disproportionate results. There are, for instance nights when we have heavy casualties, and other nights when we have none, and no amount of research and examination has yet explained the phenomena. However, the PM became very insistent on my conserving and building up strength and said he was giving me a definite direction on this that I should use smaller forces and confine myself to shorter range targets. To my mind the PM is thinking in terms of Naval forces — the Fleet in being and a strong Fleet — to sally forth every now and then to do some specific task. I told him that the effects of a bomber force were cumulative and resulted from steady and continuous pressure on the enemy. He said he did not think we had done any damage to the enemy lately, to which I replied that he had just told me how much damage he had seen in Sheffield, from which he had just returned and which has only been attacked on two occasions. I said I thought his journey would have been very different had the enemy, for the past six months, consistently thrown three thousand tons of bombs into the country and towns per month.

I can, of course, limit the maximum effort I put out, but undoubtedly by so doing good and rare opportunities will be missed. Then there is always the very important psychological factor. I am always preaching to the Command that they have a man-sized job to do; a job on which all eyes are turned; a job on which too much care and preparation cannot be expended, and above all a job which must be pushed right through to the conclusion if results are to be obtained. If, therefore, any breath that the Powers-that-Be did not consider this to be the case, or that there is any hesitation in the handling of the Force, doubt must immediately arise in the minds of the aircrew, and doubt spells irresolution. In other words it is darned hard to fight a force like the Bomber Force at a subdued tempo.

I gave Wilfrid Freeman the gist of this on the telephone this morning and hoped he would pass it on to you, as I am sure you will have to face these views from the PM in the Cabinet. Meanwhile, until I hear from you, I shall continue as I have done in the past, as I think this represents your views. It so happens, however, that as the Moon is now getting old I have reverted automatically to a one in three night effort. We had a very satisfactory night last night and everybody's tails are right up.

The PM asked for a report. He seems to think we could quite easily find out what happened, but, as you know, this is extremely difficult to do. Every attack is analysed in the greatest detail, but this will take some time. I therefore enclose a copy of a quick report I have made. Rather scrappy but I think the conclusions are as near the truth as we are likely to get.'

Now follows Sir Richard Peirse's preliminary report, prepared by his Staff. Of the 242 sorties ordered some 400 actually set out for their briefed objectives of which 169 were expected to bomb Berlin. The overall loss for the night is given as 37 aircraft broken down as follows:

No 1 Group:	7 aircraft lost attempting to attack Mannheim.
No 3 Group:	13 aircraft lost attempting to attack Berlin and the Ruhr.
No 4 Group:	12 aircraft lost attempting to attack Berlin and the Ruhr.
No 5 Group:	5 aircraft lost during Intruder and Mining operations.
Total	37 (21 out of the 169 sent to Berlin).

The Signal Logs for the various Groups controlling the missing aircraft record the following information:

No 1 Group:	2 aircraft signalled short of petrol. No fix obtained and nothing further heard.

No 3 Group: 3 aircraft signalled NAP (task abandoned) but nothing further heard.
1 aircraft reported 'landing in sea'. Starboard engine U/S. Nothing further heard.
4 aircraft not heard.
1 aircraft was given a first class fix on Hull but signal not acknowledged and nothing further heard. 1 aircraft sent SOS at position 31 90 (as written in report). Bearing was passed and aircraft told to change to MF. This was not acknowledged and nothing further heard.
1 aircraft signalled SOS but nothing further heard.

No 4 Group: 3 aircraft not heard.
2 aircraft signalled NQE (task completed) but nothing further heard.
5 aircraft sent SOS short of petrol after 8 hours in the air. Nothing further heard.
1 aircraft got a QDM when over Germany after 8 hours.
1 aircraft got a fix over Germany after five hours but nothing further heard.

No 5 Group: No signals received from any of the 5 missing aircraft.

These brief entries are illuminating but the analysis sent to HQ Bomber Command by individual Groups reveal a pathetic state of affairs. This examination is concerned mainly with the Berlin operation but the complete text is given since there are few references to individual targets.

Group Analysis of Factors Causing Losses
No 1 Bomber Group:
(a)   There are no Freshmen missing.
(b)   Eight sightings of enemy aircraft were reported but no combats.
(c)   One aircraft which returned was hit by flak.
(d)   Navigators complained of a higher wind than was expected and others that the speed and direction of the wind varied from that forecasted.
(e)   It was reported that Mannheim was difficult to find.
(f)   Five of the missing aircraft were Wellington IVs, a type particularly susceptible to high consumption unless properly handled.
(g)   Two of the missing aircraft and at least six of those which returned were short of fuel.

(h)   Signals interference might account for lack of information from missing aircraft.

(i)   Considered there are strong indications that the majority of missing aircraft ran out of fuel having misjudged the effect of high winds whilst searching for the targets. Aircraft probably flew higher than the planned height and consequently the wind was stronger than forecasted.

No 3 Bomber Group:

(a)   None of the missing aircraft reported icing trouble though this was suspected as causing 5 other aircraft to return early. This was probably due to the heavily loaded aircraft being forced into cloud when climbing.

(b)   On this night there was a very strong wind which necessitated a straight course to and from the more distant targets. The crews were briefed to fly as high as possible on the outward journey and to return as low as was compatible with safety. In point of fact aircraft were kept at a fairly high altitude due to the prevalence of 10/10 cloud which was unbroken until well on the homeward journey.

(c)   There was a bright moon which had risen approximately one hour before the attack was staged, and would therefore be in the ascendant throughout the return journey. A strong headwind reduced speed and rendered aircraft more likely to attack by fighters. Against this there were only three reports of such attacks.

(d)   It may be possible that the slow speed on the return allowed more accurately predicted flak fire. This, again, is pure guesswork and no reports were received of aircraft observed to be shot down. Though strong, the forecast winds appear to have been very accurate and, on the whole, navigation was well up to the usual standard.

(e)   In spite of the numbers concerned, those aircraft which did ask for assistance appear to have received wireless facilities without any undue delay and in cases where aircraft got off course diversion action was possible and they were directed to alternative bases.

(f)   It appears in certain instances this straying from the true course was due to evasive action and subsequent drifting, for which adequate allowance was not made — and which became effective in a very short time due to the strength of the wind.

(g)   Another cause which it is felt may have had a direct bearing on these casualties was the fact that aircraft were forced to fly high for a longer period than is perhaps normal, and that with the regrettably inefficient heating which is at present supplied in both Wellingtons and Stirlings, the crews were certainly not operating at anything like a high state of efficiency. In the case of the Stirling, complaints were almost universal. The crews stated that the temperature inside was −30°. Unless this question of internal heating is treated more seriously than it has been for the past two winters, the lack of heating facilities will continue to be a source of wastage.

(h)   There is also a suggestion that due to the time for which high altitude flying had to be maintained crews found themselves deficient of oxygen since the supply in the Wellington is inadequate for long distances; but no specific case of the lack of oxygen was reported other than the fact that one navigator from No 78 Sqdn became a casualty, and this may have been due to insufficient oxygen.

(i)   Another contributary cause may be that of late it has become well-nigh impossible to make use of enemy beacons, thereby causing crews to rely entirely on Ded. Reckoning and Astro-Navigation on the outward journey. The taking of Astro sights is fraught with considerable difficulty on nights such as the one in question. Due to the freezing up of the Astro dome it is essential to take the sights through the open window or hatch; and even then it is necessary to wipe the eyepiece of the sextant between shots. It can well be seen, therefore, that not only the navigator himself is partly frozen before endeavouring to take this sight, and completely frozen afterwards, but the rest of the crew suffer increased discomfort from opening the hatch and from the somewhat lengthy nature of the proceedings. I believe I am right in saying that research is being undertaken towards supplying some form of heating to the sextant to avoid the misting of the eye-piece between each sight. This, again, apparently is an urgent necessity.

No 4 Bomber Group:
(a)   3 aircraft probably lost through shortage of fuel.
(b)   3 aircraft certainly lost through shortage of fuel as they landed in the sea.
(c)   1 aircraft lost through engine trouble.

    (d)   5 aircraft lost through causes unknown.

    (e)   The losses through shortage of fuel are considered to be due to icing.

    (f)   There are no reports of enemy fighters.

There is a further report from No 5 Group but it adds little to the general picture and none of their aircraft went to Berlin that night. Before writing his conclusions Sir Richard Peirse adds a useful paragraph relating to the experience of the missing crews. He records this in the following manner:

No 1 Group: (7 crews missing). Minimum number of sorties per pilot — 12. Average — 26.

No 3 Group: (13 crews missing) — Not given.

No 4 Group: (12 crews missing). Minimum number of sorties per pilot — 7. Average — 11.7.

No 5 Group: (5 crews missing). Minimum number of sorties per pilot — 8. Average — 17.

Conclusions in Preliminary Report by the Commander-in-Chief

    (a)   It is probable that the losses were due to a combination of icing, heavy laden aircraft climbing through icing cloud, which calls for a higher performance from the engines and a consequent increase in petrol consumption.

    (b)   The presence of high cloud would force some aircraft to fly higher than originally intended, with a consequent change in the speed, and possibly in the direction of the wind, resulting in navigational difficulties.

    (c)   The general impression was that flak fire was normal and there were very few reports of enemy fighter activity. In consequence a large proportion of losses from enemy action may be discounted.

    (d)   A long period of operating on a much reduced scale may have had a damping effect on crews, with the result that they were most keen to make the most of their opportunity to carry out successful attacks on their objectives when the opportunity came along. It is likely that in some cases too much time was put into trying to locate targets, with the result that there was insufficient fuel to return to bases.

The operational ranges of aircraft involved in attacks on the more distant objectives was carefully considered, and in no case was there an insufficient margin of safety.

These are Sir Richard Peirse's own conclusions and he follows on with a summary:

'To sum up, it is considered that the losses, although high, are not unduly out of proportion in view of the conditions encountered. It is calculated that a loss of approximately 25 aircraft was to be expected in the light of previous experience of attacks on the same objectives. The loss of an additional 12 can be put down to keenness on the part of crews to reach their objectives after a period of comparatively light activity, and to the prevailing weather conditions.

As forecasted the weather was entirely suitable for the operation, but in fact conditions of extreme cold were experienced, and undoubtedly the prevalence of icing in cloud had the effect of causing the less experienced crews to use up more power to keep up performance, with the resulting excessive consumption of petrol. This would appear to be borne out by reports of some aircraft being given fixes over Germany after eight hours in the air.

The operational flying experience of crews is given in para 6. This is considered to be satisfactory and the flights were within the capability of all concerned.'

This preliminary report by the Commander-in-Chief was addressed to the Chief of the Air Staff — Sir Charles Portal — and followed shortly afterwards by a final and more official rendering to which the CAS raised objection. He was not satisfied and refused to accept it. In the meantime the Prime Minister, who viewed the heavy casualties sustained on that night with grave misgiving, called for a full report . . .

'The losses sustained by the night bombers . . . have lately been very heavy . . . I have several times in Cabinet deprecated forcing the night bombing of Germany without due regard to the weather conditions. There is no particular point at this time in bombing Berlin. The losses sustained last week were most grievous. We cannot afford losses on that scale . . . losses which are acceptable in battle, or for some decisive military objective, ought not to be incurred merely as a matter of routine. There is no need to fight the weather and the enemy at the same time. It is now the duty of both Fighter and Bomber Command to re-gather their strength for the Spring. Let me have a full report about the heavy losses of bombers on the night of the last heavy raid on Berlin.'

This was addressed to the Secretary of State for Air, Sir

Archibald Sinclair, who sent it to the Air Staff for action. The immediate effect of the Prime Minister's sharp observations was that of restricting further attacks against the enemy's capital and, indeed, nothing similar to the operation of 7 November took place for many months. However, Sir Charles Portal continued to press Sir Richard Peirse for a more satisfactory explanation, rejecting the official report and pointing out certain anomalies. Portal, a highly competent Air Marshal and a former Commander-in-Chief, Bomber Command, was in a difficult situation — standing between the Prime Minister and Peirse — and defended the latter though his contempt for the document is but thinly disguised. In fact he tore it to shreds. His reply to the official report is given in full:

'I have just read your official reported dated 18 November on the subject of the losses incurred on the night of 7/8 November. The Prime Minister has asked for a report on these operations and I hoped that your report could be sent to him, but I am afraid it is not suitable, because essential information is lacking and because there are certain inconsistencies or inaccuracies. It will need a complete re-write before I can submit it. The following points call for comment:

2.   You state that the average losses when attacking Berlin are about 10 per cent and the only losses which therefore call for comment are those sustained by the Whitleys. I am sure you did not intend to imply that we must complacently expect 10 per cent losses in attacks on Berlin, especially on a night of poor visibility, combining thick cloud and a waning moon, and when there was no grave threat of attack by enemy fighters. Such an admission will certainly be read into para 3(a).

3.   I gather that in your opinion the primary cause for the exceptional losses was that the crews encountered more difficult weather conditions than had been expected from the forecasts. You state that the crews were briefed to fly high on the way out and low on return to obtain the best advantage from the forecasted winds, but that they were prevented from doing so by the presence of high convection cloud causing severe icing conditions. Information supplied by D.D.M.O. at the Air Ministry shows that the probability of thunderstorms, icing and hail was generally included in the forecasts for the night of 7/8th and that the advice offered by the Senior Meteorological Officer at your Headquarters included statements during the morning, and as late as four o'clock in the afternoon, that over the Southern North Sea there would be much convection cloud with tops rising to 15,000 to 20,000 ft and icing in cloud. It appears from this that the disproportionate losses during these operations were the result of failure to appreciate fully the extent to which

icing conditions might affect endurance rather than a faulty forecast in the weather.

4.   On your own representation (para 12) the conditions on the night of 7/8 November were such as to defeat pilots whose knowledge of long range operations was defective, but I believe that the average experience of the Captains lost was 16 operational sorties. I would therefore ask for more information as to how far the real threat of icing conditons and static was known to your Headquarters and to your subordinate Commanders. I understand that at least one Group Commander regarded the forecasted conditions as unsuitable for long-range operations and asked for permission to attack the alternative objective of Cologne. Further, I have been told that one Station Commander allowed only his most experienced pilots to proceed on these operations in view of these same conditions, with the result that he sustained no losses though the amount of petrol left in the tanks proved that even these experienced pilots found they were "near the bone". I think it is important to know whether the Group and Station Commanders generally regarded the weather conditions as entirely fit for the operations ordered, and to what extent they are allowed liberty of action in carrying out the orders.

5.   I am also concerned about the narrow margin of safety in petrol-ranges which may have been allowed, having regard to the high winds which were expected on this night. Even had the cloud conditions been somewhat less severe, the forecast winds were high enough to call into question the margin of safety over the long distance to Berlin and back. It would make this report clearer if some statement could be included as to what margins of safety were expected in the light of the forecasted conditions of cloud and wind.

6.   Will you please, therefore, resubmit the report, having my comments in mind, and include information which would provide satisfactory answers to the questions I have put, and which I am sure the Prime Minister will ask.'

Sir Charles Portal signed the above letter on 23 November. It represents a balanced and logical appraisal of the official report and it should be added that the author was a practical airman and a man highly respected for his humanity and commonsense. His concern for the unfortunate bomber crews on the night in question is obvious and there was to be no brush-off. How did Sir Richard answer his questions? The criticism implied in the letter would have worried most men and yet he calmly rejects any suggestion of lack of judgement on his part. Here is his answer, dated 2 December 1941, written demi-officially and marked 'Personal':

'Thankyou for your letter . . . commenting on my official report dated 18 November. I have been through it carefully and failed to find any inconsistencies, but I have amended it in order to provide further information on the points you raise.

2. As regards our losses on BERLIN I certainly do not regard them with any complacence, but I have dealt with facts as they are, and it is certain that with our present equipment and standard of training we will incur an average loss of approximately 10 per cent in such attacks. The figures for individual attacks of reasonable magnitude in the past have varied from five per cent to thirteen per cent, and in the last big attack on 7/8 September it was nine per cent.

3. On the night of 7/8 November enemy fighter activity, as deduced from the number of interceptions reported, was only slightly less than normal, and a considerable amount of R/T traffic was intercepted, although no "Sieg Heils" were heard. The moon was only a few days after full and and the visibility above the clouds was good. It was probably a suitable night for 'Catseye' fighters. Further, very accurate anti-aircraft fire was reported over BERLIN. A loss of at least ten per cent cannot therefore be regarded as unusual or unexpected.

4. I am, of course, constantly studying every means of reducing our operational losses, and have come to the conclusion that one of the principal factors involved is the thoroughly inadequate training of our aircrew personnel. I have written many letters on this subject and I am now sending in a comprehensive review of the present situation.

5. It is true that the primary cause for the exceptional losses was that the crews encountered more difficult weather conditions than had been expected from the forecasts. The crews were briefed to fly high on the way out and lower on the return in order to obtain the best advantage from the forecasted winds, and they were prevented from doing so by the presence of a large amount of high convection cloud causing severe icing. My senior Meteorological Officer advised me that there would be considerable convection cloud in the North Sea, but in his view it would have isolated peaks rising to 15,000 feet or even 20,000 feet, and it was thought that, with the amount of moonlight available, aircraft would not find difficulty in avoiding the peaks. In fact, the general mass of the clouds, and not only the peaks, rose to about 18,000 ft and gave rise to severe icing. Also, the clouds spread all over Germany and not merely over the North Sea. In addition, it is now thought that the wind, the forecasted speed of which was 65/70 mph, was in reality about 70/75 mph.

6. I have no doubt that the conditions on the night of 7/8 November were such as to defeat pilots whose knowledge of long

range flying was defective. Unfortunately, such pilots are found not only among the least experienced of my crews. They come to me from Flying Training Command with absolutely no knowledge or experience of the principles of long range flying, or of the correct manipulation of the correct controls. I have taken a number of steps in this Command to rectify this situation and I have asked . . . that this instruction may, in future, be given in Flying Training Command.

7.   You ask how far the threat of icing conditions and static was known here and at Groups. We were all aware of the possibility of severe icing up to 15,000 feet over the North Sea, but it was not expected that the mass of clouds would extend to 18,000 feet, nor that cloud would be general over Western Germany. These two factors must be regarded as contributing to our losses.

8.   As regards the request for an alternative target for 5 Group, this was made by A.O.C. 5 Group on the question of range, and because he was not certain of his home bases and diversions would have been difficult with so many aircraft out. Recent experience has shown that the safe operational range of the Hampden is less than that of the Wellingtons and Whitleys. In fact, we nowadays regard Berlin as beyond the range of the Hampden.

9.   It has always been my rule to give my Group Commanders authority to cancel or reduce the scale of any operation at their discretion. Although I may on occasions cancel operations myself, I never insist on their being undertaken against the advice of my Group Commanders.

10.   An investigation of the amount of fuel left in tanks after the operation has shown that, for pilots who understood how to run their engines economically, the amount of fuel carried was sufficient: and in all cases the estimated time of the flight showed a reasonable margin.'

This feeble response to the vigorous demand from the Chief of the Air Staff only stirred the pot and the Vice-Chief did not mince his words. Air Chief Marshal Sir Wilfrid Freeman had a stake in the fortunes of Bomber Command and the shaping of policy for attacking Germany: he was tireless in his efforts to provide crews with the best equipment and to keep down the casualties. One of the true 'Greats', like Sir Edgar Ludlow-Hewitt, he spoke his mind, abominated 'cover-ups' and feared no one. One reads in the Official History of the Bombing Offensive that it was deemed 'unwise to pursue the enquiry further for fear of a lack of confidence spreading to Sir Richard Peirse's subordinate commanders' but eventually the reports from the Commander-in-Chief were shown to the Prime Minister.

After nearly forty years I can still recapture the atmosphere of that night when the crews of No 405 Squadron returned to Pocklington — utterly fatigued, half frozen and disgusted. Sir Winston Churchill's succinct phrase about not fighting the weather as well as the enemy comes to mind. The Canadians lacked nothing in courage or willingness to face the enemy but there was bitter resentment over their being launched on a major operation against the German Capital in weather totally unfitted for the task. 405 was to win much honour later in the struggle and the brave Fauquier survived to become an outstanding leader, succeeding to the command of both 405 and 617 Sqdns. Like many of his countrymen he could not suffer fools and invariably led from the front: he was not a rebel but at the same time he never lacked the courage to speak his mind. He possessed qualities very similar to those of Guy Gibson when it was a matter of 'getting stuck in', inspiring others by sheer example.

We may return for a brief moment to Sir Richard Peirse's letter dated 2 December. Commanders-in-Chief are not expected to be Meteorologists; expert opinion is offered by the Senior Met. Officer attached to the Air Staff and taken into account when the C-in-C makes his final decision. At the time of this operation the information available to the Met. Staff in respect of those areas lying to the east of this Island was very limited and in my experience they did an excellent job of work. Sir Richard complains: 'the crews experienced more difficult weather than had been expected from the forecasts' yet he was advised there would be considerable convection cloud in the North Sea with isolated peaks rising to 15,000 or even 20,000 feet — and it was thought that, with the amount of moonlight available, aircraft would not find difficulty in avoiding the peaks! Meteorology in 1941 was a somewhat less exact science than it is today — or even two years after these events when 'Pampa' flights in the fast Mosquitos secured vital information on weather conditions over Germany which rendered the task of the forecaster that much easier — and no blame may be attached to Dr Spence and his staff for failing to predict cloud heights more precisely. In para 5 of his letter Sir Richard Peirse admits he was aware of 'the possibility of severe icing conditions up to 15,000 feet over the North Sea. This alone would have justified the cancelling of the Berlin operation since the performance of the Wellingtons and Whitleys left little margin above that height when fully laden with bombs and fuel. Certainly, the ice accretion experienced during the climb and resulting extra 'drag' would inhibit any attempt to go much above that level.

There were relatively few 'Catseye' fighters in 1941 though no-one may dismiss the implication; it removes some of the blame from the Meteorologists' shoulders in terms of casualties but the C-in-C had already pinned the cause as 'difficult weather conditions' and I find it hard to accept. Again, the 'very accurate anti-aircraft fire reported over Berlin' affected but a small part of the attacking force which succeeded in getting anywhere near the city. In respect of the state of training of the aircrew entering the Command (para 4) Sir Wilfrid Freeman thought it a 'damning admission' and said it was the duty of the Commander-in-Chief to train them before dispatching crews on operational missions whilst Sir Richard had 'no doubt that the conditions on the night of 7/8 November were such as to defeat pilots whose knowledge of long-range flying was defective'. So why were they sent in the light of such a depressing forecast?

Finally, we come to the percentage of casualties expected from the Berlin operations. The ten per cent figure accepted by the C-in-C, if maintained for only a short time would have spelled the decline of our bomber offensive to a point where it would have no longer made sense. Later in the war we lost many more aircraft over the Ruhr, Berlin and Nuremberg and knew we could not continue in that fashion; neither aircraft nor crews could be produced in sufficient numbers. Five per cent was the limit over a period of time and when it went higher on occasions we were very worried. No Commander on land, sea or in the air admits to planning with a set casualty rate in mind; he plans his operation to succeed with the minimum loss of the lives of his men, using every means in his power to achieve this whilst maintaining his aim. The remark in the C-in-Cs Preliminary Report where he sums up his losses 'although high, not unduly out of proportion in view of the conditions encountered' infuriated both Sir Wilfrid Freeman and Sir Charles Portal who were concerned that his statement might smack of complacency: a matter which Sir Richard instantly put right in his amplifying letter of 2 December.

After all the sound and fury had died down, and it was decided not to pursue the matter further, we have to remember thirty-seven aircraft were lost and many young lives sacrificed. Only those who have flown in the kind of weather through which the bomber force flogged its way across the North Sea, over the North German Plain to the enemy's capital, can appreciate the horrors of the night of 7 November 1941. The young officers and NCOs who manned the slow Wellingtons and Whitleys of that age did indeed fight the elements as well as the enemy — in darkness, icing cloud and temperatures down to -40 they clawed their way mile by mile back to the home bases, though many fell into the sea. Amid waves up to 20 feet in height and a surface wind gusting to forty and fifty miles an hour they had little hope of survival and the eroded fuselages litter the sea-bed to this day. My friend John Fauquier's simple yet vivid recollection of 'huge waves of solid green water lifted from the surface and carried hundreds of feet by the wind' conveys something of these nightmare conditions.

And what of Berlin — how was this great attack seen from ground level? No photographs were taken by the few aircraft which got there

— thick cloud prevented this — but we have a report from an eye witness; the Assistant United States Air Attaché, no less. This most valuable account was dispatched to our own Foreign Office via Switzerland. He records two phases in the attack: the first lasting from nine o'clock in the evening until midnight and the second from 0230 to 0430 in the early morning of 8 November. In the first phase the Wellingtons of Nos 1 and 3 Groups attacked followed by No 4 Group later. Four separate areas suffered damage, namely, Mohabit, Hansplatz, Tegel and the railway station at Lehrter with much scattering of bombs. Then follows an excellent description of the defences stressing the employment by the enemy of dummy objectives and the tactical use of searchlights to draw the bombers away from the centre of Berlin.

In their references to the Berlin operation of 7/8 November, 1941, the Official Historians have been generous: the problems confronting the then Commander-in-Chief are brought to notice: in particular Sir Wilfrid Freeman's stricture requiring the Commander-in-Chief to see that his crews were adequately trained for the task is countered by the observation that he had 'for long been the unwilling recipient of crews whose training was inadequate at all stages from elementary to advanced training'. In respect of the casualties the Historians record 'Moreover, for the Commander-in-Chief to continue the strategic air offensive without from time to time incurring the risk of heavy casualties was, of course, an impossibility. Nevertheless, it seemed to the Air Staff that very grave miscalculations had been made.' And later, 'The Commander-in-Chief's handling of the force had been called into question. Bomber Command had achieved no signal triumphs, but in its lone struggle against the enemy it had been paying a heavy price in the lives of its aircrew.' All of which lays the onus on the C-in-C but what of his subordinate Commanders — the Group 'Barons' — who according to Peirse's letter of the 2 December enjoyed a degree of local autonomy?

Sir Charles Portal's letter to Peirse, rejecting the official report rendered by the latter, states in para 4: 'I understand at least one Group Commander regarded the forecasted conditions as unsuitable for long range operations and asked permission to attack the alternative objective of Cologne.'

At this point in the war their number included such famous names as Sir John Slessor (No 5 Gp) and Sir Roderick Carr (No 4 Gp) and I would have been happy to take-off for Germany at any time under their command: such was the confidence they instilled. Sir John Baldwin commanded No 3 Bomber Group from the outset of war and was the most senior of the Group AOCs: did he speak up — as he had done in the past and notably at the time of the operations over the Heligoland Bight in December 1939? We shall never know with certainty but it is most likely in view of the contents of Portal's letter.

Admirals carried in their Flagships and Generals fighting the land battle may observe at first hand the success or failure of their plans: they are close to the battle and, up to a point, share the dangers. The Air Marshal commanding a bomber force during the last contest, with rare exceptions, exercised his authority remote from the battle ground. Only later in the war did airmen possessing operational experience graduate to the higher posts armed with the kind of knowledge denied to a generation of senior officers stemming from the First World War who could not know very much about the demands of long range penetration of the enemy's country. Through no fault of their own they had to accept information at secondhand. We see evidence of this in the arguments surrounding the precise bombing of such targets as oil plants and similar small, difficult to pinpoint objectives, vital to the German war effort. This Berlin operation, from the point of view of the forecast weather, was not grasped by authority — or so it seems to this writer — though men of outstanding ability such as Sir Charles Portal seized on every single salient feature when he questioned the worth of Sir Richard Peirse's report on the operation. In Peirse's view the young captains with relatively few operations under their belts should have displayed a standard of airmanship which is not acquired save after many sorties in varying conditions of adverse weather. We have noted the difficulty attending the taking of star and planet sights under conditions of extreme cold (it was always a problem even in more favourable circumstances) whilst the matter of flying for 'range' takes second place in the struggle against severe icing — when the stuff builds up on the leading edges and the windows become opaque, when the engines lose power owing to carburettor ice choking the inlets. In the warmth of the Command Operations Room it is easy to theorise but on the frozen flight deck men fight for survival only, at such times. That so many pressed on to Berlin and actually dropped their weapons on or near the aiming points reflects the greatest credit.

So we must end this part of the long drawn out fight over the enemy's capital city and move on to another phase. We move forward by two years to a time when the Command, possessing every advantage in crews, aircraft and associated equipment — a professional force under a thoroughly competent Commander-in-Chief — fights the Battle over Berlin culminating in the Final Assault on 24 March 1944, which, like its predecessor of 7/8 November 1941, also takes its toll, though in a vastly different fashion.

Chapter 4
Berlin as a Legitimate Target

Setting aside any question of attacking the German Capital with the aim of shattering the morale of its inhabitants, and its utter destruction as a factor in bringing the war to a speedy end, there yet existed good and ample reasons for naming it a target of high priority. It was still the largest industrial city in Germany: the many factories producing war material of all kinds played no small part in maintaining all arms of the German fighting services at a high pitch of efficiency. Similarly, Berlin was the largest inland port in the Reich and a major centre for the distribution by water, rail and road of every kind of commodity. All movements of a military nature, both troops and material, including armour and heavy guns, either moved through or were controlled by the intricate and immensely efficient transport organisation with headquarters in the City. Disruption of this traffic affected both Eastern and Western Fronts alike and it may be argued with some certainty that Bomber Command was a powerful instrument in creating delay and occasionally complete havoc, amid the many huge shunting yards set in and around the capital. Finally, the high concentration of Government Departments, Ministries and various offshoots connected with the day-to-day running of the war presented a unique target — given the right conditions of weather and visibility . . . a premise rarely fulfilled.

Spread over an area of more than thirty square miles Berlin always proved a difficult target. The air of confidence conveyed in the intelligence summaries, describing the results achieved by the crews who attacked Berlin in the first years of the war, was seldom justified; yet it could not be disproved since the night camera was not carried. It was natural enough that the Air Marshal should have faith in his own men and the crew report was accepted. Captains briefed to attack the German War Ministry in the heart of the city were expected to sort it out from the mass of surrounding buildings. That it was cloud-cuckoo stuff never occurred to anyone, and in fairness to the men who struggled through wind and weather over 600 miles of hostile territory by night there is no reason to doubt that they found Berlin — there was a lot of it. They possessed the will but not the equipment for the task and bombs did indeed fall on the chosen mark occasionally: from twelve thousand feet or lower, on a moonlight night with little cloud cover the city would be seen; the target image in the mind of the bomb aimer might easily project itself into the mish-mash below and he did his best to hit it.

There were no reliable lead-marks to guide a bomber crew to a particular section of the city — nothing to compare with the kind of assistance afforded to the enemy during the blitz of 1940 when the massed Heinkels and Dorniers flew up the Thames Estuary to attack London: a target they could not possibly miss. Only the winding and insignificant River Spree plus the lakes offered any kind of datum. The latter often misled us whilst they produced little reflection or blip on the cathode ray tube of the airborne H2S. On the radar screen Berlin showed up as a mass of clutter from which it was difficult to extract any meaningful pattern and the marker crews often sought in vain for a landmark even under the best weather conditions of broken cloud. The navigators and bomb aimers studied their radar maps before take-off and a simulator was constructed with which they might practise but, somehow, it all looked different on the night. The great dummy town laid out by the Germans to the East of the city was skilfully adapted to draw the attack away from Berlin: the enemy had developed this kind of spoof to a fine art and his efforts to save his capital reached a peak of performance when he faked target indicators which lay on the ground looking every bit like the real thing. Add to the foregoing an immense concentration of heavy gun batteries and searchlights then some idea of the task confronting the Pathfinder crews may be gained.

The peacetime population of Berlin was something in excess of four millions; a figure which increased at the commencement of the war as the Government Departments swelled and additional labour was drafted into the factories. This labour included many thousands of foreign workers gathered up from Poland, Czechoslovakia and France and included women since German mothers and housewives were not permitted to work in factories on the grounds that 'factory work might inflict moral harm upon German womanhood; not only might their psychic and emotional life be affected but also their ability to bear.' Despite the war, life in the German capital continued smoothly for the first three years and according to Albert Speer:

'Whereas by 1943 England had reduced the number of maid-servants by two thirds, nothing of the sort took place in Germany until the end of the war. Some 1.4 million women continued to be employed as household help. In addition half a million Ukrainian girls helped to solve the servant problem for party functionaries — a fact that soon caused a good deal of talk among the people.'

Evacuation of schoolchildren had begun in 1942 but it was not until a year later that the majority of schools in Berlin had closed down and the children been sent to camps in East Prussia. It was only after the destruction of Hamburg that the Berlin authorities saw the red light and speeded up the evacuation.

By March 1944 the population of the city had declined by a significant figure but the foreign population was little affected. The factories had to be kept going — there was plenty of power available both from the generating stations and the coal bunkers were only occasionally a source of anxiety; this latter being occasioned by the disruption of the transport services more than anything else. Water was present in abundance — from the Spree and the many lakes in and around Berlin. Broken supply pipes were quickly repaired and in the interim water tank cars supplied the deficiency; the fire brigades had problems during and after the raids but in general the city seldom went short of water for long.

The move of various industries to the comparative safety of the Black Forest has been exaggerated. The problems were too great: the delays inherent in such a policy could not be tolerated whilst changes in the supply and transport of essential materials imposed an additional burden on the rail and canal networks. All in all it was simpler to bear the bombing and make good the damage using the plentiful supply of forced labour. Only new manufactures, such as the V weapons, were deliberately set up in remote situations lying to the east.

For those who question the validity of Sir Arthur Harris's policy in destroying Berlin the record of the United States Army Air Force should be noted. Between 4 March 1944 and March 1945 they attacked Berlin on eighteen separate occasions. The 'city area' is named as the primary target for four attacks made during May 1944 and four more were directed against the 'Berlin area': the remainder were aimed at specific industrial targets with the accent on aircraft production, diesel plants and munition works, whilst the marshalling yards and railway stations received the odd attack. All these operations were in line with the common directive sent to Sir Arthur Harris, General Spaatz and Sir Trafford Leigh-Mallory.

Chapter 5
Harris Takes Control

The long interval between the tragic events of November 1941 and the dispatch of Sir Arthur Harris's letter to the Air Ministry on 7 December 1943, when he expressed his conviction that, given a sufficiently powerful force of Lancasters the War might be brought to a close in the following April, produced sweeping changes. It has been said that he replaced Sir Richard Peirse at a moment when the fruits of years of painstaking development were about to be gathered — increased Lancaster production, new forms of radar, better weapons, night photography and a steady flow of aircrew trained overseas — but these innovations by themselves could never have lifted the Command from its amateur status in 1941 to become the most powerful single Force in the history of this Island. A catalyst was needed and Harris filled that role: his single minded approach to the defeat of the enemy, his stubbornness in the face of those who sought to deflect him into other paths and an unrelenting drive for more effective attacks on Germany complemented the numerous improvements in equipment and tactical measures. He was rarely seen out on the Stations but his personality extended to every corner of his widely dispersed command. An awareness of an iron hand at the tiller induced confidence and whilst he may not have been loved he was most certainly respected. The tasks he laid upon us were hazardous occasionally, monotonous very often, and only rarely evoked praise in the form of somewhat bizarre signals indicating his pleasure. The Force was committed to battle on an average of four nights in each week; with penetrations by small but very effective Mosquito raids in between which kept the sirens going in Berlin. Thus, he was seldom free from stress and the constant anxiety attending the safe recovery of hundreds of aircraft — quite apart from what went on over the enemy's country.

At Squadron level we did not always understand his motives — some, indeed, were puzzling whilst the cleavage between No 5 Bomber Group and the Pathfinder Force proved painful to those who at one time or another owed loyalty to both camps. The birth of the PFF carried only what appeared to be a grudging approval whilst later in the conflict his open support of Air Marshal Cochrane — to we lesser lights — seemed to run counter to the principle 'United we stand divided we fall'. I recall the astonishment experienced when Bennett was stripped of two of his best Squadrons to boost

Cochrane's own Group: they were literally whipped away at very short notice and there was gloom around the place. Was it because he was dissatisifed with Bennett or that he thought the latter's image was too great? Bennett, never one to exercise the utmost tact, disagreed with his Chief over the problems of marking Berlin; refusing to accept that a low-level marking technique proposed by Cochrane could succeed. Certainly, Bennett knew a great deal about marking that city but it made no odds whatever — he crossed his Chief on a sensitive point and that was something Harris would not tolerate. Cochrane was a brilliant officer with more faith in the rapier than in the bludgeon — a belief well demonstrated in the successful bombing of pin-point targets — but Bennett carried a far heavier responsibility and where the going was rough the Pathfinders were sent in. The elite force so firmly rejected by Sir Arthur was to find ultimate expression in Cochrane's Group, whilst the matter of Berlin did not lie within its capability.

The Battles of the Ruhr and Hamburg during the summer of 1943 had demonstrated the immense striking power of Bomber Command employing the latest forms of radar equipment. The phenomenal accuracy of 'Oboe' had resulted in the devastation of Essen and similar cities lying within the huge conurbation set in the Ruhr Valley. Over Hamburg the airborne H2S, though less accurate than 'Oboe', had played a part since the geographical features, combining clearly separated areas of land and water, produced the best possible conditions for its use. In four major heavy bomber operations the city and port had been incinerated whilst the casualties had been relatively light. Neither of these Battles was fought as a single engagement though the Hamburg operations were more concentrated than those directed against the Ruhr when weather and other considerations precluded such a course of action. However, following the resounding success of the Hamburg operation Bomber Command was approaching the high noon of its offensive: Berlin, lying hundreds of miles to the east would, during the four months in which it lay under repeated attacks, demand a great sacrifice of bomber crews; whilst Nuremberg would ring down the curtain on 30 March with nigh on a hundred crews killed or missing. Never again would we sustain the cruel losses which marked the early months of 1944.

Sir Arthur's conviction that he could end the war in the space of a few months was total; otherwise the final battle for the enemy's capital city would not have taken place. The forces ranged against us were increasing daily and the margin between a monthly production figure of two hundred and twelve Lancasters and an expected loss rate of one hundred and seventy-one was narrow indeed allowing little for a shortfall in production or an increase in casualties. And what of the American contribution? They could do nothing to help at this stage: such a long penetration in daylight without escorting fighters would have been murderous. Fighter Command was power-less — the transition from defence to attack, in terms of carrying the offensive deep into Germany, had produced no change in their posture — and this was a source of frustration to General Arnold who could not 'reconcile the helplessness of his own bombers with the relative inactivity of "thousands" of aircraft in Fighter Command'. There were fifteen hundred aircraft in Fighter Command largely retained for the defence of this country but the day had long since passed when a second mass onslaught by German bombers was to be feared. The Americans were critical of our inability to provide cover for our bombers beyond the French coastline and even more outspoken concerning the lack of co-ordination between Bomber and Fighter Commands: 'Why,' asked General Arnold, 'were not the Mustangs of Fighter Command used offensively?' He had good reason to be sore — the October attack by the 8th AF on Schweinfurt had cost them sixty Forts lost over Germany and a further hundred and twenty suffered battle damage: their Thunderbolt escort withdrew on reaching Aachen, the limit of their range. Thus, in the absence of an adequate number of long range fighters the Americans could do nothing in support of Harris's plan to wipe out Berlin. Bomber Command had no choice but to go it alone.

Why was it so important to wreck Berlin 'from end to end'? From the point of view of the Air Staff in Whitehall it wasn't: there were other priorities with Schweinfurt at the top of the list yet Sir Arthur was not persuaded that any single one of these targets matched Berlin in importance: ball bearings at Schweinfurt and oil installations at various other locations, even if the object of successful attacks, could never make the same impact on German morale as that stemming from an all-out effort against Berlin. And so, despite the opposition encountered from the Deputy Chief of the Air Staff and the Director of Bomber Operations who sought to tie the Commander-in-Chief to his current Directive, the Battle commenced in mid-November, 1943. It was to last for four months culminating in the operation of 24 March: no less than sixteen heavy attacks were made and an equal number of minor attacks by Mosquitos of Bennett's Light Night Striking Force. During this period other attacks, interspersed with those on Berlin, were made on a variety of targets including the major cities of Frankfurt (four attacks), Stuttgart (four attacks), Leipzig (twice), the Ruhr, Schweinfurt, and several more culminating in the dispatch of seven hundred and ninety-five bombers to Nuremberg on 30 March from which no less than ninety-seven failed to return. All these are grouped within the period of the Battle proper and are reckoned part of it.

Whilst the strongly reinforced fighter Squadrons of the GAF took their toll this was not the only cause of the casualties sustained and on the night of 16 December thirty-four bombers crashed on return to this country whilst attempting to find their bases in foggy conditions. This was one of the few occasions when the 'heavies' were dispatched in extremely dubious weather — even at take-off visibility was poor — and a cancellation was expected — but they went to Berlin. On the return low cloud with poor visibility beneath produced the worst situation I can recall and crews baled out at low height with the inevitable result . . . one hundred and thirty officers and NCOs lost their lives over England. These were early days in the Battle and as time went by the pace accelerated; there was no shortage of crews and replacement Lancasters and Halifaxes were flown in to fill the gaps.

From the outset of the Berlin battles strong pressure by the Deputy Chief of the Air Staff, Sir Norman Bottomley, had been brought to bear upon Bomber Command to attack the ball-bearing industry at Schweinfurt: this was a sensitive target since the output of these indispensable components affected every facet of the German war effort — and in particular the production of aircraft engines. Thus, a successful raid on the heart of this process could help in no small measure to reduce the flow of fighter aircraft from the German factories, which were turning out replacements at the rate of between six and seven hundred a month. The Americans had seized on this supposedly key manufacture quite early and suffered massive casualties in their daylight attacks — through lack of protective fighter cover on 17 August and 14 October. They were unlikely to make a further attempt until such cover was forthcoming but in the meantime Schweinfurt was well within the competence of Sir Arthur's force operating by night.

Prior to the opening of the Berlin onslaught on 18 November 1943, Sir Arthur Harris wrote two important letters — one to the Prime Minister spelling out the record of the Command to date in destroying German towns and the second to the Air Ministry detailing his plan for bringing the war to an end through an acceleration of the bombing offensive.* The first letter, dated 3 November, commences with a reference to a suggestion made by the Prime Minister after the '1,000' raid on Cologne, whereby twenty German cities should be proscribed by public announcement — and to proceed thereafter with their systematic destruction. For various reasons this suggestion was not followed up — weather and tactical considerations plus the inevitable build-up of enemy defences once apprised of our intentions. Instead a more elastic procedure was adopted and Sir Arthur continues with a long list of targets divided into three sections, viz., Those 'Virtually Destroyed', those 'Seriously Damaged' and a third selection of those merely 'Damaged'. In addition he states: 'many industrial targets in occupied countries serving the German war effort have been very heavily damaged,

* PRO Air 20/842

e.g., Renault, Gennavilliers, Le Creusot, Montlucon, Montbeliard etc, etc, and stresses the fact that 'most of this damage has been done since March this year, when the "heavies" came into full production and Oboe, H2S and the Pathfinders served to concentrate the effort.'

After that he lists the order of priority further targets commencing with Berlin and ending with: 'tidying up the Ruhr — Solingen, Witten and Leverkusen'.

'I feel certain that Germany must collapse before this programme which is more than half completed already, has proceeded much further. We have not far to go. We must get the U.S.A.A.F. to wade-in in greater force. If they will only get going according to plan and avoid such disastrous diversions as Ploesti, and getting "nearer" to Germany from the Plains of Lombardy (which are further from 9/10th of war productive Germany than is Norfolk) we can get through it very quickly. We can wreck Berlin from end to end if the U.S.A.A.F. will come in on it. It will cost between 400–500 aircraft. It will cost Germany the war.'

Sir Charles Portal received a copy and was invited to pass it to the Secretary of State. It is not a normal procedure for even a Commander-in-Chief to write directly to the Prime Minister — unless the CAS agrees the draft beforehand and Sir Arthur's action is evidence of the degree of confidence reposed in him by Mr Churchill. The string of successes which had marked Sir Arthur's eighteen months in command, to which we may add a forcefulness and strength of character in dealing with every possible contingency, had secured for him a unique position. Mr Churchill on more than one occasion had invited certain highly placed individuals to write to him personally (General Wingate provides an example) short-circuiting the 'usual channels' which might, possibly, have killed a good idea stone dead or at least delayed consideration, and in this case Sir Arthur cut clear across the bows of the Air Staff: their priority list did not begin with Berlin but with Schweinfurt; a very significant point. Nevertheless, that was not how Sir Arthur saw it. In his view victory could be achieved speedily by crushing attacks on a range of cities, with Berlin bang in the centre.

Schweinfurt bounced back and forth over the net: Sir Arthur was aware of its importance and equally aware of the interest of Sir Charles Portal and his Deputy Chief of Air Staff Sir Norman Bottomley — a former Senior Air Staff Officer at HQ Bomber Command. With Sir Norman it became almost a crusade: he dispatched a number of 'Directed' letters to Sir Arthur, skilfully prepared by The Director of Bomber Operations — Air Commodore Sidney Bufton — all of which received cool replies from Sir Arthur who refused to budge an inch from his declared belief that his own way was best. The Directive of 14 January, signed by Sir Norman is a masterpiece of drafting, explaining the background in the first section, coaxing in places and containing a firm request for the Commander-in-Chief to get on with the destruction of 'the town of Schweinfurt and the ball bearing factories it contains'. Any objections raised by Sir Arthur to this document were finally overruled by a Directive dated 28 January equating the German aircraft production (fighters) with ball bearing production. This was a Combined Offensive Directive addressed to Sir Arthur Harris, General Spaatz and Sir Trafford Leigh-Mallory but at para 6 Bomber Command was instructed to accord first priority to Schweinfurt. Sir Arthur was not moved. He had no faith in quick remedies: Schweinfurt was an obvious target and had been so for a long time; the ability of the Germans to disperse their key manufacturing plants to more remote areas was well known and in any event he viewed all studies by the Ministry of Economic Warfare with the gravest suspicion and cited other examples such as the German Railway system and even the Möhne Dam. In his opinion there was no easy solution — no lynch pin to knock out which might end the war quickly. There was but one method — and that to hammer the Germans into submission by repeated attacks. His fame and stature were such that few cared to challenge his belief — and the Chief of the Air Staff was reluctant to cross swords with a Commander-in-Chief who had prosecuted the offensive so vigorously that his name was a byword for offensive action where it hurt the enemy most — at the heart and sinews of his homeland. The nation as a whole was solidly behind Sir Arthur and he received much encouragement from within the Whitehall corridors; as the following message would seem to indicate,

Immediate. 24 Nov. 43.
'Following for AOC-in-C from Secretary of State.
My warmest congratulations to you and all ranks serving under your command on the two crushing attacks upon the Nazi citadel. Berlin is not only the home of Prussian militarism and the capital of Nazi Government but it is also the greatest single centre of war industry in Germany. Often before your Squadrons have struck it hard. The most convincing measure of their success has been the huge deployment of the enemy's resources for its defence. Nevertheless, your attacks these last two nights have reached a new level of power and concentration and have proved that however much he may marshal his guns, searchlights and fighters, the enemy cannot match your skill and resource or the valour and determination of your crews.'

The above refers to the attacks of 22 and 23 November on

consecutive nights; the first being an exceptionally heavy assault off-loading 2,500 tons over Berlin: a night I recall without difficulty because Wing Commander John Hilton, DSO, DFC, to whom I handed over command of No 83 Pathfinder Squadron only a week earlier was lost over the city, and I returned to hold the fort for another two weeks until a replacement in the shape of Jock Abercrombie arrived. He too, alas, lost his life not long afterwards — during the Berlin attack of 1 January. Both these officers were exceptional men: John Hilton was among the very first to volunteer for Pathfinder duties and completed a full tour of duty with 83 Sqdn as a Flight Commander. His pleasure at being picked to command his old Squadron was quietly evident and his loss deeply felt. Abercrombie, a forceful Scot, came from No 5 Group where he had already made his mark as an outstanding leader.

Returning to the arguments surrounding Schweinfurt as a priority target, Sir Maurice Dean, Permanent Under Secretary in the Air Ministry, and earlier in his distinguished career Deputy Secretary, Control Office for Germany and Austria immediately after the War sets the seal on Sir Arthur Harris's belief. He writes:*

'After the great but disastrous American attack on Schweinfurt in October 1943 the Germans became convinced, reasonably enough, that a concerted attack was to be made on their ball-bearing industry. They at once took three important steps. They ordered new machinery, they arranged for the industry to be dispersed, and they also arranged for a census of existing stocks, with severe penalties for false returns. The result of the census astonished them. There were eight million bearings in stock, enough with appropriate redistribution to keep the armaments industry going for months. The Germans had had no idea of this. Other attacks on the factories followed, notably those by Bomber Command and the United States Air Force in February 1944, but as far as military needs were concerned the outcome was nugatory — not a truck suffered from lack of bearings. A number of important reflections arise from this episode:

1.   The basic reasoning was wrong. Had Schweinfurt been a real Heel of Achilles for Germany, and had it been destroyed in toto, Germany would not on this account have been gravely or even seriously embarrassed. As Webster and Frankland comment, the resources of a brave, determined and resource-ful state would have been concentrated on the problem. Buffer stocks or not, Germany would soon have had bearings running out of her ears.

2.   The limits of knowledge. If Germany in 1943 was ignorant of the basic statistics of her own ball-bearing industry it was

* Extract from *The Royal Air Force and Two World Wars* by Sir Maurice Dean.

scarcely likely that British Intelligence authorities, including
the Ministry of Economic Warfare could do better.
3. The effect on Bomber Command. The Commander-in-Chief
put no trust in economic predictions about ball-bearings.
They were professionals, he was not. Nevertheless in the
event, history shows that in this matter they were wrong and
he was right. Anyway, from this, as from other experiences
such as with molybdenum, he was led to a deep distrust of
what he called 'panacea' policies; that is short cuts to
victory.'

Albert Speer, however, regarded the attack on the ball-bearing
industry as a serious blow to the German war effort. Following the
American attack of 17 August 1943 he records the loss in production
as 38 per cent and stresses the difficulties attending any relocation of
the factories. He makes no mention of any huge stocks held against
such an emergency but bewails the fact that their reserves were
consumed in six to eight weeks; after which

'the sparse production was carried daily from the factories to the
assembly plants, often in knapsacks. In those days we anxiously
asked ourselves how soon the enemy would realise that he could
paralise the production of thousands of armament plants merely
by destroying five or six relatively small targets.'

Speer was correct in his assumptions. The second attack by the
American 8th Air Force on 14 October 1943 proved devastating;
enormous damage was done to the Schweinfurt plants which lost over
sixty per cent of production though not without the heavy loss of sixty
Fortresses out of a total of two hundred and ninety-one attacking.
Considerable pressure had been exerted on our Commander-in-Chief
by the Air Staff to make follow-up attacks, but he resisted all
attempts to deflect him from his aim of destroying the major cities on
the road to Berlin. Schweinfurt he believed to be a 'panacea' target
only; his goal was the 'Big City' and it was not until February of the
following year that Bomber Command attacked the ball-bearing
industry.
By his somewhat contemptuous dismissal of the Ministry of
Economic Warfare assessment of the importance of Schweinfurt and
the ball-bearing industry Sir Arthur strengthened even further his
right to determine what was best for Bomber Command and the
conduct of the Strategic Air Offensive in particular. In respect of the
second paragraph of the Combind Directive, which accorded equal
priority to ball-bearings and fighter aircraft production he could fairly
claim that Berlin was a most legitimate target. The eight major
attacks delivered during November and December 1943, involving

3,646 successful sorties and a bomb weight of 14,000 tons had wrought enormous damage over a wide area of the city. No less than ninety-eight industrial concerns had suffered varying degrees of destruction including many factories engaged in the manufacture of aircraft engines and components, electrical and wireless equipment and a whole range of products essential to the German war effort. In addition rail and road communications, public utilities, Ministerial and public buildings and military installations had all sustained appreciable damage. Devastation, as confirmed by day photographic cover, extended over an area of 2,757 acres representing approximately twenty per cent of the fully built up zones. The aircraft firms of BMW, Argus, Dornier and Heinkel had all been hit. The total of aircraft missing from these operations was one hundred and eighty-three.

The Bomber Command Quarterly Intelligence Summary covering this period forecasts 'a long and arduous fight' with indications that

'victory in one of the greatest battles of all time either on land, sea or air, is going to be won, and won at a very reasonable cost in relation to achievement.' Further, 'in view of the greatly strengthened German defences, it would not have been unreasonable to expect an increasing rate of loss as the battle progressed, but, in fact, the loss measured in percentage of aircraft missing to those despatched since the beginning of November is less than three quarters the rate that obtained prior to November.'

The figure of one hundred and eighty-three was indeed small for Berlin but these were early days: with the turn of the year the situation changed markedly as the Germans put forth everything they had in terms of night fighters and by the end of March the North German Plain was to be littered with the bones of burnt-out Lancasters, Halifaxes and Stirlings. Nevertheless the Summary exudes confidence . . . 'Damage throughout the city is so vast that it is not practical to enumerate it here in detail . . .' This Summary was for distribution to the higher staffs both inside the Command and Whitehall and if it was to be believed the omens looked promising.

The Opposition

The destruction of Hamburg had made a profound impact on the Germans and it was only logical to assume that Berlin would be next in line for an all-out assault. In the past great reliance had been placed on the Flak Regiments of the Luftwaffe which boasted huge establishments to man the 88mm, 105mm and later the 128mm batteries sited along the approach paths and around the perimeter of the city. The heavy armaments had a psychological effect; Krupps guns had outshot all competitors since the Franco-Prussian War of 1870 and the slick '88s' had filled a universal role since the beginning of the present hostilities; originally designed for tank warfare they had been quickly adapted for anti-aircraft use and there was none better at the business. Predicted fire up to 20,000 ft could be lethal and the grouping of batteries, loosing off salvoes of a dozen or more shells, brought down many a bomber; a near miss was often sufficient since the razor edged fragments moving at high velocity penetrated the wings and fuselage with comparative ease. Over a million men were employed in the many flak and searchlight formations to which we may add the requirements of a vast civil defence organisation: thus, Germany was, in effect, fighting a war on three fronts — in the East, in Italy and over the homeland. Hard pressed to offset the appalling casualties on the Russian Front whilst keeping Kesselring's army at strength in Italy, any dilution in the quality of her manpower must necessarily fall on the home front, where the deficiencies were met by the use of prisoners of war and the drafting of boys aged fifteen and sixteen years of age. Similarly, the urgent need to increase the strength of the Luftwaffe night fighters resulted in the switching of bomber pilots to this role; this latter measure proved very successful.

The superiority of the fighter element over the ground defences had been clearly demonstrated over the past two years: the flak gunners, previously occupying a primary role, could never hope to achieve the successes which marked the advent of the fully equipped radar guided Me 110G and the powerful Ju 88 in ever increasing numbers. Their Naxos radar, designed to 'home' on the H2S transmissions from the bombers proved a thorn in the side of the Command and one not easily removed despite the ascendency of 100 Group, a formation created solely for the exploitation of Radio Countermeasures, and one which contributed vastly to the reduction of various forms of German radio and radar identification, early warning and control of the searching fighters. Despite these advances there were occasions when the heavy Flak came into its own once again. Firstly, in a situation where a small number of Pathfinders — ahead of the main force and thus presenting single targets for the massed ground artillery — drew unto themselves the full orchestra of searchlights and guns, predicted accurately on the approach and followed through to the 'kill'. The best example I can quote occurred over Cologne in 1943 when a succession of marking aircraft were singled out and held in the top of a giant flat cone of white light. Rapid salvoes aimed into the intersecting beams destroyed two Pathfinders, missed the third and took the fourth in line — a unique display of co-operation between these two elements and a night to remember. My own crew, backing up the early markers, came through without a scratch: we were lucky. The arrival of the main force of bombers quickly swamped the defences and then it was a case of 'the mixture as before' with the heavy flak firing a box barrage into the bomb release point.

Ground speed was an important factor in the success or failure of the flak gunners on a given night. A strong headwind for the return favoured the gunners, increasing the time bracket in which the aircraft's course, height and speed could be assessed and fed into the predictor. The straggler, flying over a cloud layer and unsure of his position, was often an easy victim: the first indication of danger being the arrival or six or more heavy anti-aircraft shells which ringed or 'bracketed' the aircraft — an ugly situation and one to scare the pants off most of us. A second salvo followed the first so quickly that evasive action was barely possible though on one occasion I dropped wheels and flaps turning on to a reciprocal course with the control column thrust forward to lose height in the minimum time. This foxed the enemy and by the time he had sorted out the situation we had got clear. Heavy flak was calculated to be a deterrent — the crack of the bursting shells accompanied by a ruddy coloured flash was something we all remember long after other features of the bombing-run have been forgotten whilst its counterpart, the light flak weapon was murder at low altitudes and responsible for the death of numerous crews 'letting down' over the enemy coast on the way out, believing all was safe . . . and by low altitudes I mean anything up to four thousand feet. I recall one such incident — a Stirling flying below me as we cleared the French coast in bright moonlight with the waters of the English Channel visible — a few miles to go and another 'Op' behind us. I was at about six thousand feet, nose down and showing 240 knots on the air speed indicator with the Stirling slightly ahead and below me. I saw the line of the tall cliffs and the flurry of foam beneath — then a single light flak gun opened up, the red and green blobs of his incendiary shells streaming ahead to catch the lumbering Stirling which burst into flames and went into the sea only a few hundred yards from the shore. After that I was more cautious when approaching such a coastline: but these were early days and there were lessons to be learned.

Flak was something we could see — it lay ahead, the twinkling bursts clearly observed through the forest of waving searchlight beams — and because it was seen it lost something of its frightfulness. Like the Ruhr, the Berlin defences were disposed in depth, increasing in intensity as we neared the city, and we knew the form; the night fighter was another matter entirely — the unknown quantity in the equation. He could be anywhere — above, behind and below or, as I experienced on one very special occasion, flying parallel only a few hundred yards away. By January of 1944 the night fighter element had swollen massively: the record of 'kills' over the past few months was impressive and, though late in the day, the enemy began to realise the full potential of his single and twin engined fighters. In the first three months of the year they offered a challenge we could barely answer; 'window', that splendid gift from the scientists, had but a short life and served us well at Hamburg and other targets attacked in that period. We did, in fact, continue to drop it throughout the Battle for Berlin but its powers declined as the enemy varied his wavelengths and brought new devices into service. Thus, whilst the directed twin engined fighter continued to be employed, though in smaller numbers, a new generation of night-fighters — single engined and free to operate at discretion — entered the struggle: the 'free-lance' Me 109 and the Focke-Wulf 190 would, finally, swing the defensive battle against us.

Although new techniques and fresh tactics, such as cleverly devised 'spoof' raids to mislead the enemy, had been introduced, and the strength of the Command was approaching the 1,000 mark, the performance of the bomber remained static, and no improved armament was forthcoming to replace the antediluvian turret guns of .303 calibre. The heavy turrets — hydraulically operated — contained little more than pea-shooters when set against the effective cannons of the attacking night fighter. It was too late in the day for a wholesale change and higher authority was more concerned with increasing the bomb load of the Lancaster than improving its defences. This evident weakness was to outlive the war.

The increase of another three thousand pounds of bomb load affected the Lancaster markedly at a time when an improved performance in terms of speed and manoeuvrability could have been a factor in reducing the casualty rate. Much time and effort had gone into an endeavour to produce a more offensive attitude on the part of the crews — notably at the instigation of Air Marshal Cochrane in No 5 Group — and particularly among that stalwart breed — the air gunners of Bomber Command. Fire first, freely and often was the cry but, like the philosophy of the 'mutually defensive' bomber formation of December 1939 over the Heligoland Bight, it wasn't the answer: in fact, we might have been much better off relieved of the heavy turrets but given another thirty or forty knots at altitude. As it was the Lancaster groaned its way to Berlin incapable of any fast evasive action when opposed by the nimble free-lance fighters which appeared in ever increasing numbers as the Battle progressed. It was, indeed, a very uneven contest and once detected, followed and attacked the future for the bomber crew was bleak. The margin of speed enjoyed by the night fighter gave him every advantage. On a dark night he could follow his contact at an interval of a thousand yards abiding his time and choosing his moment then — opening his throttles slide quickly beneath the unsuspecting bomber and open up with his twin cannon — set to near vertical — and rip it apart.

Positioned where nothing could touch him, it was a matter of cold calculated destruction of his opponent.

I saw the early free lances over Dortmund in mid 1943 — two Focke-Wulf 190s flying at my own height amid the flak and searchlights, seemingly indifferent to what was going on around them, and at the time I thought it madness — a 'one-off' — but the idea was to grow and by January 1944 they were operating in droves on the road to Berlin. Whilst they possessed little in the way of radar guidance they had no difficulty in locating the bomber stream given general direction from ground control. The size of the bomber force alone made it relatively simple and a single transit of the long drawn out procession of four engined bombers was enough — the succession of slip stream air turbulences revealed all and they could turn into the trailing air bumps to follow up the attackers some distance ahead. Again, once near the target their prey would appear stark against the fire and smoke of the burning city and from then on it was murder — legitimate, certainly, and simple in execution.

The kind of Directive sent to the Commanders of the British and American Bomber Commands, which named the German fighter aircraft producing factories as an equal 'first priority' with the ball-bearing plants at Schweinfurt, made good sense. The mass production of fighter aircraft was Germany's last throw: the damage done by both ourselves and our American colleagues was significant and yet the enemy never faltered in the dispatch of replacements for his front-line Squadrons. In their determination to defend Berlin the Germans were fighting their own Battle of Britain — and fighting it with the same tenacity and guts which had characterised that famous engagement. Nothing was left undone which *could* be done by human effort — even the creation of a dummy city some miles away from Berlin, complete in all major features including the open space of the Templehof airfield. Dummy target indicators were set off in the centre of this dummy city — to draw the bombs away from Berlin and overall swarmed the mass of night fighters — both twin and single engine. The kind of offensive action we offered to reduce the bomber casualties was small — Serrate equipped Beaufighters and Mosquitos, never more than a handful, flew in the bomber stream — and were successful in the face of great difficulties. We, in the heavies sweating it out, were grateful but the scale was too small: we had reached a stage where we needed to be escorted by night as, later on, we would be escorted by daylight over the invasion beaches and against short range targets in support of the Armies.

The Crews

The Battle raged from November to the end of March and some thirty-nine major attacks were made including the sixteen on Berlin.

What of the men who fought it? More than a thousand aircraft lost represents more that seven thousand young men lost and as the Official History puts it the Command 'turned over its strength'. It is for the record that the final attack on Berlin by a massive force was conducted largely by 'hostilities only' officers of very junior status and the non-commissioned officers, who formed the bulk of the bomber crews. In many instances their experience of flying generally was not great, whilst their experience of operational flying was small indeed. Trained initially in the overseas establishments provided by Canada, South Africa, Australia and New Zealand they filtered through the Operational and Conversion Units in this country before arriving at their front-line Squadrons. Flung into this, one of the most savage of all Bomber Command's many battles, they yet maintained the honour and record of Squadrons wearing insignia and mottoes dating from the First World War. A young bomber captain setting out for Berlin with six crew members behind him carried a great responsibility for the lives and well-being of the men who flew with him. Determination and courage we take for granted but coolness under fire and an instinctive reaction to danger come more easily with experience — even a 'second dicky' trip with the Flight Commander meant much but at the height of the battle few possessed this advantage. The best Squadron Commanders were loathe to send a totally inexperienced crew into the maelstrom but when a maximum effort was called then all had to go. The days of the casual-seeming Short Service Officer who took on all comers were long past and it was another generation of Pilot Officers and NCOs who flogged their bombers to the 'Big City'. All of which brings me to the matter of morale and I doubt seriously whether it was ever in danger: there was no lack of volunteers for Bomber Command. I know of one instance only of an officer captain off-loading his 'cookie' over the Channel — but he was no tyro: he was a Flight Lieutenant of mature years who insisted his aircraft was performing badly on the outward crossing and he used his discretion. Subsequent to this incident I had no further grounds for complaint concerning this officer and he went missing eventually. On the other side of the ledger I know of at least half a dozen instances of captains carrying on after failure of quite important pieces of equipment including an engine! Turret failures were common, leaving the aircraft minus half its guns but these were not reckoned serious enough to abandon the sortie whilst failure of the gunners' heated suits, the inter-communication circuits and even oxygen supply were all accepted as part and parcel of the game. I recall clearly the morning after Nuremberg — when I visited a squadron which had suffered heavy casualties — and nobody wished to discuss it: if Nuremberg had been called again that night every man would have gone cheerfully.

Some writers have dwelt at length on the subject of morale among

Harris's men viewing it objectively and expressing commendable concern for the attitudes and state of mind of crews dispatched night after night to bomb Germany. Many endured terrible ordeals but in my experience morale was never a problem in Bomber Command and cases of LMF (lack of moral fibre) were exceedingly rare. Considering the many thousands of young men who crewed the Lancasters, Halifaxes and Stirlings — the Wellingtons, Hampdens and Blenheims of the earlier period and the Mosquitos of the Pathfinder Force it is certain that not all were cast in the same mould — yet the Commander-in-Chief was well served. Squadron and Flight Commanders set the pattern, occasionally backed by a Station Commander of the calibre of Group Captain Gus Walker, that paladin among senior officers of his day. Air Marshals and the like meant little to the bomber crews — they came and they went — back to Group or Command HQ, to the warmth of the Ops Room and the solid comforts of a Headquarters Mess — but the Squadron Commander was a live, thrusting individual who flew, ate and drank with them. He was the man who briefed them for the night's operations: he called the tune and had the power to make life hell on occasions. He knew the form. Men like Don Bennett and Sir Basil Embry were exceptional and much respected for their past achievements but for the most part the Air Marshal remained a distant personage remote from the blood and guts of the road to Berlin. Cochrane was outstanding as a Commander, possessing great talent, but he enjoyed unusual privileges and contrived to set his own Group apart: I served under him on two occasions and admired his ability to shake sense into what seemed at first to be insoluble difficulties. The coldness attributed to his character stemmed from reserve: I never heard him raise his voice or display any kind of emotion but he was as friendly as they come and a good listener.

Our Commander-in-Chief did not visit his Stations and Squadrons save on very rare occasions — he came to Syerston at the time I had 106 and there must have been other visits — but for the whole of his tenure of command he remained a legendary figure — unique and awe inspiring — to John Smith and Bill Brown on the muddy East Anglian airfields. I have seen four thousand pound bombs (cookies) standing beside the Lancaster, prior to winching up into the long bomb bay, bearing crudely written slogans such as 'from Bert to Adolf with love' and others less printable. Few had ever seen 'Bert' yet they scrawled his name on the steel casing as if he lived just down the road — and in a sense did so.

The aircrew called him 'Butch' and I have known a captain fly sorties over and above his statutory limit out of pure affection for the burly Chief he had never clapped eyes on. I do not exaggerate nor does this statement come out of the fog of nearly forty years — it happened and it was a Pathfinder crew whose captain led by five sorties over and above his crew total. This was the result of his flying a number of second pilot trips early in his operational career. He asked me if he might see his crew out to sixty sorties, and pleaded hard, so that it was done and all went off on their end-of-tour together. For reasons I cannot explain the crews went along with 'Butch' — they admired him — and I doubt whether the many thousands of documents lying in the Public Record Office will assist the earnest researcher looking for the answer: it isn't on paper and never will be. You had to be there to gauge its significance.

The Battle which raged from November to March 1944 drained the life-blood from the Command: cold facts support this statement. In the face of steadily mounting opposition losses were inevitable though none the less grievous and as a consequence some dilution of quality was to be expected. The raw crew who arrived one morning only to be posted missing a few days later were not always victims of their own lack of experience: our casualties were evenly distributed. The old hands, now few in number, would react quicker to a situation but in the thickly concentrated bomber stream chance played a big part. The will to fight on when attacked, to use every trick and turn to defeat the enemy fighter; to stay with the aircraft when there was the least possibility of getting the crew home was strong in all the young captains and it often paid dividends. Nursing a battered Halifax or Lancaster back across the North Sea with dead or wounded men in the fuselage was common enough and the experiences of Flight Lieutenant R. I. Hudson, rear gunner of a Lancaster are memorable . . .

'With the exception of a near miss with a Halifax crossing from starboard to port at the same height on leaving the English Coast the first leg of the course to the target had been quiet. Once across the enemy coast some random flak was encountered and twice below us a stream of pin points of light indicated an air combat in the lower level of the bomber stream. We had plenty of height and my sympathy went out to the Halifaxes doomed to fly at a lower altitude. This false feeling of security was to be shattered within the hour — and mercifully unknown at the time.

As we turned on the final leg to the target there was plenty of evidence that the enemy was well aware of the location of the bomber stream. Anti-aircraft fire was getting heavier and more concentrated: enemy night fighter activity was becoming more marked. On either side of us air combats were taking place in increasing numbers — mid-air explosions took place and the slash of lights on the ground below from jettisoned bomb loads became frequent. Just ahead of us the Mid-upper Gunner reported a Lancaster coned by searchlights and bracketed by heavy flak bursts: from my position in the tail I felt the movement as the skipper eased away to port to keep us in the dark part of the sky. Then the centre of activity moved toward us and the mid-upper gunner warned us of a night fighter out on the port side. Swinging my tail turret I carefully scanned the starboard side — to avoid being caught unawares by his buddy coming in from the dark side — a favourite ploy. I was right — a Ju 88 swung in to attack from less than 500 yards — the old trick was working and although I was not properly sighted I pulled the triggers in a vain attempt to intimidate the attacker but the stream of .303 from my four guns was well behind the fighter as he closed on us. I saw the flicker of fire from his wings and a solid stream of 20mm cannon shells hit the starboard tail and fin — ran down the fuselage and across the mainplane. So close were the explosions of his shells that for a split second I was blinded by the flash. I remember thinking that the sound of the striking shells was as if a child had run along a paling fence with a stick. Above the increased roar of the engines, as the skipper reacted to the attack, I could hear explosions inside the fuselage and the aircraft shuddered with the impact. I doubted whether our aircraft could remain in the air after such punishment and consoled myself with the thought that this mattered little if, by chance, the 'cookie' was hit.

The aircraft was still in a steep dive to starboard; it should by now have changed to a climb as the next sequence of the defensive corkscrew manoeuvre and I realised that matters were taking a turn for the worse. My turret was still swung to starboard and out beyond the fin I could see, through the clear vision panel, a streak of flame from a burning engine. The intercom was dead and there was no reply when I pressed the attack-lights buttons. It was time to get clear of my turret. My parachute was stowed in a container near the rear spar and the first thing was to get into the fuselage. Momentarily, I experienced panic when the hydraulic controls failed to rotate the turret but by pressing down the manual rotation handle I was able to engage it in the rotation ring and swing the cupola into the fore and aft line of the fuselage. Hampered by my bulky Taylor heated-suit I reached for the wire which tripped the sliding doors at my back; one slid open but the other refused to budge. With a massive effort I screwed half round and felt a wave of relief as I got my shoulder behind the edge and forced it open. The Lanc. was still hurtling down and the force of the dive tended to pull me back hard into my turret seat. I pushed back, lifted my feet clear of the ammunition servo unit and kicked out wildly in an effort to get free and at that moment the aircraft gave an almighty lurch and came out of the dive so that I shot out into the fuselage, coming to a halt with a sickening crunch up against the step under the mid-upper turret. In the process I lost my helmet and one flying boot. The latter was of little consequence but the loss of my oxygen mask could be serious. I pulled myself up and looked around.

Up front I saw the glow of lights from the navigator's position and took comfort; there was still life aboard the aircraft and I had not been left to my fate. Absolute chaos reigned in the fuselage. The rear door had been opened by the Wireless Operator who was standing ready to abandon the aircraft. In the glow from the burning wing I spotted that he had hooked on his 'chute by one clip only and it was resting slantwise across his chest. Whether by accident or in the confusion he had pulled the D ring and the silk from his chute was billowing about his feet. He now stood by the door, holding himself by one hand and vainly trying to gather his 'chute together with the other. He had lost his helmet and was suffering from lack of oxygen. I staggered across and grabbed him by the harness to hold him back shouting to him not to jump but to wait for me: he seemed dazed and did not understand but I managed to get him away from the door. He seemed relieved that someone had him under control. Now that the aircraft was on an even keel I tottered back to the main spar to get an oxygen bottle where I met the bomb aimer and between us we fixed up the Wireless Operator with oxygen to which he reacted and gave me the thumbs up sign. At that moment there were a series of explosions and I felt an impact across my back as if a sledgehammer had hit me. My legs gave way and I fell to the floor: I realised I had been hit and probably quite badly as I lost the complete use of my left arm. The aircraft had gone crazy and was bucking all over the sky — I was thrown from one side of the fuselage to the other and in the darkness I had the impression I had lost my left arm. Terrified out of my wits I waited for the end — giving up the struggle for self preservation and accepting the inevitable.

As the nose of the Lanc. went down again I slid forward, coming to rest near the flare chute. My shoulder was beginning to hurt like hell and I felt a warm liquid around my face and down my neck. I attempted to get to my feet but something was trapping my feet. Then I became aware of the bomb aimer who, not realising I was wounded, was attempting to move me. I screamed with the pain and fought him off but he succeeded in getting me into a sitting position and tried to make me comfortable. It was then I realised why I could not move — damage to the long ammunition trays which ran down the side of the fuselage had allowed the belts to run free and they were wrapped around my legs — trapping me. The liquid on my face and neck which I thought was blood was hot hydraulic oil

escaping from the supply pipes. By now I was feeling the effect
of shock and hovered between hazy bouts of unconsciousness. I
still lay against the flare chute and resisted all efforts to move me
into a warmer part of the fuselage. The aircraft was on an even
keel and my breathing was easier and I knew we were at a lower
altitude.

By screwing my head round I could see the feet of the mid-
upper gunner and I was worried about him. When the Flight
Engineer came back to see if I was all right I indicated the legs
and feet hanging from the turret — he obviously needed help
and I motioned to the Flight Engineer to help him down but he
shook his head — the gunner was beyond help and dead in his
turret. I remember little of the flight home. I got colder and
colder and the pain in my shoulder sent me into bouts of silent
screaming, but I still refused to be moved. I don't know why but
perhaps I registered the fact that I was in my emergency position
for a crash landing and safer there than anywhere else.

I can dimly remember a faint light filtering through the
fuselage as the dawn broke and an occasional burst of heavy flak
as we crossed the enemy coast. Then the navigator came back
and told me we were safe and would soon let down to a landing
at the first airfield that would have us.

With a crash landing imminent, the Navigator and Flight
Engineer came aft and without further ado dragged and carried
me up to the restbed against the main spar — remaining to hold
me in position for the landing. I felt the aircraft surge as full
power was applied to the remaining starboard engine to prevent
the wing dropping on the approach to the landing strip. We must
have been low on fuel as I heard the engine splutter long before
we reached the runway, and the Captain decided to put the
aircraft down as soon as possible. He literally flew it into the
ground and we hit with a resounding crunch — leapt 20 feet into
the air and then settled again. The nose reared up, and lifting my
head, I saw the awesome sight of the fuselage break away aft of
the flare chute — and this whole section bounced away behind
us, turning over and over as it did so. What was left of the
Lanc. came to rest in a water course of the marshy salting which
we had struck.

My last recollection of this remarkable flight is of the Station
Sick Quarters at Tangmere. I watched as the Bomb Aimer
pointed out to me the left hand clip of his parachute harness —
smashed and unrecognisable. He removed this harness and his
battledress top — then he pulled off his heavy woollen flying
pull-over. There was a clunk as something heavy hit the floor
and there, for all to see, lay two thirds of 20mm cannon shell.
How lucky can you be?'

Flight Lieutenant Hudson made a full recovery and, at his own express desire, returned to operational flying with another crew where he completed an extended tour of duty. He makes little of this but recalls sadly that the gallant captain and the other members of his first crew were shot down and killed on 6 June 1944. His affection for these men remains: they had fought their way home under terrible conditions only to die two months later in the face of the enemy.

A premonition of coming disaster was not unknown among the bomber crews and was not confined to the more sensitive: an ugly doubt as to how long the luck would hold was natural enough and the last sortie of a tour of duty tended to concentrate the mind on the chances of pulling it off to enjoy the 'end of tour leave' and a few months free from the mounting horrors of life on the Squadron. I am indebted to Flight Sgt A. F. C. Smith, rear gunner of a 90 Sqdn Lancaster shot down on the last sortie of his tour of duty for the modest, yet unique, phrase — 'No operation was easy — all were noisy, cold and uncomfortable' by which he sums up the lot of every bomber boy. Smith had a premonition and though this flight to Germany took place after the Berlin struggle was over — and was flown in daylight — it bears out his fear that this was to be the eclipse of a stout crew.

'We were a well balanced crew . . . memory is a strange thing and now, thirty years later, those nights and days are still clear in my mind — the comradeship and co-operation of seven men — but nothing sticks out so vividly as our last flight together. During our tour we had several traumatic experiences including being attacked eight times by fighters on the way to Nuremberg and getting away with it.

We were called early from our beds by the duty NCO with the raucous shout 'Ops are on — get moving' and I remember thinking what a beautiful morning as we went to the Briefing Room, but I had this feeling — a premonition, and it was deep rooted, nothing would shake it — in my mind. When I entered the room and saw the Skipper's face I knew I was not alone in my premonition. He greeted me with a wry grin and "This is it Chum". We were given the usual stuff about weather, signals etc., and special instructions for the new run-up procedure using two huge roman candles fixed aft of the rear turret and fired by the rear gunner: this device was intended to concentrate the bomber stream when near the target and level flight was maintained in a follow-my-leader manner, with no weaving whatsoever, and this was the second time it would be tried-out. On the first occasion Wing Commander Peter Dunham was leading the stream when he received a direct hit in the bomb bay and blew up. Then we were told that 90 Sqdn would be leading the stream and as it was Flight Lieutenant Aldhous's last operation he and his crew would have the honour!! of leading the Squadron! This was our skipper and turning to two other Captains I heard him say "With yellow flames shooting out of our backsides anything can happen!" We went out to our aircraft and I checked the infernal contraption fitted to the rear end.

The trip out was uneventful and we crossed the English Coast at St. Osyth in Essex where two weeks earlier I had spent my last leave. After crossing the Dutch Coast we flew over 10/10ths cloud and the bomber stream made a beautiful sight behind us. Eventually, I heard Mac, our Navigator, call out "Twelve minutes from target now" and in accordance with my briefed instructions I pressed the red button . . . and with a mighty "Whoosh" a huge yellow flame shot out from the first rocket. I watched the stream creeping in toward each other, into a close-knit box — over three hundred bombers on course to flatten a synthetic oil producing plant at Datteln. Mac call out a second time "Four minutes to the target" and I pressed the green button when the second rocket burst into yellow flame. We flew on dead straight and level with the bomb doors open until I heard "Bombs Gone" over the intercom and the rocket burnt out. At the same time there was a bloody great bang and I felt pains up my legs. I looked out on the port side and saw flames and smoke pouring past my turret. I tried to rotate the turret but the hydraulic control didn't work so I used the manual lever. Flames were belching out on the port side and leaning out from my turret I saw both engines on fire. I tried to call up front but the intercom was dead. Then with another mighty bang we were hit again — no hydraulic control — no intercom and no oxygen. I peered up the inside of the fuselage to see a mass of smoke and flame creeping towards me — and it was time to go. I was then very thankful that I always wore a pilot type parachute — as I knew I could never have had time to move the turret round once more by hand to where the "chest type" chute would have been fitted in the stowage, and anyway by this time it would have been burned up.

Feeling dizzy from lack of oxygen I opened the turret doors and with difficulty and pains in my legs I pulled myself up and out. I looked up towards the front of the aircraft and the mid-upper turret was empty — perhaps Roddy was attempting to escape. I noticed that both starboard engines were also on fire and the diving speed of the aircraft was increasing rapidly. I stood at the rear door — looked behind and up when I saw, diving behind us, another Lancaster — white faces of the crew peering at us — and with a wave I jumped — counted ten (very quickly) and pulled the rip cord. With a feeling of relief I felt the chute pull up my back and it opened. I looked up at the canopy and saw that it was full of holes. I discovered afterwards that this chute saved my life twice that day: the sorbo cushion was full of shrapnel after it had passed through the pack! And so I went through the cloud into Germany.

After the war when I reported back to the Squadron I met the pilot of the Lancaster who followed us down who told me he had reported me as having jumped without a parachute — not seeing one in the usual place on my chest and he assumed I had taken the easy way out. He told me we were hit twice with three bursts of flak each time and that the other members of my crew had no chance of getting out of the blazing inferno. Whenever I visit their graves I can still see them as they were; and I wonder if my premonition of disaster had softened the initial shock of being hit, and had given me extra impetus to get out. I shall never know.'

The members of his crew killed in action that day were:

Flight Lieutenant B. T. Aldhous	— Captain
Pilot Officer C. D. Palmer	— Navigator
Pilot Officer C. Foy	— Bomb Aimer
Pilot Officer R. South	— Mid Upper Gunner
Sergeant S. Power	— Flight Engineer
Flight Sergeant A. Smee	— Wireless Operator

Flight Lieutenant Aldhous and his crew went into action with the knowledge that once the rockets were fired his aircraft would be a certain mark for the heavy ack-ack below — and his predecessor, Wing Commander Dunham had been blown out of the sky — yet they pressed on, dead straight and level, to accomplish their task. The rocket technique was discontinued.

There is no mention of morale, fear or any kind of objection to tackling the job for which they had been briefed — in either of these straightforward accounts by survivors. Flight Sergeant Smith's premonition did not stem from fear though his apprehension is evident — most felt the same on a last sortie of the tour. Fear is everyone's lot in varying degrees: the man who tries and fails is still more worthy than the individual who studiously avoids the action, seeking a secure staff job which will see the war out nicely — and I don't doubt there were some of those around. The relatively few instances of LMF (lack of morale fibre) which came to notice were dealt with swiftly but it was rare for a captain to demand a replacement crew member: once in the swim the crew as an entity took care of itself.

Confidence in the skill of the navigator came second only to that placed in the captain: this aspect of the work of the crew has not always received the prominence it deserves though somewhat earlier in this narrative I have made the statement that Bomber Command stood or fell by the quality of its navigators; and this is true. To be 'lost' over enemy territory was a frequent occurrence in the early days of the bomber offensive, as we have seen, but the consequences were nothing like so frightening as later on when the night sky was stiff with opposition. With a multiplicity of aids available after 1942 and in the context of a streamlined technique with Pathfinders to light the way home and back such incidents were few. However, on some occasions, when wind speed at altitude was unusually high, it could happen and could be damaging in the sense that security of the crew was impaired — seemingly — and those not in the know such as the gunners were entitled to feel anxious. We all took the navigator for granted — both captains and the remainder of the crew alike — he had the answers and was expected to produce them at the drop of a hat. A competent and confident navigator was a powerful factor for morale from first to last — courage, determination and the will to press on in the face of flak and fighters was one thing; but only the skill of the navigator could ensure that the effort was taken to the vital spot. The demands on his services were frequent and we all heard with relief the familiar voice over the intercom on the way home: 'Dead on track Skipper — you should see the coastline in a few minutes — you can start letting down any time now.' A shaky navigator could be an uncomfortable thought in the minds of the rest of the crew — so much depended on him and, whatever the situation, he must remain cool and capable of using his head quickly to calculate the new course to get us out of trouble. With punctured tanks, and the fuel running low, a single mistake on his part could result in a 'ditching' on a winter's night with a rough sea below: likewise, he could run us over heavily massed defences such as the Ruhr perimeter by a miscalculation. When the unexpected arose he was the first to be asked if we were still on the correct track and if not, then why not? Like the policeman — his lot was not a happy one. The following story from Flight Lieutenant Moore of 83 Sqdn bears this out:

'We were just leaving the target when another Lancaster above us sustained a direct hit and dived down at us with exploding petrol tanks, filling the sky around us with confusion and coming uncomfortably near to taking us down with it. On this particular night we had serious problems with the wind (the meteorological variety) and on the return trip things went terribly wrong. German night fighter activity was the fiercest I had ever known it to be and so many aircraft were being shot down in our vicinity that we stopped recording them and detailed all available crew members to maintain a sharp look-out. After more than an hour of this an unusual and most heated argument blew up between our Captain (Bill Siddle) and the Navigator (Dick Lodge) concerning our position. Siddle insisted we were heading for the heart of the dreaded Ruhr and the Navigator insisted this was far from being the case: he was using the latest wind speed and direction radioed from Bomber Command, anyway, we were in the centre of the bomber stream — we couldn't all be wrong and off course!

The fear and anxiety generated by what was taking place around us was beginning to affect the confidence of an efficient and experienced crew. Finally, the argument ended with the Navigator being invited up to the flight deck to "see this bloody lot ahead for yourself". There followed a brief pause in the dialogue after which the Navigator was heard to remark, "You're dead right Skipper, that is the Ruhr — let's get to hell out of it . . ." He quickly calculated a fresh course and as we flew into a safer area we witnessed the sad spectacle of dozens of our aircraft, the victims of night fighters and flak, spinning down into the smoke and haze of the Ruhr Valley.'

This was 24 March and the total casualties sustained was no less than seventy-two bombers. Flt Lieut Moore completed two full tours of operational duty including six sorties to the 'Big City' volunteering to fly as a 'stand-in' spare rear gunner after his own crew was stood down. Pilot Officers Siddle and Lodge were killed in action at a later period, likewise Dick Jones the mid-upper gunner on this occasion. Moore operated in both 9 and 83 Sqdns and from the manner in which both he and his mid-upper volunteered, despite having finished a tour, to stand in for men off sick it seems there was little wrong with morale in either Squadron. In respect of Moore's remark about the high wind at altitude this was indeed a feature of the operation of 24 March; our bombers were always at a severe disadvantage *vis-a-vis* both flak and fighters when they flew the return journey in the teeth of strong westerly winds which pulled the groundspeed down by as much as eighty knots on occasions.

The experiences of these crews, as related by the survivors, are by no means isolated events: they were repeated in varying forms on hundreds of occasions and I have introduced them at this stage as evidence of the spirit of Harris's men. Weariness, utter boredom, fear and desire to walk away from it all are commonly encountered: as the casualties mounted not a few questioned the wisdom of a policy which cost a Squadron fifteen crews within a few days; but they went just the same; day after day the familiar routine, the briefing, the dressing up, the take-off and the long haul over a route, scarred by the blackened remnants of a thousand Lancasters, Halifaxes, Stirlings and Wellingtons — to the 'Big City'.

Chapter 6
The Battle of Berlin
18 November 1943 —
24 March 1944

The massive operation of 24 March was the sixteenth in the series. These attacks were spread among the nineteen raids carried out over major cities including Leverkusen, Frankfurt, Ludwigshaven, Stuttgart, Leipzig, Stettin, Brunswick, Magdeburg, Schweinfurt, Augsburg and Essen. Small attacks by both Mosquitos and 'heavies' were fed in between and the Battle would conclude with the last Berlin operation followed a week later by the distressing losses on Nuremberg. Thus the bomber crews were well aware of the mounting casualty rate whilst the pressure was never relaxed and day followed day with the customary routine of briefing, bombing-up and personal preparation for the night take-off. The interval between 15 February and 24 March was the greatest in the sequence of raids on the enemy's capital city but the Command had been far from idle in that period. After the mid-February attack where we sustained a loss of forty-three bombers it was believed by some that we might well have finished with Berlin. Leipzig had claimed no less than seventy-eight four engined Lancasters and Halifaxes on the night of 19/20 of that month and the long awaited assault on Schweinfurt cost us thirty-three crews: this latter figure was not reckoned high, in the scheme of things, yet it was occurring too often for comfort. Table 1 illustrates the size of the effort and the cost in trained crews, between January and the final week in March, for the major attacks only: smaller operations are not shown whilst the Mosquitos dropped 4,000 lb 'cookies' on Berlin nearly every night in the week!

Each of the foregoing was a set-piece battle in the fullest sense: every circumstance which was likely to influence the operation was checked and rechecked. The Ops Staff at Harris's Headquarters were competent, tireless and thoroughly professional; the underground Operations Room, known as 'the hole', functioned smoothly. Bennett, at his Pathfinder headquarters, was responsible for marking the targets and there was nothing routine about the planning; each operation was separate and on the occasions when a target was attacked two nights on the trot he rang the changes, using his Mosquito force to the best advantage; diversionary attacks to draw off the enemy fighters from the main objective were in his province and whilst it was not possible to mislead the Germans on every occasion he had more successes than failures. Too little has been written about the work of the Light Night Striking Force but it saved many lives in addition to its special role of making persistent attacks, including occasions when it was virtually impossible to launch the bomber force as a whole.

Table 1. Bomber Command Major Attacks on Germany — January to March 1944.

Target	Date	Aircraft Dispatched	Aircraft Attacking	Bomb Tonnage			Aircraft Missing
				HE	Incend.	Total	
Berlin	1/2 Jan	421	386	772	629	1,401	28
Berlin	2/3 Jan	383	311	658	458	1,116	27
Stettin	5/6 Jan	358	348	633	490	1,123	16
Brunswick	14/15 Jan	498	472	1,125	1,101	2,226	38
Berlin	20/21 Jan	769	697	1,164	1,237	2,401	35
Magdeburg	21/22 Jan	648	585	1,016	1,224	2,240	57
Berlin	27/28 Jan	530	481	1,067	694	1,761	33
Berlin	28/29 Jan	680	596	1,086	868	1,954	46
Berlin	30/31 Jan	540	489	1,069	892	1,961	33
Berlin	15/16 Feb	891	806	1,230	1,413	2,643	43
Leipzig	19/20 Feb	823	730	1,202	1,352	2,555	78
Stuttgart	20/21 Feb	598	552	1,077	976	2,053	9
Schweinfurt	24/25 Feb	734	662	1,226	1,036	2,262	33
Augsburg	25/26 Feb	594	528	1,034	794	1,828	21
Stuttgart	1/2 Mar	557	502	1,022	756	1,778	4
Stuttgart	15/16 Mar	863	813	1,226	1,519	2,745	37
Frankfurt	18/19 Mar	846	769	1,367	1,820	3,187	22
Frankfurt	22/23 Mar	816	774	1,318	1,915	3,233	33
Berlin	24/25 Mar	810	726	1,070	1,423	2,493	72
Essen	25/26 Mar	705	675			2,798	9
Nuremberg	30/31 Mar	795	702			2,473	97
					Total Aircraft Missing		771

The autumn and winter months, from November to March, favoured deep penetration of the enemy's homeland; an important factor in the case of Berlin and other targets lying far to the east. Unescorted heavy bombers depended heavily on the long hours of darkness for cover: a situation which was changing rapidly as the Battle progressed and the greatly strengthened night fighter element interposed itself between attacker and target. The very size of the bomber force, exceeding the eight hundred mark in March of 1944, lent itself to rapid location and the deployment of both free-lance and directed fighters along the approach lanes. Whereas in the past their attacks on our bombers had been mainly in the target area, and on the return route, a new situation developed whereby interceptions took place long before the actual target became apparent to the defenders. The 'spoof' raids which had so often misled the enemy in 1943 lost credibility to a great extent and the task of the planners became that much more difficult.

It will be observed that the gaps in the launching of the big raids during these early months of 1944 extend to days and sometimes longer — and, exceptionally, up to two weeks. These intervals result from the prevailing weather systems — both in the target area and over the home bases. The bigger the force the bigger the problem of ensuring a safe return when the weather proved tricky; fog and reduced visibility in low cloud and rain with eight hundred heavy aircraft flown by tired crews — or the spreading of the force over fifty airfields from Cornwall to Scotland if caught out by bad weather — could become a nightmare. Valuable lives and aircraft could be lost by an error of judgement. A small force was more easily insured against bad weather over the home airfields so that these apparent intervals of no activity were, in fact, filled by the dispatch of Mosquitos and small pockets of 'heavies'. Thus, the pot was kept at the boil and the sirens drove the Berliners and Stuttgarters to the shelters; there would be no let up for the fire and ambulance services, for the gun crews, searchlight operators, radar controllers and fighter pilots at standby. Again, when the weather was favourable the opportunities were not missed and the Command operated two nights in succession — missed a third for recovery and maintenance then went on with the business.

In respect of casualties suffered it will be seen that these were always heaviest when long-range attacks were made over Central and Northern Germany, Berlin being the outstanding example with Nuremberg and Leipzig following suit. Nuremberg is a special case though the exceptionally strong headwind for the return applied to other targets on occasions and the 'Big City' in particular; but there were other factors which doomed the Nuremberg operation. German night fighter strength, an unfortunate choice of the outward route and clear skies over enemy territory combined with condensation trails of unusual clarity to cause the disaster, whilst the small Mosquito diversion attacks on Kassel and Cologne lay too near the stream of bombers heading due East.

The fact that Bomber Command had lost more than nine hundred crews since the commencement of the Battle in mid-November meant some dilution of quality: replacement crews in many instances lacked the experience of the men who had gone before and were flung into a situation where the enemy fighters were fast gaining the upper hand. This was a time where a split second could determine survival or an exit; the old hands were quicker to react to the call from the men in the turrets.— hesitation spelled certain death.

Flight Lieutenant Basil Leigh, radar operator in No 156 Sqdn attacked Berlin no less than ten times. His crew completed forty-six operations with Squadron Leader Hopton as captain and were lost after D-Day 1944. Leigh was sick at the time otherwise he would have gone down with them. On 27, 28 and 30 January they went to Berlin:

> . . . 'and the Squadron lost 14 or 15 aircraft in those three nights. Crews came and went, never really having belonged to the Squadron or so it seemed. In the hut where I slept I was the only person left. So the following morning I packed up and moved elsewhere.'

He was philosophic as to the outcome

> '. . . just as all bomber crews we had our ups and downs — our good and our bad times. I think that from the time the target was announced there was some psychological effect — because it was the 'Big City' with the prospect of a seven and a half hour flight — and the thought of what was to be expected — the terrific defences of the city, the ring after ring of searchlights, the gunfire which had to be penetrated and the bombing run into the target . . . we were attacked and hit by a night fighter after leaving the target, setting fire to the starboard engines. The Captain gave the order to bale out but the rear gunner found his turret doors to be jammed: instead, the Captain put the aircraft into a steep dive, losing height from 20,000 to 12,000 ft in a matter of minutes. Miraculously, the fire was blown out but as three of us hauled back on the control column it seemed as if the wings would never take the strain — but, gradually, we eased her out. Then the long journey home on what engines we had left.'

Leigh's crew had flown as a unit for many months. Their pilot, an outstanding Pathfinder, had risen from NCO Pilot to Squadron Leader and Flight Commander of 'A' Flight 156 Sqdn — 'mainly due to the heavy losses sustained in January of 1944', as Leigh puts it somewhat modestly. In fact Hopton was a born leader, a young Canadian with plenty of spirit and a high courage leading his men on forty-six consecutive 'Ops' and volunteering for Pathfinder duty. The crew, less Leigh who was taken off sick, crashed near the village of Les Mesnuls, Seine et Oise, and were buried by the Mayor and helpers from the village. Leigh, who was at some pains to discover their fate, received the letter, shown as an Appendix to this volume, from the French patriot — a worthy tribute to a stout bomber crew.

Deep penetration attacks invariably produced a higher incidence of failures than sorties to the Ruhr and similar targets lying nearer to the bases. Intense cold at height affects both aircraft and crew — guns freeze up and under certain conditions ice accretion forces a bomber down to a lower level; a greater physical and mental effort is expended by everyone in performing the various tasks and I have on record the case of a wireless operator using his elbow to tap out messages on his morse key — both hands were frozen. Warrant Officer Randolph Rhodes describes his experiences on the night of 28 January 1944, in Halifax 'L' of No 35 Squadron, PFF:

'Icing began shortly after we crossed the enemy coast and due to the rapid build-up the Skipper decided to lose height in an attempt to reach the warmer air below. From the mid-upper turret I could see the heavy ice layers and realized this might well be my third and last operational flight. Down we went and soon became a target for what appeared to be every flak battery on the Continent of Europe. Searchlights illuminated the cloud through which we were flying and the stuff came up thick and heavy from the batteries below. Such was the weight of ice we carried that our journey downwards was no longer a matter of choice and we jettisoned the bomb load and returned to base.'

Rhodes was eventually shot down over Gelsenkirchen and became a POW.

'Early returns' for whatever cause were a bug-bear and never taken lightly: the loss in effort — preparing the aircraft, fusing and winching up the bomb load and its eventual jettisoning — was serious. Mechanical and electrical failure were the chief causes but few captains accepted the situation without some attempt to rectify faults. Having gone through all the trauma of the briefing, air testing, the long wait before the final call to Flights and dressing up, to say nothing of the mental strain (and it could be heavy), once in the air, they were reluctant to abandon the sortie. So much work had gone for nothing and an early return to base tended to throw a crew out of gear. There are instances of crews losing an engine but pressing on to the target regardless and this occurred in my own Squadron — and the target was Berlin! The Captain was reproved and got a pat on the back in the same breath. Such was the spirit in the PFF.

As stated earlier thirty-five major attacks took place on various targets during the period between November and March and if we isolate the sixteen Berlin operations from the rest some idea may be gained of the effort and cost sustained in attempting to take out the enemy's capital. It was enormous. In Table 2 it will be observed that almost thirty thousand tons of bombs were off-loaded from the eight thousand odd sorties flown and the casualties amounted to nearly five hundred. Roughly fifty per cent of the bombs carried to Berlin were high explosive and the other half incendiary bombs of various types. Since it had become the practice to drop the high capacity 'cookie' or blockbuster on nearly every occasion more than eight thousand of these weapons fell on or near Berlin which will account for the HE

Air Commodore
John Searby
DSO, DFC

Lancasters of 5 (B) Group en route to Le Creusot on a daylight raid, October 1942.

Moving a 4,000-lb 'cookie' into position for winching into the bomb bay. The bomb had no aerodynamic shape and literally tumbled to earth.

A Lancaster bomber ready for take-off.

The crew of a ditched Stirling of 149 Squadron are picked up by a rescue launch in the North Sea in June 1942. The Stirling had first been hit by a Wellington that had been shot down over Holland, then hit by flak and cannon shells from a Ju 88.

A Stirling bomber in flames after crashing at Oakington.

A target map of Berlin locating the railway mars

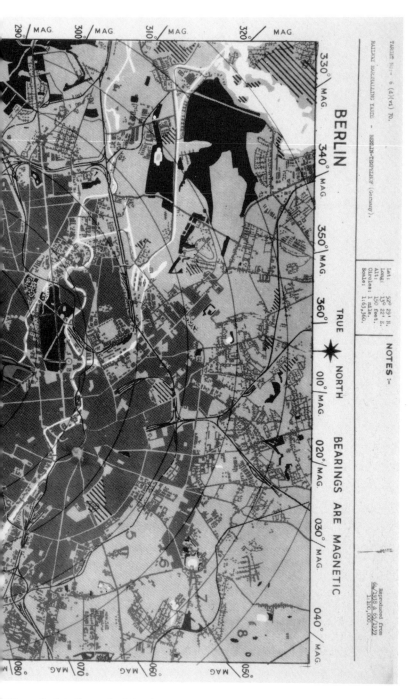

Reproduced from
64/1918 & 65/1922
1:126,000.

NOTES :-

Lat: 52° 29' N.
Long: 13° 22' E.
Alt: 150 feet.
Circular: 1 Mile.
Scale: 1:63,360.

TARGET No:- 6 (d)(vi) 70.

RAILWAY MARSHALLING YARDS - BERLIN-TEMPLHOF (Germany).

BERLIN

290° /MAG.   300° /MAG.   310° /MAG.   320° /MAG.   330° /MAG.   340° /MAG.   350° /MAG.   360° /MAG.

TRUE NORTH

BEARINGS ARE MAGNETIC

010° /MAG.   020° /MAG.   030° /MAG.   040° /MAG.   050°   060°   070°   080°

t Tempelhof, to the south of the city centre.

An aircrew is debriefed at Oakington following a raid on Berlin, 28 November 1943.

The funeral of Sgt J. C. Shaw, shot whilst trying to escape from Stalag Luft I in northern Germany.

An aerial reconnaissance photograph of Berlin taken on 8 March 1944 shows extensive damage in the central area of Berlin. Blocks surrounding the Lutzow Platz (left centre) are gutted — evidence of the devastation caused by uncontrollable fires.

Group Captain K. Rampling with section officers of 7 PFF Squadron at Oakington in February 1944. Over the next three months all of them would be killed in bombing raids. Rampling himself was shot down over Frankfurt a few days before the Berlin raid of 24 March (see p120).

Flt Lt Ralph Edwards (far left) and his crew of 7 PFF Squadron at Oakington who took part in the raid on Berlin on 24 March 1944.

total of 15,254 tons. (A 'cookie' weighed four thousand pounds.) The bulk of the incendiary load would be made up from the tiny four pounder carried in containers forward of the 'cookie' station in the bomb bay. Despite its shortcomings — it could not be 'aimed' and possessed no ballistic qualities — it proved the most effective weapon for destroying buildings and in combination with the four thousand pound HE bomb was responsible for the destruction of Hamburg and other cities. Ideally, this weapon should have been dropped in clusters, thus providing a means of aiming it, but no satisfactory answer was found to the problem: the scatter was accepted and corrected to a certain extent by deliberate 'overshoot'. The path in to the target became a familiar sight to the later arrivals — a glittering carpet of burning magnesium.

Table 2. Details of Bomber Command Raids on Berlin — 18 November–24 March.

Date	Dispatched	Attacking	HE	Incendiary	Total	Casualties
18 Nov	444	402	708	796	1,594	9
22 Nov	764	670	1,133	1,332	2,465	26
23 Nov	382	332	710	625	1,335	20
26 Nov	450	407	859	717	1,576	28
2 Dec	458	401	882	804	1,686	40
16 Dec	492	450	947	868	1,815	25
23 Dec	379	338	710	578	1,288	15
29 Dec	712	656	1,099	1,216	2,315	20
1 Jan	421	386	772	629	1,401	28
2 Jan	383	311	658	458	1,116	27
20 Jan	769	697	1,164	1,237	2,401	35
27 Jan	530	481	1,067	694	1,761	33
28 Jan	680	596	1,086	868	1,954	46
30 Jan	540	489	1,069	892	1,961	33
15 Feb	891	806	1,230	1,413	2,643	43
24 Mar	810	726	1,070	1,423	2,493	72
Totals	9,105	8,120	15,254	14,550	29,804	500

The difference between the totals of aircraft dispatched and those reporting as having attacked the target varies, and in some instances the gap is large. From these figures the casualties must be extracted and the remainder failed for different reasons to reach the objective. Mechanical or electrical failure accounts for a proportion and weather proved a significant factor. The winter of 1943/44 provided few opportunities for a clear run at Berlin. I know of no better description of the conditions pertaining night after night than that written by our Commander-in-Chief, Sir Arthur Harris in his book 'The Bomber Offensive':

> The whole battle was fought in appalling weather and in conditions resembling those of no other campaign in the history

of warfare. Scarcely a single crew caught a single glimpse of the objective they were attacking and for long periods we were wholly ignorant, except for such admissions as the enemy made from time to time, of how the battle was going. Thousands upon thousands of tons of bombs were aimed at the Pathfinders' pyrotechnic sky-markers and fell through unbroken cloud which concealed everything below except the confused glow of fires. Scarcely any photographs taken during the bombing showed anything except clouds, and day after day reconnaissance aircraft flew over the capital to return with no information . . . Then after six attacks a reconnaissance aircraft did bring back some not very clear photographs which showed that at last we were hitting the enemy's capital hard . . . Then the clouds closed in again over Berlin and the Command made eight more attacks without any means of discovering whether all or any of them had been as successful as the first six raids. It was not until March was far advanced and the nights were too short for any but Mosquito attacks that an aircraft brought back more photographs and it was possible to assess the results of the Battle of Berlin as a whole.'

In the conditions described above the Pathfinders faced a formid-able task. The precise 'Oboe' technique which had served them so well over the Ruhr and similar short range targets was useless over Berlin. The airborne radar, independent of ground control, invariably produced a clutter of reflections which defied the efforts of the most experienced operator on occasions but, short of actually seeing the ground below, it was all they had. It was used to the maximum possible extent for marking the area, releasing both the customary target indicators and for the dropping of coloured flares . . . in the expectation that one or the other might succeed in the attempt to mark the area for the main force behind them. Whilst they did not always pull it off later photographic cover of the city revealed a fair degree of accuracy. The coloured flares, or 'Wanganui' technique as it was known, was a very approximate method since the wind effect at height was such as to blow them quickly away from the objective whereas the ground markers spewing from their containers at a height of three thousand feet burned for several minutes. If the cloud was not too thick the ground markers could be seen as a blur but for the most part they were not seen at all and the sky markers dropped by relays of Pathfinders filled the gap. Bennett's strong objection to Cochrane's suggested low level marking was justified: the persistent cloud, often several thousand feet thick, would have obscured any marker bomb planted by a Mosquito flying at rooftop height — whilst the survival of its crew was a matter for conjecture. In the hugger-mugger of gunfire, smoke and searchlights to find the mark would have been chancy and to return and put down a 'pink pansy' or some similar long-burning pyrotechnic virtually impossible.

By the time these operations were directed against Berlin we had reached almost the limit of tactical planning. The enemy was no longer fooled by small spoof raids conducted against other targets in the hope of misleading his fighter controllers. There were only two roads to Berlin — direct, or roundabout Denmark to the Baltic and then on south to the 'Big City'. Minor switches were possible such as dog-legs where the bomber stream appeared to be thrusting its way to a town or city maybe a hundred miles from the capital and then a sharp turn to the real objective, but we were scraping the barrel for ideas. All the novelties were deployed — every possible form of electronic jamming commencing with the coastal radars to the interruption of the fighter controller's messages to the aircraft positioned at the various 'beacons'. The 'Windowing' or release of strips of metallised foil was faithfully performed by Mosquitos flying ahead of the main force of heavy bombers but the enemy had switched his frequencies and much of this effort became ineffective. The H2S scanners were not permitted to rotate en-route to the target since the Germans were capable of homing on the radiations. By splitting the Force and sending large numbers of aircraft to bomb widely separated targets some relief was obtained. The fact remained that a big force is hard to hide and the greatly increased strength of the enemy in fighters of all kinds — FW 190, Ju 88 and Me 109 — meant he enjoyed a flexibility previously not possible.

The last of the great raids on Berlin was laid on after a gap of five weeks during which heavy losses had been sustained over Leipzig on 19 February (seventy-eight bombers) whilst less costly attacks had been made on Stuttgart, Schweinfurt, Augsburg and Frankfurt. Weather was the reason for this hiatus and it was not until this last fateful week in March of 1944 that Berlin became a possibility once more. 'Fateful' because in the space of seven days the Command would suffer its worst disaster ever, with a combined casualty total of 178 Lancasters and Halifaxes. It was indeed the end of a long and very painful episode — but not by any means the end of the offensive — and the preparations for 'Overlord' — the invasion of Europe — took precedence over all else. In any event the arrival of the shorter nights precluded any further deep penetrations into Northern and Central Germany. When the autumn came round again the Command would resume its customary role.

Chapter 7
The Final Assault —
Operational Planning
24 March 1944

At his planning conference on the morning of 24 March Sir Arthur Harris was confronted with the old old problems of clear weather over the target and poor visibility at the bases. Over the past week he had launched major attacks on Stuttgart and Frankfurt (twice) dispatching more than 800 aircraft in each case with relatively few losses — thirty-seven on Stuttgart and thirty-three on Frankfurt. These figures followed the usual pattern for targets at short range in South West Germany where both fighter and ground defences were less thickly concentrated. Leipzig on 19 February had been a disaster with seventy-eight aircraft lost following Berlin on the 15th, when forty-three bombers had failed to return. It was estimated that the bulk of these losses had occurred en-route and over the targets whilst few interceptions had taken place on the homeward journey; an indication that the enemy was adopting fresh tactics, and deploying his fighter strength between the bomber force and its objective. As mentioned earlier it was becoming more and more difficult to mislead him and a partial solution to this problem was the dispatch of more than one group of aircraft to widely separated areas in Germany. The road to Berlin had been trodden so often that the approach of a single large force was sufficient for the defence to pull out all the stops and think first in terms of their capital city. With more than 1500 fighters, equipped with the latest radars, for detecting and closing the bombers they had good reason to believe the pendulum was swinging in their direction. The secret of making interceptions early in the fray lay in the positioning of the defending night fighters using radio beacons as rallying points — a technique which was proving ever more effective. Once the main stream of Bombers had been identified as making for Northern Germany the Controllers would bring up aircraft from as far afield as Paris and similar areas lying far to the south: the precise objective might not be assessed in the early stages but once they had gathered their strength in the area under threat correct deployment would follow.

Five weeks had elapsed since the last big attack on Berlin. Weather had not favoured further raids and the Command had been employed elsewhere, taking advantage of clearer skies to the south. On this particular night an encouraging forecast for the Berlin area was given by the Met. Staff at Headquarters Bomber Command and the Commander-in-Chief saw it as a rare opportunity to put out his full strength, but against this he had to balance the high probability of fog at the bases for the return. This is what the Senior Meteorological Officer offered:

> *Bases*. Fog will develop at 0300 in Lincolnshire and East Anglia, and in Yorkshire and the Training Groups after 0400 hrs. All Groups will have at least half their bases fit until 0200, with 1500 yards visibility or more; and many airfields will hold until 0400.
> *Germany*. Belt of strato-cumulus along front. East of the front, patchy medium cloud with little or no low cloud. East of 15E. on the Baltic Coast broken strato-cumulus and good visibility. Berlin, good chance of clear skies; but possibility of 10/10 thick strato-cumulus. Better prospects of Brunswick.
> *France*. Little cloud — patchy strato-cumulus in NE.

The overall weather picture was described in the following terms:

> Feeble warm front from 60N. 03E. — 55N. 05E — Frankfurt, becoming cold to Vienna.

This was the general situation and a more detailed forecast was always given at Briefing on the various Stations. In particular forecast wind speed and direction for the various sections of the route from the English Coast to the target and return was specified by the local Met. Officer. The gathering and distribution of weather information improved greatly after the formation of the Met. Reconnaissance Flight in early 1942 and the dispatch of a Mosquito or Spitfire to report on conditions over enemy territory prior to the launching of a big raid represented a significant advance. Obviously, such sorties were undertaken at great risk to the pilot or crew: like their opposite numbers in the photo recce business they were quickly picked up by the German radars and became a target for any German fighter possessing the speed and climb to catch them. Fortunately both the Mosquito and Spitfire proved exceedingly difficult to intercept but it was a dangerous assignment calling for the utmost in courage and skill. I regret we took both the Met. and Photo Recce boys for granted in those days: they performed extraordinary feats.

Air Vice-Marshal Don Bennett, who controlled No 1409 Flight as part of his Pathfinder Force, wrote:

> 'No 1409 Flight flew by day or night as and when required . . . their total time in the air often covered most of the twenty-four hours of the day. Their penetrations into Germany were quite

deep even in broad daylight in clear weather. Naturally, they flew high and fast but the danger was extreme and it was a nerve-racking job . . . they would plan their routes with suitable changes of course to throw off enemy fighters and pass through the area required making a full record of the weather at the appropriate positions. They had no guns — nothing offensive. I often wonder whether it was appreciated at Headquarters Bomber Command . . . that in doing so they were asking an unarmed aircraft to proceed deep into the heart of enemy territory in broad daylight without any cloud cover. The ease with which they called for a 'Pampa' was quite frightening.'

Once the decision had been taken the action signal to Groups followed swiftly and within a few minutes every bomber station had received it. The target was named, the size of the effort and bomb-loads was all that was needed at this stage; the long and intricate Form 'B' would arrive some time later. Early information indicating 'Ops' were laid on for the night enabled the maintenance crews to get going whilst the armourers could begin the laborious work of fusing the bombs and loading the trailers for delivery to the dispersal pans. The servicing of the aircraft was one thing but the fusing and movement of the heavy 'cookies', thousand pounders and incendiary bombs was no simple exercise. One could never have too much time.

Form 'B', the detailed and complex series of instructions covering every single aspect of the operation, formed the basis of the crew briefing. For the night of 24 March 1944 it extends to several feet, meshing in various activities from target-marking to radio counter-measures and diversionary attacks in addition to the normal information relating to numbers of aircraft, wave timings and heights, signals and navigation instructions and much more besides. Group Headquarters compiled and dispatched these orders to each airfield under their control with copies to all interested parties likely to be affected. (The Pathfinder Form 'B' for this operation runs to seven feet in length!)

It was usual for the Deputy C-in-C or the Senior Air Staff Officer to speak directly to Commander of the Pathfinder Force immediately following the departure of Sir Arthur Harris from the Operations Room. Such discussions were conducted over a 'scrambled' line and covered not only the method of marking the target but the tactical aspect involving 'spoof' raids and diversionary targets: routing and timing were agreed and the employment of Bennett's Mosquito Squadrons in support. The latter enjoyed pretty well a free hand since he carried full responsibility for marking the aiming point whilst his intimate knowledge of the many problems associated with the use of radar (H2S and Oboe) was respected. Nevertheless, there were other Group Commanders involved and it was not unusual for one or other to put his particular point of view. The Deputy, Sir Robert Saundby, was uniquely qualified to oversee these brief conferences both by virtue of his experience and his impartial attitude. Deeply versed in every facet of the bombing war he maintained strict control, never once 'blowing his top' but skilfully probing the weak point in the argument with his customary quiet authority. Looking back one realises now just how great was Saundby's contribution to the success of the Command. Both he and Ralph Cochrane had served under Sir Arthur in Iraq as Flight Commanders in No 45 Sqdn in the early 'twenties' when the RAF maintained law and order in addition to flying the Cairo-Baghdad air mail: an association to be repeated on a much larger stage in the future.

At Pathfinder Headquarters Bennett conducted his own planning conference assisted by the Senior Air Staff Officer and various experts. Each operation was personal to Bennett. There must have been an odd occasion when he delegated responsibility to Air Commodore 'Bruin' Boyce though Bennett took no leave during the whole time he had command of the PFF — from August 1942 until the war ended — and he was tireless. No detail, however small, was missed and he was out on the Stations attending briefings and the subsequent interrogations after his aircraft had returned. Efficient, dedicated and abreast of every aspect of the job he had the advantage over his opposite numbers in command of the main force Groups in that he had flogged a Halifax to war as a Squadron Commander in No 4 Group. This was important — to us — and he was much admired in consequence. He led from the front and whilst reference has been made by eminent writers to Bennett's 'abrasive' manner we had little to complain about. Certainly, he was intolerant of idiots and laid on the line precisely what he had in mind. He had his faults but if you got on with the job and showed a bit of zeal he was well satisfied. Boyce, the Senior Air Staff Officer, was a 'regular' and very competent: he had an easy manner, was no snob and cheered us all up when he visited the Squadron. He, too, had a good record; he came to the PFF from the Middle East where he had a Blenheim Squadron and the going had been rough. He flew with the Pathfinder Squadrons when possible and he was popular with the crews; he had the knack of stripping the nonsense — possessing an easy assurance of his own powers and background and a somewhat caustic wit. His relationship with Bennett was strained at times since they were both strong characters but he was a significant factor for success and we enjoyed his outspoken comments on men and matters. Not much has been written about Boyce — and that would cause him no pain whatever — since it was inevitable that he should be overshadowed by the brilliant Bennett but it was sometimes a comfort to know he was around.

Bennett's immediate Staff was handpicked. Operational experience was the first qualification and as time went by and the pioneers became tour-expired he contrived to retain their know-how by appointing a number to his HQ Staff. This worked very well. Pathfinder planning sessions such as that on the morning of 24 March 1944 were never routine and it was not unknown for Bennett to be challenged: he welcomed new ideas though at this stage there could be little in the way of innovation in the marking of the main target. However, some scope existed in the employment of the Mosquito Squadrons, dropping 'window' ahead of the main force, and other aircraft were to attack enemy airfields known to deploy fighter aircraft. In these attacks Bomber Command called in the Mosquitos of the Second Tactical Air Force (belonging to No 2 Group) whilst a massive diversionary raid was staged by the Operational and Conversion Units in an attempt to draw the enemy fighters to the South. We may add to all this the inclusion of Mosquitos of No 100 Group — fighter aircraft fitted with the special Serrate equipment which enabled the crews to home on the intercepting single and twin engined night fighters. This is but an outline of the Pathfinder programme for the night; the detailed timings and trimmings came later.

The early broadcast from Bennett's Headquarters to the main force Groups was confined to the method to be used. Briefly, this was the form:

(a)   Method will be Newhaven groundmarking. Wanganui sky marking will as an emergency if cloud obscures target indicators.

(b)   Pathfinders will open the attack at Zero hour minus five with sticks of illuminting flares and green target indicators dropped in the target area. The aiming point will then be marked with large salvoes of mixed red and green TIs and kept marked with red TIs.

(c)   In addition if cloud obscures target indicators the release point will be marked with flares — red with yellow stars.

(d)   Main force aircraft arriving early in the attack should aim their bombs at the large salvoes of mixed red and green TIs if visible. Otherwise all main force aircraft should aim at the centre of all red TIs. Care must be taken to avoid the weaker and shorter burning red decoys which may be dropped by the enemy.

(e)   If cloud obscures target indicators main force aircraft should aim at the centre of all flares — red with yellow stars — while holding a heading of 217 Magnetic. In this case bomb sights should be set for true height and zero wind.

(f)   Aircraft must not drop incendiaries before zero hour.

(g)   All crews should be warned to listen out on 'darky' frequency when near the target area. A Mosquito and a

Lancaster will act as Master Bombers and will broadcast comments and advice to all crews throughout the raid. The call signs will be as follows:
　　Mosquito — Pommy
　　Lancaster — Redskin

The above was Bennett's Pathfinder plan for the attack. It will be observed that he combined both ground and sky marking — a form of insurance against adverse weather with cloud hiding the burning ground markers. This was known as the Berlin method. So often the bomber force battled its way to the enemy's capital only to find it blanketed by cloud layers. 'Wanganui', the code-name for sky marking could never hope to achieve the accuracy of ground marking and it was a last resort. In an earlier phase of the bombing offensive the sky marking flares had been released from Mosquito aircraft under the control of the 'Oboe' operator, during attacks against Ruhr targets, but Berlin was beyond the range of the equipment and reliance was placed in the airborne H2S in the case of Berlin — a much more difficult technique. Nevertheless, it was infinitely better than 'bombing on ETA' — a desperate measure whereby the bomb aimer dropped his load on the instructions of the navigator estimating his position to be over the target after a long period when no sight of the ground was possible. Navigators received intensive instruction on the use of the H2S when they arrived at the Navigation Training Unit and achieved a high degree of skill before being let loose on a live target, but Berlin was tricky: the picture on the cathode ray tube varied with direction of approach, with height and frequently for no reason whatever. The vast spread of the city resulted in a mass of reflections — bright dots of light on the screen — but at least there was no mistaking the fact that Berlin lay beneath the bomber, though the selection of precise aiming points proved difficult and sometimes impossible.

Given moderately clear conditions — the sky only half covered or even less — the sticks of flares released by the early Pathfinders served to assist the observer in the nose of the bomber to pick out ground detail and mark the area for the crews dropping the distinctive 'aiming point marker' — a responsibility given only the most experienced Pathfinders whose reliability had been proved in many similar operations. An error of judgement on the part of these picked crews could mislead the following main force of bombers and though more than one aiming point marker would be released by other pathfinders the 'stray' always attracted attention and bombs would be wasted. Thus the onus of dropping the final marker was heavy indeed and if there was any doubt in the mind of the operator the special target indicator must not be dropped. There were occasions when an aiming point crew was hit by flak and, inevitably, the markers tucked up in the bomb bay were blown out of the stricken aircraft and nothing could be done about that. It happened from time to time since the early bombers over a target became a mark for every six-gun battery below — virtually alone in a hostile sky lacking the support of the massed bombers thundering along behind them. This was reckoned an occupational hazard in the PFF and no one made much of it.

The increasing pressure by Bomber Command on the North German cities, and Berlin in particular, had resulted in a reinforcement of the enemy night fighters and ground defences. These measures included the masking of certain features reckoned to assist the attacking bombers and the introduction of such novelties as dummy fires and decoy target indicators. Whilst it was barely possible to reproduce on the ground an exact imitation of our own coloured target indicators the enemy got fairly close and the red decoys mentioned in the Pathfinder plan above became a feature of later attacks on Berlin. These pyrotechnic displays were sited in areas away from the city and fired as the bombers approached whilst a few were actually dropped by aircraft short of Berlin. They lacked the deep red colour achieved by the famous firm of Brocks Fireworks in this country but were good enough to deceive the uninitiated hence the caution expressed in the Pathfinder broadcast on 24 March. Bennett frequently added another warning to his plan for the night and this referred to the release of incendiary bombs — the small 4 lb type — which often fell short of the target resulting in a long trail back in the direction of the oncoming bombers. The effect was cumulative, pulling back the release of the weapons and wasting significant quantities of high explosive — the 'fringe merchants' as Bennett termed them were not always to blame but he was justified in ramming home to all and sundry the resulting loss of effort. The paragraph relating to incendiaries stems from this experience: a 'virgin' target must not be spoilt at the outset by a careless or misguided individual who might well mess up the work of thousands of ground airmen, baffle the perspiring aircrew and waste thousands of pounds of the tax-payers' money.

The release of the Wanganui flares — the sky markers — was precomputed according to the forecast wind values at height, thus the main force crews were required to do nothing more than set the corrected altitude and zero wind on the bombsight. It might seem odd to the reader — the catching of a rapidly disappearing flare in the bombsight lens — but, as I have indicated it was a last resort and sometimes paid off surprisingly well. Taped recordings of the language of the bomber crews pursuing the red flares with coloured stars do not exist, alas, and something has been lost to posterity. Whereas a number of crews might deem it sufficient to let go — aware of the activity and taking this as evidence of location —

without chasing the flares the majority made a conscientious attempt to back up the Pathfinders: having got to Berlin with a full load they did their best to see it was not wasted.

Finally, the task of the Master Bombers — and they could do nothing if cloud obscured the target — detailed to co-ordinate the attack by sitting it out until the job was done. Amid the hugger-mugger of the attack the Master Bomber attempted to concentrate the bombing on what he assessed as the correct aiming point. Regardless of what was happening around them they were committed to stick it out from first to last, encouraging, prompting, ordering — bending their energies to getting every single bomb on the target. Enemy fighters, heavy flak and searchlights were totally disregarded and invariably the returning crews remarked on the help and satisfaction which accompanied the sound of an English voice amid the holocaust. The Master Bombers who directed the Berlin attacks took on the toughest of all assignments and deserve the highest praise: the enemy defended his capital with a ferocity unequalled in previous engagements and their survival amid the fury of both ground and air opposition was pure chance.

The action signal from Headquarters Bomber Command, following Sir Arthur Harris's morning conference carried the code word 'Goodwood'. This denoted a maximum effort on the part of all Groups requiring the dispatch of every available aircraft capable of getting to Berlin and back. If necessary scratch crews were to be made up to offset the absence of a man sick or otherwise not available for duty. Generally, this was the highest priority although another existed and had been ordered on very rare occasions: this was 'Grand National' used at the time of the Thousand Bomber Raids. 'Grand National' brought in the Training Units which supported the Command; providing the steady flow of replacements to offset casualties and tour expired crews. The four engine Conversion Units disposed of a large number of Lancasters and Halifaxes and were manned by experienced instructors drawn from the Squadrons on completion of operational duties. The new crews completed the last stage of their training at the Con. Units before joining the Squadrons and in an emergency might be used to swell the bomber force on a particular occasion. A combination of operationally experienced instructors and pupils could provide a reasonably competent crew and this was preferred to the dispatch of a raw crew. Nobody liked a 'Grand National' since it brought a complete disruption of training and could, on occasions, bring dire consequences. If casualties were heavy, and instructors lost, replacements produced a problem whilst lost or damaged bombers from the training programme affected the flow of aircraft to the front line squadrons. A 'Goodwood' affected only the latter, but this prefix to an action message implied rather more than just increasing the numbers: it meant that the C-in-C was looking for something special from his crews and, invariably, he got his way. The Lancaster on scheduled inspection in the hangar — a mass of ladders, gaping inspection panels and all the paraphernalia of the testing equipment — became the focus of maintenance gangs supervised by bustling NCOs and took its place in the line later in the day for bombing up. Somehow it was done and we watched the serviceability board as the numbers crept up from nine or ten at the outset to sixteen serviceable Lancasters by late afternoon. Such was the spirit of the ground staffs, and by take-off time 811 heavy bombers were ready for the final attack on the 'Big City'.

In addition to the large force of 'heavies' ordered to attack Berlin diversionary attacks were ordered against Kiel (11 Mosquitos) and a total of 150 aircraft from training units were to make a feint attack in the Paris area carrying no bombs but calculated to turn the attention of the enemy to a posed threat far to the south of the main stream of bombers passing over Denmark and the Islands at the entrance to the Baltic. A group of PFF Mosquitos attacked Duisburg in the Ruhr and others bombed Munster and the airfield at St Trond. No 2 Group Mosquitoes attacked night fighter airfields at Venlo, Juvincourt, Twente and Leeuwarden. No 100 Group (Radio Countermeasures) provided the customary 'Mandrel' chain and 10 Mosquitos equipped with the special 'Serrate' radar mingled with the bomber stream. There was little which was new in this overall plan: the use of the training establishments added something but this was not a deter-mined thrust at another recognisable target such as Stuttgart or Nuremberg which would have certainly divided the enemy fighters. In the event it was not the fighters which scored the victories, as we shall see when we come to the weather aspect, but the greatly strengthened heavy anti-aircraft batteries. The penetration by the training aircraft was too short to attract much attention and, anyway, the enemy must have been aware of the main bomber stream crossing the North Sea: he may well have estimated Berlin to be the bombers' goal in the light of previous attacks in Northern Germany: the Duisburg diversion followed a familiar pattern — a small number of high flying Mosquitos so often employed in such a role — and it was the eight hundred pounding 'heavies' approaching Denmark which occupied the German controllers. The north-about route to the German capital was always reckoned the best; it was longer but offered less chance of interception: the danger areas were those around Kiel and Berlin itself, a fact well demonstrated in the past. Having rid themselves of the heavy bomb load and much of the fuel aircraft handled well, possessed a good rate of climb and could defend themselves very much better under these conditions. The cursed Lancaster overload of an extra three thousand pounds (on top of an already significant bomb tonnage) imposed by Headquarters Bomber Command irked the crews more than somewhat but all these troubles disappeared once the target was left behind: no one feared taking on a night fighter with a nimble aeroplane under control, whereas the chance of survival was less than slight with an overload and the aircraft wallowing at eighteen thousand feet.

Maintaining a precise track all the way from the English coast to the German capital was essential if the narrow limits on timing imposed by Bennett were to be implemented. He demanded an accuracy which only a couple of years earlier might have been reckoned impossible — but it was done. With eight hundred heavy bombers to be passed through the target in the short interval of twenty minutes the tolerance was small indeed. A minute was not acceptable and fifteen seconds was the outside margin whilst even that small error made Bennett wince. Certainly, on occasions, since man may not control the weather, things went awry, but rarely, in my experience; and always the accent lay on timing, timing and again timing. Thus, the timing of the several parts of the Pathfinder plan, and those for individual aircraft, reflect a delicacy of touch in keeping with the complex drill created to take care of every possible contingency. In this connection we may take a look at the Operation Order dispatched from Pathfinder Headquarters to all Stations under command, with copies to the main force Groups and other interested parties.

The 'Who, Where and When' had a wide circulation — was Top Secret and sent out on the secure teleprinter circuit. On the Operational Stations it was received in the Intelligence Section and studied by Station and Squadron Commanders in advance of the actual crew briefing later in the day. As for the crews themselves they knew nothing save that 'Ops' were 'on' for that particular night but one was aware always of a change in the atmosphere and speculation as to the target was bandied about in the crew rooms. Leipzig on 20 February had been a disaster with seventy-eight bombers out of a total of 823 dispatched — night fighters had been responsible for this heavy casualty rate — and whilst the memory of this ghastly night faded somewhat with the switching of the assault to Stuttgart and Frankfurt, where the loss rate was lower by far, Leipzig had not been forgotten. The strain on our crews had been heavy throughout the Battle and it was commonly believed that we had finished with Berlin after the mid-February onslaught where forty-three bombers had fallen victim to the defences: evidence of a massive build-up in the German fighter element had been supported by the Leipzig attack which, contrary to the customary pattern, had suffered its worst casualties *on the approach* to that city. The ability of the enemy to interpose his night fighter element between Bomber Command and the designated objective was something entirely new, pointing to increased numbers and greater flexibility on the part of the opposition.

Discarding the earlier system of control whereby night fighter aircraft were virtually tied to a specified area or 'box', and freeing all aircraft, wherever based, for deployment over a threatened locality, the enemy sought to achieve a significant concentration of force where it was most needed. In this he was mainly successful, although there was a high risk factor since a mistake in forecasting the likely target for the approaching bombers could result in hundreds of single and twin engined fighters being diverted to the wrong spot. The use of radio beacons around which the defending forces could gather awaiting the final instruction from the controller was a feature of this system and amounted to the setting up of standing patrols. As reports came in from the long range radars on the coast, of the approach of our bombers, the fighter airfields were alerted and dispatched their aircraft to await orders at one or other of the beacons set up for this purpose. From then on the chief controller took over the responsibility for getting them to the correct area. Our own experts in the Signals Branch of the RAF quickly got on to this and devised methods of jamming the orders broadcast from the controller though this could never be entirely successful and various stratagems were employed on both sides. However, there was another factor which became prominent as the Battle progressed: as the size of the attacking force increased it became more and more difficult to conceal it from the enemy.

At the time of the Battle of Berlin Bomber Command was putting more than eight hundred four engined bombers into the air: a figure which was to increase steadily throughout the year until by January 1945 the strength shown on the availability board in the Command Ops Room stood at fourteen hundred Lancasters, Halifaxes and Mosquitos. Even eight hundred aircraft flying in waves separated only by a few minutes in time made a fair sized blob in the night sky and were readily identified on the enemy radar screens so that the task of the German controllers was not all that difficult. Diversions, or spoof attacks in the shape of a small number of Mosquitos were an accepted part of the overall tactical plan but it was unlikely they would attract more than passing interest from the Germans when there were 800 'heavies' pounding the route either over the Danish Islands or taking the more direct path over the flat North German plain. Sir Arthur liked the big numbers: they stood for all that he had planned and hoped for but it might have been better to have recognised there was an optimum figure if an element of surprise was to be achieved. Splitting the Command and striking at targets widely separated plus the use of Bennett's Mosquito Squadrons might well have made the Germans tear their hair on occasions quite apart from reducing the casualty rate among the crews. A brief study of the big attacks such as Leipzig, the Berlin series and Nuremberg reveals the ease with which the enemy identified and flung everything he had into the bomber streams. Bomber Command, in 1944 en-masse, and flying by night, was, though in a lesser degree, approaching a situation not unlike that which faced the USAAF 8th AF after Schweinfurt. We needed protection if the broad front policy was to be pursued — and that was not forthcoming.

The few Serrate fighters, stoutly led by officers such as Wing Commander Bob Braham and Squadron Leader Freddy Lambert, represented a drop in the bucket. We needed all the Mosquitos in Fighter Command and anything else which might have helped; but the gulf between Bomber and Fighter was immense and, seemingly, nobody tried to bridge it. The greatest help we got from our fighter brothers was the use of their splendid airfields when diverted through bad weather — and that was truly something. The luxury of a Fighter Mess is still a fond memory after all these years. If there was the least chance of getting into a fighter establishment rather than a bomber or OTU airfield the crews went for it; in the latter case one might be lucky to get a bed (a chair in the Flying Control building was my lot on one occasion) but at Middle Wallop they laid on the best for us: breakfast in bed produced by a neat WAAF wearing a chintz pinafore. That was the deal at a Fighter base. Guy Gibson's own views on this are well set out in his book 'Enemy Coast Ahead'. He had flown a full tour of duty in Beaufighters in between bomber tours of duty.

Immediately following the plain statement '688 heavies of 1, 3, 4, 5 and 6 Groups and 112 Pathfinders will attack Whitebait'* comes a reference to thirty supporting aircraft of No 1 Gp. Whilst they form a part of No 1 Group's total these aircraft had been asked for by Bennett to join a further forty supporters from Pathfinders briefed to be over Berlin five minutes before H hour. Their task was simple enough — to mask the Blind Marker Illuminators, twenty-five in number — whose duty was to open proceedings well in advance of the actual bombing. H hour was set for 2230 and by filling the sky with an extra seventy bombers the novelties sent up by the opposition would be shared.

Not everyone rejoiced in the role of 'supporter' — joining the early Pathfinders before H hour, when the gunners serving the heavy flak batteries around and inside the city perimeter were flexing their muscles, aware of the importance of these few isolated marker crews and bending to the task of disrupting the marking sequence. The preliminary salvoes fired in the first phase of the attack were invariably more lethal than the barrage which built up with the arrival of the main force of bombers; thus the duty of the supporters was one of swamping and absorbing the shot and shell so that the marker crews would suffer less interruption. Despite the release of clouds of 'window' the bombers' best hope of getting through lay in the

* Codewords, PRO F.14.

concentration which characterised this form of assault, when the gun and searchlight radars would experience difficulty in 'locking-on' to individual aircraft; but the opening and critical preliminaries involving a relatively small number of marker crews offered single targets and the flak came up thick and fast.

Whilst the support element aiding the Pathfinders did their best to get over the target at the stipulated five minutes before H hour varying skills and experience affected the outcome. The severe casualty rate suffered by the Command over the past three months had, inevitably, brought about some dilution of efficiency; and the numbers of battle-hardened crews had diminished. It was not to be expected that replacement crews with only a few operations under their belts could perform with the same accuracy and reliability as the old hands. With all the pressure which Bennett put on his picked men and his constant emphasis on precise timing he could never guarantee a one hundred per cent kick-off at the appointed hour and whilst the majority of the PFF captains made it there would always be some who for reason of weather, aircraft serviceability or enemy action either arrived late or not at all.

The release of 'window' in advance of the opening phase of the attack was designed to confuse the defences and whilst all heavy aircraft carried this countermeasure Bennett's Mosquitos were sent ahead to 'salt' the area beforehand. Nineteen of these aircraft were ordered to commence dropping many thousands of the metallised strips on the aproach and over the target between 10 and 11 minutes before H Hour. The 'window' screen could not be fully effective: experience had shown that only a high degree of concentration could blanket the enemy radars, but Bennett did his best with the small force of Mosquitos available.

In his preliminary signal describing the method for the night Bennett adds a paragraph . . . 'Aircraft must not drop incendiaries before Zero hour'. The risk of spoiling an attack through the careless or accidental discharge of these little fire-raisers has been discussed earlier and to make quite certain, these were not included in the early bomb loads. All supporting aircraft from the PFF and from No 1 Group were loaded with high explosive but no incendiaries.

The possibility of a marker crew being hit and scattering its load of target indicators could never be discounted and it had happened in the past. Such an event could mislead a proportion of the main force and the presence of a Master Bomber was the only form of insurance against a wastage of bombs. Certainly, he would be on the look-out for an incident of this nature and broadcast a warning to the on-coming bombers; if he was heard all would be well but in the heat and fury of the attack coupled with the likelihood of interference, or jamming of his transmitter there was no absolute certainty. A Pathfinder aircraft suffering a direct hit created a spectacle on occasions with the red and green candles blown from their casing as the 'cookie' exploded — great slashes of bright colour mingling with the smoke and flame, and drifting slowly downward amid the searchlight beams and the flak bursts to burn briefly amid the fires below.

The Commander of the Pathfinder Force carried a heavy burden. A successful attack would be taken for granted but failure invited criticism. From past experience 'reasonable conditions' were hard to come by; Berlin was invariably covered by a layer, or several layers of cloud, and during the whole of the Battle to date our aircraft had not encountered clear skies over the city. The best for which one could hope was half-cover or broken cloud with useful gaps through which the aiming point might momentarily be glimpsed. Nevertheless, fifteen attacks had been launched to date whilst photographic reconnaissance had failed to establish the degree of destruction achieved: overcast conditions prevented any clear view of the city. The reader might well wonder why Sir Arthur Harris persisted: the record of casualties sustained was daunting whilst there were other and more profitable targets to claim his attention. The answer may lie in the fact that time was running out: preparations for Overlord, the coming invasion of Europe, were well in hand and in the near future the Command would be committed to the support of the armies crossing the Channel. Preliminary operations would be ordered for the sealing off of the beaches and Sir Arthur would be compelled to accept the priorities decreed by the Supreme Allied Commander. All of which is true enough but one must allow for the resolute character of our Commander-in-Chief: Berlin was the very heart of Nazidom and he intended to destroy it piecemeal. It was a crusade with Harris and he would never admit defeat.

To return to Bennett and the task of marking Berlin . . . after so many attempts in the bad weather a lesser man might have sought to persuade his C-in-C to lay off but this was not in character. It is apparent that Harris became dissatisfied with Bennett's methods and was looking to Cochrane for ideas. Air Marshal Cochrane possessed a fertile brain and offered a new concept: his stand-off technique for marking had been successful on certain selected targets but never tried in the blood and muck of the 'Big City' — in the welter of massed heavy batteries and searchlights covering a vast area. Sir Arthur Harris was impressed by the performance of No 5 Group which was setting a high standard of accuracy under the leadership of Group Captain Cheshire VC, whose gallantry and devotion to duty was above local loyalties, but Bennett doubted whether these tactics were suited to the Berlin operations.

Bennett was asked to use Mosquitos at low level 'to find the exact aiming point and mark it with target indicators'. He refused to adopt Cochrane's methods. Weather and good visibility are prime factors in low-level marking whereas Berlin rarely met this criterion. Persistent low and medium cloud would, in any event, hide the target indicators if the Mosquito crews were successful in identifying the aiming point amid the clutter of buildings, the harassing light anti-aircraft fire and searchlights — this last being a most formidable weapon against aircraft flying at roof-top height. Bennett argued his case over the telephone but failed to convince Sir Arthur who was not pleased and a personal interview followed later in the day. According to Bennett he was

> 'received with a frigid and formal notification that I was to send immediately 83 and 97 Squadrons (Lancasters) back to their parent Group together with one Mosquito Squadron and that in future No 5 Group would adopt the method which I had refused to accept — namely, the low level marking — and would then mark a large number of their own targets themselves. This was, in itself, a tremendous slap in the face to a Force which had turned Bert Harris's Bomber Command from a wasteful and ineffective force into a mighty and successful one. It seemed, in the eyes of the rest of the Command that, in the opinion of the C-in-C the Pathfinders had apparently failed.'

The date of this interview is not recorded in Bennett's book; only that it took place 'towards the end of the Battle of Berlin'. Action followed swiftly and Bennett lost two of his 'founder' Squadrons plus a Mosquito unit to the AOC No 5 Group — Air Vice-Marshal Ralph Cochrane — never to return, though he was still required to train and man them with replacement crews! The shock-wave was felt throughout the Command. I mention this incident only to emphasise the strain on Bennett. Harris was not a man to take half-measures whilst Bennett could ill brook interference or criticism, and in a clash of minds he was accustomed to winning hands down. His unique experience and the fact that he was the only Group Commander to date with an operational background in this war set him apart, but the deed was done; though not until the last great battle over Berlin had taken place, when Bennett's methods were used. This was just as well in the light of the prevailing weather on that night.

Considering Bennett's statement as to when the interview took place we may fairly assume it happened before the final raid on the enemy's capital. There is no evidence to suggest that Bennett took unusual steps to make this last assault a 'do or die' effort: his planning was always meticulous and every contingency was provided for in the event of the weather over the target turning sour. With twenty-five experienced crews opening the attack — illuminating the target area — followed by five Visual Markers to clinch the marking and eighteen Backers-Up to keep the pot boiling throughout, there was nothing more to be done. The crews allotted the crucial role of identifying and marking by eye alone were selected with a view to their success and past performance — there were none better in the whole of the Pathfinder Force and included Squadron Leader Keith Cresswell, Flight Commander in 35 Squadron, whose reputation for pressing home the attack had created something of a legend.

The Visual Marker represented the highest skill and proven reliability over many sorties against 'hard' targets. Men like John Fauquier, Pat Daniels, Hamish Mahaddie and Frazer Barron, to name but a few, had won their laurels over the toughest targets in the German Reich beginning with the early days when distinctive flares (the Aiming Point Flare as it was known) were dropped from a low level without the aid and backing of radar equipped Lancasters or Halifaxes lighting up the area. These captains went in among the exploding novelties 'naked' to find the mark, releasing a green flare over the spot which burned for only as long as it took to reach the ground, and was not very satisfactory, but better by far than anything done previously. The elaborate ritual described in these pages was the ultimate refinement using the excellent target indicators — so sophisticated in design that they could be triggered off at predetermined heights — manufactured by a British firm with experience of making fireworks going back to the days of George the Fourth. The vast spread of Berlin with its hundreds of heavy and light gun batteries, dummy fires and imitation target indicators, to which one may add the smoke and confusion which characterised any major raid called for the utmost in dedication on the part of the Visual Markers — and many were lost in the pursuit of what often seemed the impossible. The inclusion of a Master Bomber to control the attack (described in 5 Group circles as 'the personal representative of the Air Officer Commanding over the target', whatever that may have meant) had only limited effect for obvious reasons — after the first few minutes he was, in some instances, blind as a bat as to what was going on below and his main contribution was one of exhorting the on-coming waves of main force aircraft to bomb what seemed to him the most accurately placed markers. By sticking it out to the bitter end he lent encouragement and authority over a grim panorama of devastation. I say this only of Berlin: the control by Master Bombers after the invasion of Europe when attacks were delivered against marshalling yards and similar objectives was taut and effective in nearly every case, achieving a degree of precision seldom possible over the North German cities. The immediate aim of the Master Bomber on arrival over the target was one of establishing a datum — a lake, river or prominent landmark such as the Tempelhof airfield (heavily camouflaged and virtually undetectable) or buildings on easily recognised thoroughfares like those leading to the Brandenburg Gate. The River Spree wasn't much help — winding and narrow with few prominent bridges — and one of the many lakes in and around the city was usually chosen. The opportunity would not last long and it was important that the accuracy of the first markers dropped should be assessed at once: undershooting or overshooting, whatever the error, he had quickly to grasp the fact and pass the information. He could attempt to correct the marking using his own target indicators carried for that purpose and occasionally this was done but time was against him: once the bombs began to fall on a badly placed marker his chief task was one of instructing subsequent markers or backers-up to recover the situation with all speed. Failing that he would order crews to bomb on the centre of the pattern of marker bombs. To haul off and commence his own fresh bombing run from a predetermined datum point in an attempt to recentre the bombing required several minutes and in that interval the attack might stray well away from the chosen aiming point. Any 'creep-back' would be apparent by the carpet of bright incendiary bombs trailing along the line of approach as the bomb loads fell short: this he would attempt to stop immediately regardless of the exact objective. It was a feature of many attacks and one which cost us many wasted bomb loads.

Whilst all this was going on the enemy was doing his very best to defend his city and knock down the attacking bombers. By March 1944 his defences were indeed formidable, augmented by a horde of night fighters often clearly seen amid the holocaust — both controlled and free-lance they flew among the shell bursts though their best opportunities were taken on the approach path and as the bombers left the city on their return journey.

One last reflection on planning — the 'Wanganui' or sky marking technique provided in the method for the night was a last resort and by its very nature could never replace ground marking. On finding the target obscured by cloud the radar equipped crews released the distinctive flares — red and yellow stars — at a predetermined height. They drifted quickly in the wind and yet considerable damage was done to Berlin by this means: the main force crews with bombsights set to zero wind, true height and speed picked up a flare and pressed the bomb release. What happened after that might only be revealed in subsequent reconnaissance photos since the night camera carried in the bomber would not be effective.

No route markers were planned for the outward or return journey though in the past they had been used with discretion on targets at long range. As the enemy fighters gathered strength these markers provided a means of locating the bomber stream; originally, it had been done with the aim of assisting main force navigators, and perhaps more importantly, concentrating the force. In view of their use to the enemy no one was unhappy when they disappeared.

The Pathfinder Marking Sequence

The 'Berlin Method' designed to cover all eventualities was necessarily somewhat complex and if we include the 70 supporting aircraft which had no marking role, but were necessary to mask the twenty-five Pathfinders opening the attack, a total of one hundred and thirty-nine bombers appeared in sequence over the city:

Zero hour — 2230

(a)	Blind Marker Illuminators	25	commencing at	Z−5 minutes
(b)	Supporters	70	commencing at	Z−5 minutes
(c)	Visual Markers	6	commencing at	Z−3 minutes
(d)	Blind Backers-Up	18	commencing at	Z−1 through to Z+15
(e)	Visual Backers-Up	20	commencing at	Z−1 through to Z+15

'Blind' means releasing target indicators and flares solely by means of H2S, the airborne radar equipment.

Main Force Waves and Timings

Form 'B' dispatched by each Group HQ to the various Stations under command constituted the executive order for the night's operation. The Pathfinder Form 'B' contains more detail than that of the main force Groups whilst following the same pattern in layout. It is too long to be included here, but an extract from the signal dispatched by No 5 Group is given below:

A. Form 'B' No 197
B. 24 March 1944
C. 192 A/C of 5 Group and 520 A/C of other Groups assisted by 72 A/C of PFF Group will attack the target,

Wave 1	27 Lancs 1 Gp 12 Lancs 3 Gp 24 Hals 4 Gp 39 Lancs 5 Gp 18 Hals and 4 Lancs 6 Gp	Z to Z+3
Wave 2	27 Lancs 1 Gp 12 Lancs 3 Gp 24 Hals 4 Gp 39 Lancs 5 Gp 18 Hals and 4 Lancs 6 Gp	Z+3 to Z+6
Wave 3	27 Lancs 1 Gp 12 Lancs 3 Gp 24 Hals 4 Gp 8 Lancs 5 Gp 18 Hals and 4 Lancs 6 Gp	Z+6 to Z+9
Wave 4	26 Lancs 1 Gp 13 Lancs 3 Gp 24 Lancs 4 Gp 38 Lancs 5 Gp 18 Hals and 4 Lancs 6 Gp	Z+9 to Z+12
Wave 5	26 Lancs 1 Gp 13 Lancs 3 Gp 24 Lancs 4 Gp 38 Lancs 5 Gp 18 Hals and 4 Lancs 6 Gp	Z+12 to Z+15

The above is followed by a breakdown of numbers of Lancasters

(5 GP was an all-Lancaster Gp) required from each Station, bomb and fuel loads together with special instructions regarding the dropping of 'Window' and a resumé of the Pathfinder method of marking on this particular night. Since No 5 Group performed certain special tasks and enjoyed a degree of autonomy not extended to other formations this order is not without an oblique reference to that happy state. A glance at serial C gives the key — the word 'assisted' is deliberate: any admission to being 'led' is thus avoided. After all these years I find this amusing.

The 793 heavy attack bombers and seventeen Mosquitos which crossed the North Sea on the night of 24 March 1944 represented Sir Arthur Harris's final bid to destroy the German capital. It was not the largest attack; he had sent out nearly 900 bombers in mid-February at a cost of forty-three missing: a figure which was just below the maximum acceptable loss rate of five per cent. Leipzig, four nights later had proved disastrous with a missing rate in excess of ten per cent — a unique success for the German night fighter crews in that most of the interceptions took place before the bombers got into the target area. After this calamity Sir Arthur switched to targets lying further south where the night fighters were not so thickly spread. The Frankfurt operation had cost us thirty-three aircraft out of a total of more than 800 dispatched, and it was believed the enemy was less sensitive in respect of his South Eastern territories — a belief soon to be shattered when Nuremberg was attacked at the end of March. In fact the great increase in the enemy's fighter defences, coupled with his readiness to transfer significant forces wherever the threat appeared, ruled out what had been moderately 'safe areas'. Skilful planning embodying the use of spoof targets was no guarantee of success provided the weather conditions were favourable for the fighters. In the past we had waited on clear weather for a successful Berlin operation and when, as was believed, it finally came the advantage lay with the augmented German squadrons equipped with the best in search radars and fire power, to which may be added droves of 'Wild Boar' or free-lance gentlemen willing to sacrifice all for the chance to knock down a single Lancaster. That the writing was on the wall for Berlin was a fact seen most clearly by the German High Command whilst the identification of a huge force of bombers crossing to lower Denmark in this March evening had the warning bells ringing from the Jutland coast to Berlin itself. It seems that the decoy element of our training aircraft proceeding to a point south-west of Paris barely registered; the business of the night lay in the north and the enemy made ready.

Sir Arthur had long recognised the vulnerability of his night bombers to the increasing strength and skills of a resolute Luftwaffe but he had no recourse to new tactics: the barrel was empty. We sorely needed escort fighters. In the conditions now obtaining his crews went virtually naked to the slaughter, their plight barely eased by the presence of 11 Serrate Mosquitos of 100 Group and the assistance of a few aircraft of Fighter Command and Second Tactical Air Force whose mission was one of attacking enemy airfields along the route — with the aim of keeping their heads down. It was late in the day, but he made a strong case for an escort fighter possessing sufficient radius of action to stay with the bomber fleet. The Western Air Plans drawn up immediately before the Second World War* postulated daylight raiding but no long range fighter was envisaged; fighter aircraft were strictly for home defence. One of the great tragedies of the Bomber Offensive was the lack of interest and the piddling assistance contributed by other formations who were loath to lend their aircraft — save in tiny packets on occasion. After 1941 this Island was no longer under serious threat and yet hundreds of aircraft sat on lavishly equipped airfields from the Channel coast to the Firth of Forth, with no real commitment. The Americans acted with commendable promptness after Schweinfurt to produce the splendid Mustang: they were not content to suffer the kind of casualties which marked the early daylight raids. Without fighter escorts they would have been beaten into pulp. As for Bomber Command it took more than four years and thousands of lives to come to a decision — that the night fighter could master the lumbering bomber. With the turn of the year (1944) we needed a balanced force whilst the proof lay in the savage losses on the road to the Big City. We needed fighter pilots to maul the Luftwaffe over Germany proper — by night; and it could have been done. The shining deeds of Wing Commander Bob Braham and his little band of stalwarts — small though they may have been in terms of the actual number of German fighters downed — will be remembered by some of the bomber crews of that era. After the long years of going it alone this faint taste of honey, in the shape of the Serrate boys' efforts was sweet indeed.

Put quite simply 'Serrate' was a device which identified the opposing night fighters and enabled our own fighters to follow their transmissions. In a sense it represented full-circle, for the enemy was equipped with Naxos and the improved SN2 search radars, by which means they trailed the bombers using H2S and Monica — a situation long deplored by our own Scientific Intelligence under the direction of the brilliant Dr R. V. Jones. Similarly, he had endeavoured to convince our own Air Staff of the dangers inherent in the use of the IFF carried in every bomber (Identification Friend or Foe). This last device had been in constant operation since the beginning of the war — an effective, familiar and recognised 'must' which carried its own legend as being useful against searchlights and flak batteries — distorting the enemy director radars. In fact it did nothing of the

* 1.9.39 *Strategic Air Offensive Against Germany*, Webster and Frankland

kind: instead it provided the enemy with a useful clue as to the whereabouts of the bomber. In his book 'Most Secret War' Professor Jones lays emphasis on what he terms our prodigality in handing to the enemy the means of locating the whereabouts and strength of the attacking bomber force, and points out the seriousness of the situation. Eventually, the use of H2S was restricted and Monica cast out by Sir Arthur, but IFF seemed almost impossible to eradicate; the notion that this instrument harassed the enemy died a lingering death. Indeed, some reckoned it a morale factor — 'if you think it works then derive whatever comfort you may — it may even strengthen one's resolution.' Seemingly, we had no reason to suspect the IFF, much as in the early days the tossing out of empty beer bottles by the rear gunner was reckoned a sovereign remedy against searchlights. This enjoyed considerable vogue.

Over enemy territory the bomber crew's best protection was absolute silence coupled with unrelenting vigilance, radar and radio silence and no words spoken over the aircraft's inter-com. save when necessary. Experienced captains rigidly enforced this rule with regard to speech over the intercom; the need is obvious; a split second delay in acting on warning from a look-out could make the difference between survival and a swift exit, but the flood of replacement crews fresh from the training units took time to adapt to the disciplines of bomber 'Ops'. This was another world and survival of the first five sorties to Germany was reckoned an achievement; a time to work up and apply the lessons driven home by the Flight Commander. The extra sense — the instinctive reaction in emergency — could only come with a mounting total of 'Ops' and at this stage of the bomber offensive twenty under one's belt was veteran stuff.

Chapter 8
Briefing and Preparation

'We went into Briefing not knowing what lay in store for us. The
aircraft had their overload tanks on, so we guessed we were in
for a long night. Up on the rostrum the target map was
unveiled . . . a thin red line commencing at Hull ran across the
North Sea to Denmark, then out over the Kattegat and on to a
point just South of Sweden — making a turn into the Baltic and
the Island of Bornholm. From there in a straight line to Berlin.
Another red line was pinned to the map which ran Southwards
into France.'

These are the words of Kenneth Grantham, a member of No 640
Sqdn stationed at Lissett in Yorkshire and later we are privileged to
read his account of what followed after take-off. He uses a language
every bomber crew could well understand and at this distance in time
it touches a chord long silent.

The crews came from the domestic sites seemingly indifferent to
what lay ahead: no whisper of the nature of the target had reached
them but the old hands could put two and two together — full petrol
loads, a 'cookie' winched up into the bomb bay plus a big load of
incendiary bombs. Guesses ranged from Munich to Stettin and
Berlin. Five weeks had elapsed since the last assault on that city and
it seemed a likely prospect in view of the fact that a maximum effort
had been ordered. There was a time when crew briefings were
lightened by the odd shaft of wit; when losses were few and
Squadrons acquired a homogeneity stemming from long association
one with another, but that lay in the past. The daily advent of fresh
crews to replace those killed and missing made for new faces at each
briefing session. The likelihood of surviving the first few sorties was
very much a matter of luck — and everybody knew it. After two years
of hard training during which they were educated in every single
aspect of their final task they joined a front line unit — happy to have
escaped the pressures and disciplines of the Operational Training and
Conversion Units. Here at long last was the 'real thing' and any
nervousness they felt dissolved in the pride of belonging to a
numbered Squadron. Not every Squadron Commander was willing
to include a freshman crew in his battle order for the night; a
mine-laying operation in the Heligoland Bight or off the Dutch
Coast, and sometimes as far afield as the Baltic port of Gydinia,
provided an opportunity to break them in but, inevitably, they

would face their first sortie against a 'hard' target. It might well be Berlin.

Crew briefing was the responsibility of the Squadron Commander assisted by officers possessing specialist knowledge — navigation, signals, gunnery etc; each had a part to play but the personality of the Wing Commander and the manner in which he drew it all together — summing up the essential points, outlining the tactics, ramming home the business of getting stuck into the target regardless of what the enemy was doing was the chief ingredient for success. The morale of a unit is a direct reflection of the character and powers of the man who leads it and this was amply demonstrated in both the Pathfinder element and the main force of Bomber Command; particularly during the period from November through to the following March of 1944, when the going was very rough indeed. Whilst there were no 'aces' in the Pathfinder Force there were officers who bore a reputation for thrusting home the attack: others served Bennett equally well by the consistency of their marking and flying accuracy. John Fauquier and 'Tubby' Baker, both Squadron Commanders, ranked high in the establishment along with Harry Bufton (Mosquitos and pioneer of the Oboe technique) and Fraser Barron. There were 'characters', such as 'Pluto' Cousens and Guy Lockhart; the former being the first navigator to command a PFF Squadron and the latter renowned for his 'press-on' attitude to bombing the enemy. Losses were heavy among the Squadron Commanders — a sore subject with Bennett, outwardly cool and dispassionate, but who suffered agonies over the loss of so many of his friends in the battle over the 'Big City'. I believe we were closer to one another in the Pathfinder Group than in any formation and I remember well the shock I received at the news of the death in action of Group Captain Kenneth Rampling, Royal Australian Air Force, then in command of No 7 PFF Sqdn at Oakington. He was killed over Frankfurt a few days before the Berlin operation of 24 March and the circumstances of his death were witnessed by a member of his own Squadron. It was rare for anyone to say with a degree of certainty that the aircraft he saw shot down belonged to a particular crew but there seems little doubt in this instance. The following is an eye witness account by Flight Lieutenant Ralph Edwards who was over the target at the same time.

'At the briefing Group Captain Rampling led off the proceedings as usual; his name and those of his crew stood at the head of the Squadron Battle Order for the night — Primary Blind Markers, to be over the target six minutes before 'H' hour.

My own crew was named to be over Frankfurt at H−6 in support of the early markers. The route led over the North Sea turning south at the Frisian Isles and then straight to the target.

It was still daylight as we took off and climbed to set course for the Frisians; the light began to fail and we turned on to the final course in complete darkness, flying at 18,000 ft. The crew were keyed up to maximum alertness keeping a sharp look-out but it was so dark that the blackness seemed to close in on us like huge velvet curtains. With no cockpit light burning the luminous instruments reflected brightly on the windscreen and the four Merlins made a deafening roar — the exhaust ports spitting back red streams of flame. We flew on steadily south waiting for anything that might happen; hands gripping the control column and feet braced ready on the rudder bar — drawing nearer to whatever was waiting for us — adrenalin glands working overtime and with a feeling that it was all too quiet for comfort. We were to be in early at six minutes before the show opened and in small numbers. No moon, only blackness overhead as we drove steadily on to the target and then — suddenly — it happened . . . "My God we're on fire" was my first thought when, without warning . . . instantly . . . we were in the midst of blood-red blinding brilliance — bathed in an orange-red incandescence. The whole aircraft stood out amid the conflagration. Right alongside us a Lancaster was on fire — flames engulfing her from nose to tail. Every detail of her from the front turret, cabin, mid-upper turret, the H2S blister, engines and tailplane all so clear — and we were very close — bathed in the reflection of her agony — shimmering in the baleful glare.

The inter-com. came to life and I heard the urgent voices of my gunners. I was talking to them . . . "Can you see anyone getting out — any parachutes — what are the aircraft letters?" Then again, "Watch out for the night fighter — he must be still around — keep your eyes peeled." The blazing Lancaster gradually slowed and lost way as we watched — flame and smoke covered her — then she sank gradually downwards with bright red explosions tearing her vitals. My gunners saw brilliant coloured flares erupt — and this must have been one of the blind markers whom we were there to support — and who could that be? Another flash and she exploded — showering fragments to the earth below.

We pressed on to the target and all went normally; then we flew back to Oakington. At the de-briefing there were many questions asked about this incident . . . because the Squadron Commander, Group Captain Rampling and his crew were missing — and they were Blind Markers ordered to be over the target at H−6. Theirs was the only aircraft from No 7 Squadron to be missing that night.'

The above is Edwards' account and he kept a diary during this time. In the circumstances it is reasonable to assume that he saw the demise of his Squadron Commander — a man whom he both respected and admired. Most of us saw such incidents at one time or another though not necessarily quite so terrible as that related by Edwards. Squadron Commanders were expendable; they took precisely the same risks as any other member of the Squadron and were just as likely to go missing. Wing Commander Guy Lockhart who assumed command immediately following Rampling was lost a month later and a similar fate overtook the gallant New Zealander who stepped into his shoes — Wing Commander Fraser Barron. Number 7 Sqdn lost three COs in a very short time. Barron was the Pathfinder *par excellence*. One of the early volunteers, he had come up from Flight Lieutenant; surviving the fiercest attacks to achieve the distinction of commanding a Squadron to which he had given everything that duty and honour required.

On the day of the Berlin operation — six after Rampling's death — Flight Lieutenant Edwards sat again in the briefing room. Lockhart was known only by reputation to the Squadron; having previously commanded No 692 Mosquito Sqdn of the Light Night Striking Force. Rampling's going had left a gap — 'I will always proudly remember him — every inch the CO — tall, ramrod straight and upright with keen gimlet eyes. He possessed great courage, together with sympathy and understanding. Our loss was tragic indeed'. It takes time to win the confidence of men and the kind of confidence they had in Rampling helped every man-jack of them to go into battle at a time when the Command was being torn and savaged by the Luftwaffe's fighters. Bennett's choice of Lockhart was shrewd and timely: he had been shot down sometime earlier, evaded capture and made his way to the South of France — crossing the Pyrenees in bitter weather only to be captured by Spanish Frontier Guards and consigned to the notorious prison at Miranda in Northern Spain, where he spent the best part of a year. I met him for the first time in the George Hotel at Buckden where he was spending his leave with his wife and small daughter. He had broken out of Miranda and succeeded in getting to Gibraltar to be returned to England with all speed. A faded and creased snapshot taken at the time of his escape showed a gaunt figure in a ragged battle dress — head shaven, hollow-eyed but far from being dejected — standing with a group of other prisoners. Somehow he had kept himself fit enough to make the break-out but he assured me that he would never get into that kind of situation again — anything was better than another spell in Miranda. The hospitality of the Spanish prison left much to be desired though he was not ill-treated. When he got home he applied immediately to return to operational flying and since he had not been a prisoner of war in the hands of the Germans permission was given. He could have spent the rest of the war in modest comfort — and not everyone would have rushed back into the conflict — but elected to do what he believed was right. He was a strange individual — well educated, French speaking and on occasions an attractive personality; he had a certain magnetism and like all brave men was only content to be in the lead — others could follow but he had to be first into the fray. In another age he would have been the officer to lead the Forlorn Hope. Bennett, in his account of the Pathfinders had this to say:

> 'This Wing Commander commanded one of the Squadrons with such enthusiasm that it was positively dangerous . . . I never, throughout the entire war, met anyone so fanatically courageous and "press-on" at all times and in all circumstances. Virtually nothing could stop him. For example; on one occasion he took off in a Mosquito carring a four thousand pound bomb and after take-off had a complete failure of one engine: nevertheless, he went all the way to Berlin and back on the other . . . his determination passed all bounds and the inevitable result was that eventually he lost his life.'

Squadron Commanders had access to Bennett at all times: he treated everyone alike and the relationship was easy and pleasant: he expected the best and any criticism was constructive. He could not abide time-servers — in for a quick tour and a medal — whilst the role of his Squadrons precluded such a possibility. Though sometimes attacked for his methods and independence — and sorely tried, as in the case of the swift removal of 83 and 97 Squadrons — he bore up well, though Berlin caused him anxiety.

> 'This battle was the bitterest part of the war for me . . . not only was it gravely important that we should succeed, and thereby confirm the effects of Hamburg, but it was also bitter because of the great losses we suffered — particularly serious because they included a large proportion of experienced and good Pathfinder crews. I lost a number of Squadron and senior Flight Commanders and at one stage I thought the backbone of the Pathfinder Force was really broken.'

The loss of most of the senior officers who had given him the utmost in loyalty from the very beginning was hard to bear: they had supported him when the PFF came under fire from some of the 'Barons' and their faith in Bennett's ability to succeed remained unbroken. Wing Commander John Hilton and Group Captain B. V. Robinson (Robbie) were lost; the former on his first operation as CO of 83 Sqdn after a period as Staff Officer in the Group HQ and the latter as Station Commander at Graveley where he flew as second pilot with a new crew, to give them confidence.

On 24 March 1944 weather at the Pathfinder bases was poor.

Visibility was around a mile, improving slowly by mid-morning but with a promise of fog after nightfall — or so we estimated the chances. Berlin was laid on but the prospects were far from good so that a cancellation was expected around noon. It didn't come. A maximum effort was required by Command and the Squadrons went through the customary routine but right up to an hour before take-off many believed the show would be called off. Experience of local weather and the vagaries of the East Anglian climate justified such a belief and a certain uneasiness prevailed. Cancellation just before take-off was a miserable business, anyway, and once geared up to the task in hand the sense of anti-climax was strong: crews hated it. Dressed up and waiting for the transports to take them to the dispersal areas it was better always to crack on with the job. Once in the air nobody gave a thought to the return; that was for others to worry about; the Command Dispersal plan invariably worked well, sending all aircraft to clear-weather landing grounds from Cornwall to Scotland, though it posed a problem in terms of recovering the force. An unserviceable or battle damaged Lancaster sitting on a remote airstrip several hundred miles from the home base was lost to the front line for days on end.

The Met. forecast for the route and target area was promising. It spoke of strato-cumulus with tops at five thousand feet over much of the North Sea diminishing to broken cloud near the Danish Coast with a good chance of clear weather over Berlin — though the forecasters covered themselves by saying there was a possibility of 10/10ths thick stratus right over the target; a situation common enough at Berlin on occasions. It was going to be cold at height and strong north-westerly winds would be encountered up to 60 mph at cruising altitude. For the assembled crews in the many briefing rooms throughout the Bomber Groups it was very much the mixture as before and the navigators shrugged their shoulders — a strong headwind pulled back the groundspeed on the way home but it was nothing new. The Intelligence Officers spoke of increased night fighter strength and the Squadron Commanders and Gunnery Leaders dwelled on the tactical aspect — constant vigilance and snappy on the firing buttons. The Pathfinder method received close attention — 'Newhaven' plus 'Wanganui' to suit the weather over the city. The crews heard it in silence — the old hands knew it backwards and the new boys made careful notes. Some had never seen 'sky marking' before — the release of brilliant red and yellow flares to be caught briefly by the bombsight lens before they shot away from the target area at the whim of a sixty-mile-an-hour blast. The ground marking was easy to understand — reds and greens burning for several minutes and these must be bombed if seen — they would be dropped by skilled crews after visual identification of the aiming point — disregarding all other marks including the feeble dummy target indicators laid by the enemy to draw the attack away from the city. The Master Bomber would guide them if needs be and they were to listen out for his voice over the target area; he would be in full control. Some comfort could be drawn from the size of the force; eight hundred plus across the target in fifteen minutes, with three minute intervals between the five waves, would swamp the defences; at least that was how it had happened on previous occasions: but that applied strictly to the ground defences.

The concept of concentrating the bomber force had been well established over the past two years — since the 'Thousand' raids against Cologne, Essen and Bremen in mid-1942 — and the duration of our attacks had been squeezed to very narrow time brackets. The further the objective the greater the likelihood of scatter and failure to meet the strict timekeeping essential if such tactics were to succeed. The dropping of route markers by the leading Pathfinders helped at a time when the enemy fighter opposition was not so fierce but was stopped immediately the Luftwaffe began to make use of them: they drew the fighters like a magnet.

Inevitably, the skills of the navigators varied: some were better than others, whilst that of the pilots caused some of the former category to tear their hair on occasions. Despite the facility of a Distant Reading Compass, with the master unit suspended on gimbals at the rear of the fuselage, and the provision of a Gyro Compass at eye level in the Lancaster, the holding of a constant course demanded great concentration on the part of the pilot. The 'corkscrew' manoeuvre was widely employed by all Bomber Groups and this, coupled with evasive action in emergency undoubtedly produced errors in track-keeping however hard the Captain endeavoured to steer a mean course; all of which worked against the perspiring navigator. Whereas, in theory, the bomber stream remained a narrow well-compacted body extending many miles in length, once out of 'Gee' cover, or in the absense of well defined land marks, the combination of the foregoing and the weather tended to spread the aircraft over a broad front. In the case of bombers flying from widely separated bases — from Yorkshire in the north to Norfolk in the south — the naming of a rendezvous point in the North Sea was essential if they were to approach the Dutch coast in anything like close company: and the RV for the night of 24 March lay in Gee range with the purpose of gathering the various groups together before launching them into enemy occupied territory. The Danish coast would offer a further opportunity for fixing position and the bomb aimers lying prone in the nose would use their utmost endeavours to secure a pin-point from which the navigator would expect to find the wind velocity — review his calculated course — and stick to the planned route.

The North Sea was both friend and enemy to the bomber crews. To get clear of the attentions of the enemy when returning from a sortie over Germany was fine — we all remember the feeling of relief — but in terms of weather during the winter months and in the case of a limping bomber with the captain struggling to make base before the aircraft was forced on to the sea's surface, where a black night and twenty foot waves spelt disaster, the prospect was grim. Even under the best conditions a 'ditching' was tricky — too high and she might break up on striking the water — wheels first instead of the tail — and the aircraft could do a cartwheel, arriving on the sea upside down! Blind save for a single light out on the mainplane, and no prospect of finding the line of the swell or the precise wind direction at the surface it was a matter of 'joss' — lucky if you made it — and got the crew clear before she sank. Housed in the starboard mainplane the dinghy was released by an immersion switch whilst a manual control in the cabin made doubly certain. Inflation was automatic and the dinghy remained tethered to the aircraft until cut free by one of the occupants. Every second counted once the aircraft came to rest on the surface and much depended on the state of the sea: the crew left the positions taken up prior to ditching and a mad scramble followed to get out and into the life raft, tossing and pitching in the waves. A wounded man could present a problem: most certainly he would not be left whatever the circumstances but time was of the essence. The dinghy painter was long enough to allow the use of the main door to the fuselage and the injured crew member would be passed out into the bucking rubber contraption. A hand torch was the only means of finding one's way and the whole operation was fraught with difficulty from first to last. Despite this there were successes, though what came after was in the hands of Providence. If the wireless operator transmitted the aircraft's position in good time there was a chance they would be picked up, but in winter somewhere in the North Sea death from exposure might well be their lot. Coastal Command and the fast launches of the Air/Sea Rescue Service manned by Royal Air Force crews brought off many rescues in appalling conditions but the difficulty of finding a tiny rubber dinghy in the waste of waters needs no emphasis. The hand operated transmitter in the dinghy sent out signals on which the aircraft attempted to 'home': a signal pistol was available in the craft for use when an aircraft was either heard or, in daylight, sighted and an airborne lifeboat could be dropped if the dinghy was located, but with a strong wind blowing and the crew weak from exposure it was well-nigh impossible to secure it. Such were the hazards of ditching — it could happen to anyone — and did so. A small percentage of our crews were saved from the sea but a large number perished; they are recorded as missing — with no known grave. Thus, enemy territory apart, the weather over the North Sea was always a factor — if routed the long way round to the 'Big City': the comment of Group Captain John Fauquier after the catastrophe of 7 November 1941, comes readily to mind . . . 'I have seen the North Sea in many moods but never more ferocious than that night . . .' Well, history was to repeat itself in March 1944 — as we shall see.

The first weather reconnaissance of the day took off from Wyton forty minutes after midnight on 24 March — following a request from the Americans who were planning a big daylight attack in the Berlin area. Flight Lieutenant J. M. Briggs with Pilot Officer C. Baker as navigator penetrated as far as Nordhausen, some eighty miles south-west of Berlin to find solid strato-cumulus, unbroken from the German coast onwards. They returned after four hours in the air and on the basis of their report the American attack was cancelled, whilst the substance of this reconnaissance was available for Sir Arthur Harris's morning conference, but did not affect his decision to lay on a full scale operation that night. It was far too early in the day and his Chief Met. Officer held out the likelihood of an improvement later. Planning went ahead and another weather sortie was ordered. At 1030 Squadron Leader J. M. Birkin, Officer Commanding the Weather Reconnaissance Flight, took off with Flight Lieutenant Cowan to cover the route across the North Sea and Lower Denmark where they found frequent gaps in both the medium and low stratus cloud — an obvious improvement over the past few hours supporting the forecast produced by the Command Met. Staff.

At the midday review of the weather the situation was deemed good enough for the work of aircraft preparation and crew briefing to go ahead. Nevertheless, the threat of poor conditions over the home bases persisted and the risk was, for the time being, accepted. So often in the past this kind of situation had obtained, but with the distinct possibility of Berlin being free of the customary blanket of thick cloud the chance of hitting it was not to be missed. Cancellation was simple; and could be effected right up to the time of take-off with all the frustration and cursing on the part of the crews wound up for an operation over the past eight hours; but once in the air a huge force of four engined bombers might not be turned round easily to land back at the various bases; thousands of tons of high explosive and petrol would first need to be dumped — jettisoned over the sea — whilst the accident risk among aircraft endeavouring to get back on the ground before fog obscured the runways might be high. Loss of precious bombs, waste of equally precious fuel, damaged Lancasters and Halifaxes — scattering of the force — a calamity of vast proportions might well be the result. All this lay on Harris's broad shoulders — time and again — but the period of the Berlin Battle was probably the worst of any.

Reverting to the Met. forecast for the night . . . 'Fog will develop at 0300 in Lincolnshire and East Anglia . . . all Groups will have at least half their bases until 0200 with visibility 1500 yards or more.'

The threat left little margin for the recovery of 800 heavy bombers: the return from Berlin would take place between 0130 and 0200 whilst the stragglers might not show up for another hour or more. Again, this kind of timing derived from the forecast winds for the night; strong winds would be encountered beyond 04E — but there was no certainty as to the precise strength and in the event they exceeded the forecast value by a significant figure. Thus, the interval between 'safe' landing conditions and the airfields being 'socked-in' by fog was too narrow for comfort, and a further small drop in temperature — a matter of a couple of degrees — could change the situation with disastrous results.

The Command Operation Order for the night had named Berlin as the primary target and Brunswick the alternative. The same briefing served both objectives in terms of routing and fighter opposition whilst the final decision was not taken until late in the afternoon; and in some instances as the crews were out on their way to the aircraft. Cloud conditions over Berlin was the deciding factor: Sir Arthur had experienced too many disappointments in the past four months to go 'nap' on the Big City and he did not intend on this occasion to send his crews so far into Germany only to return empty handed with another Berlin failure to report. The likelihood of one or the other, of Berlin or Brunswick, being clear of cloud was enough to keep the operation in being until the latest meteorological evidence could be obtained and assessed. Brunswick did not rank with other cities as a prime target for Bomber Command although it was an important transportation centre lying on the direct rail link between Berlin and the Ruhr: the South Marshalling Yard was one of the biggest in Germany and was attacked during the night of 14/15 January 1944 by 500 'heavies' incurring a loss of thirty-eight bombers. Whilst the ground defences were nothing like as formidable as those surrounding Berlin it lay in an area stiff with night fighters grouped for the defence of the German capital; hence the relatively high casualty rate of nearly eight per cent on his occasion. Nevertheless, in the briefing rooms the crews kept their fingers crossed — better Brunswick than Berlin — an hour less over a particularly dangerous section of the Reich and a short run back to the coast. Night fighters were one thing and the 600 heavy flak guns with their complementary searchlight batteries defending Berlin were another: the fighter was the unseen menace but the horrors of the flak barrage were both seen and heard whilst the last agonies of a stricken bomber — a common sight under these conditions — scarred the minds of the more sensitive. This was a bad time for the bomber crews — the Battle commencing in the previous November had been long and costly in lives and aircraft and despite the fact that the force was approaching its peak in the numbers of aircraft dispatched, the experience of the crews was small in many instances, the all-up weights had been increased and the severity of the opposition exceeded anything known previously. Berlin was in many respects a latter day Passchendaele for the Royal Air Force — on a much smaller scale and with a less well defined objective — there would be no breakthrough or territorial acquisition, only a hoped for psychological victory over the minds of the defenders: a legitimate aim if it would shorten the war, as Harris firmly believed it would. Back in the bomber bases John Smith and Bill Brown were more concerned with the fact that Brunswick was infinitely better than Berlin as a target for the night, as they drew on their Mae Wests, shouldered their parachutes and grabbed a seat in the vehicle which carried them to the Lancasters and Halifaxes sitting on the round concrete pans; bombed-up and ready to go.

Chapter 9
The Operation

'The main target was the Big City but weather conditions were uncertain and an alternative was laid on: the final decision would be made just before take-off as to which we would attack. If the choice was 'A' we would go for Brunswick; if it was 'B' then it was the big one. We hoped for the lesser evil. At dusk we were dressed and ready, standing by our aircraft, laughing and joking among ourselves. The CO's little car drove fast into our dispersal bay. He said two words:

"It's B".

We climbed aboard and it didn't seem funny any more. As we taxied into position at the end of the runway the ground staff and WAAF were lined up on either side to wave us off. It seemed a nice gesture — nice to know some wished us well.

Engines run up to full revs — brakes hard on — final check and then we were rolling, leaving the runway at 1900 hrs exactly and heading for the first turning point over Hull; then out over the North Sea but keeping low to stay beneath the German radars for as long as possible. After two hours or so came the words which put everyone on the alert — "Enemy Coast Ahead." We flew over Denmark just north of Esbjerg at 14,000 ft, climbing and turning slightly to avoid Copenhagen. There was little enemy activity at this stage — isolated flak and tracer shells climbing skywards. Time to start windowing. I pulled up the little bundle of foil strips — jerked the string to tear the wrapper — and pushed the lot into the chute which would send the strips flying into the slip-stream to jam the German radar scopes. One a minute — pick up — tear — throw; a monotonous rhythm which would not end until we were clear of enemy territory. In between times I spun the dial of the radio receiver over the short wave band searching for the voices of the German fighter controllers. When I picked one up I tuned in the transmitter quickly and sent out a burst of noise stemming from the microphone located in one of the engine nacelles. If it was done quickly the instructions from the German controller to his waiting fighter were blotted out by the racket from my transmitter.

Then, below us, lay neutral Sweden and we saw something we had not seen for a very long time — towns and villages lit up! There was no blackout anywhere and I was fascinated to see twinkling lights. Suddenly, one of the gunners reported fighter aircraft on our beam; and he was puzzled because they made no attempt to engage us. We could see them quite plainly — ghostly white aircraft flying alongside the bomber stream. We watched them for a while as they came and went and concluded they were Swedish — making a token gesture of defending their neutrality. To the north of our track we saw streams of light flak and assumed this to be from Swedish ground batteries — not trying to hit us but performing a similar duty. The fighters accompanied us well out over the Baltic, perhaps curious to see where we were going. Then they vanished.

It was about this time that our navigator started to have serious doubts about the wind speed and direction being put out on the Group broadcast. By their recokoning it was in the region of 80 mph but our navigator was calculating wind in excess of 100 mph. Later we discovered he was much nearer the mark. We had encountered the phenomenon now known as the 'jet stream'. This was a wind of very high velocity blowing at a particular height — something like a tide-race at sea — but at that time nothing much was known about it and the bomber stream was straying all over the sky due to the conflicting opinions. By now the enemy had guessed our destination and the fighters we had seen previously had changed to dark prowlers in the night sky. Hundreds of fighter flares were coming down to light up the bombers and assist the Messerschmidts and Focke Wulfs to attack from the darkness whilst our own gunners were blinded by the powerful lights, and we met heavy flak which increased in intensity. Almost before we realised it we were over Berlin. Now the heavy Ack-Ack was the menace and a veritable curtain of bursting shells faced us. Up front the Canadian bomb aimer was exclaiming over and over in a broad Canadian accent,

"Jesus Skipper — look at that flak . . . just look at it will ya . . . we'll never get through it . . . Jeez, just look at it." Then the Skipper's tense voice silenced him.

Berlin was already burning when we arrived. My own view of events was mercifully obscured by the bulk of the navigator and bomb aimer. At times I preferred not to look and the glimpses I got were frightening enough. It was mayhem down below — bombs bursting — photoflashes blinking and a pall of firelit smoke over everything. Nothing can ever recreate that moment. The tight muscles, the dry mouth and the buffeting the aircraft received whilst the Skipper fought to keep it steady as we swam through the slip-streams of a hundred other aircraft and bounced to the Ack-Ack bursts. It was an unbelievable experience. Three years of training — hours of circuits and landings — nights spent on cross country navigation exercises — all leading up to this moment — to *Berlin* — and we were *there*.

The bomb aimer spotted the PFF flares and adjusted his sights. There was silence in the aircraft as he went through the familiar routine . . .

"Steady . . . Steady . . . Left a bit . . . Right . . . Hold it . . . Steady." Then the moment when everyone lets out a sigh of relief . . . *"bombs gone"*. The aircraft leapt as the weight dropped from her belly, then the Skipper's Texan voice over the intercom . . .

"OK. Bomb doors closed — let's get the hell out of here."

Weaving slightly to throw off the fighters we flew south, pushed along by a vicious tail wind until near Leipzig we were in a belt of searchlights — great pillars of blue light weaving back and forth like flying through a vast cathedral . . . cones of several lights coming together to trap some poor devil while the flak batteries pumped their shells into him. We turned northwards on to track, as we thought, for a more lightly defended route out via Emden. Flying at 24,000 ft the navigator again queried the broadcast wind since we were rapidly drifting south of track. Then we were once more into heavy concentrations of flak and searchlights and realised we had drifted over the Ruhr — the most heavily defended area in Germany. Struggling to make headway at one stage our groundspeed was down to a mere 30 mph and once again the searchlights hit us — the aircraft suddenly lit up as if the sun had risen and the flak started to pound us as the Skipper put us into a steep dive; the light was left behind and we plunged earthwards in total darkness. We didn't complain.

We left the enemy coast by Texel — well to the south of where we should have been — opened up the flasks of coffee and ate our Mars bars. England slid beneath us near Yarmouth and we landed at base after seven hours in the air. We had been to *The Big City*.'

The crew whose exploits are recounted above were making their sixth war flight — and first trip to Berlin — from RAF Station Leconfield. No 640 Sqdn, formed in January 1944, was an offshoot of No 158 based at Lissett, Yorkshire. The author of the story was the wireless operator of a unique crew — unique in the sense that it was captained by an American who had come to Bomber Command via the Royal Canadian Air Force and his crew included two Canadians, two Scotsmen, a volunteer from Brazil and a Londoner. After only a month with No 640 Sqdn (Halifax B.IIIs) they were recruited for the Pathfinder Force by Group Captain Hamish Mahaddie who had an eye for talent and in the face of strong opposition from the Squadron Commander. They were not very experienced at the time of this operation and Ken Grantham, the wireless operator, states:

'With less than a month at Leconfield we were still new to the game. So far we had been lucky: we had survived the crucial first five on which so many crews came to grief . . . but we were still green . . . a tight crew, well disciplined and well led which made us confident, but not unafraid.'

Captain	: Lieutenant 'Doss' Kornegay. RCAF	
	and later Captain USAAF	
Bomb Aimer	: F/O G. Williams	
Navigator	: F/O G. Prosser	(This crew completed a total
W/Op/AG	: Sgt K. Grantham	of 56 sorties, 48 of which were
R/Gunner	: Sgt R. Chapman	flown with the Pathfinder Force
M/Upper	: Sgt H Wilcox	— and survived the war)
F/Eng	: Sgt A. Wooler	

This account was chosen from many similar stories to illustrate the effect of a Berlin operation upon a relatively untried crew. Berlin was without doubt a 'bogey' to some and to return safely after a battering seemed nothing short of a miracle. They had tasted the worst and what came after could never match it in horror — or so it seemed at the time. Their previous targets had been Trappes (French marshalling yards), Le Mans, Stuttgart and two operations over Frankfurt — but Berlin was different.

★　★　★

In falling darkness I watched No 156 Squadron take off for the Big City — twenty-one Lancasters crawling round the perimeter track maintaining a precise distance between successive aircraft. The noise of the Merlins was clear and distinct — the moist atmosphere accentuating the roar of their exhausts as one by one they drew into the runway threshold, paused for a moment for the customary brake test and then opened up to take-off power — plus seven boost and 2850 revs. Flight Lieutenant Blamey was first away and the remainder followed at minute intervals. In the Flying Control tower the departure times were chalked up on the wall display and the airfield became silent — empty, not merely empty of aircraft but seemingly stripped of life. This was true of all bomber airfields for the Squadron was both heart and sinew: the airfield and its complex organisation existed only to serve the fighting unit and would return to life with the sound of the homing Lancasters. Back in the Mess the atmosphere was subdued, such was the effect of the departing Squadron. Off duty personnel glanced at the clock in the ante room . . . in seven and a half hours the Lancs would be back.

Across the North Sea the enemy was already alerted and preparing for another night of battle in the air and on the ground. He, too, had given the synoptic charts careful study. The growing power and frequency of our attacks on his major cities and ports was plain evidence of the will to destroy him piecemeal and his Signals Intelligence organisation operated at maximum efficiency throughout twenty-four hours in every day. Every squeak from a radio transmitter whether a bomber carrying out a night flying test earlier in the day or a routine coded transmission on the network linking the Groups with Command Headquarters was faithfully recorded whilst his long range search radars swept all approaches to his coasts. The trick of crossing the North Sea at an altitude reckoned below the optical scan of his radar worked well in the beginning but was not a hundred per cent effective. In any event the German fishing boats off the coast were all equipped to report hostile aircraft and did so. At two thousand feet above the waves and a hundred or more miles from the coast we became blips on the cathode ray tube, and from then on were closely monitored in an attempt to assess the likely objective.

Whilst the enemy paid the greatest attention to our own radio transmissions the Royal Air Force 'Y' Service worked even harder to gather valuable intelligence. Not enough has been written about the devoted band of officers and other ranks, including a high proportion of women belonging to the WAAF, who operated this vital service day in day out from numerous locations along the south and east coasts of England. Intercepted messages were recorded and passed to the Bletchley Headquarters for decoding and study by expert crypto-graphers. Nothing escaped this net and when Bomber Command was out over Germany the 'Y' Service listened for the reactions of the enemy — and in particular to the German controllers directing night fighter defences. On the night of 24 March 1944 they intercepted numerous messages commencing almost immediately after our aircraft crossed the coasts of Yorkshire, Lincolnshire and Norfolk en-route to the rendezvous point in the North Sea.

At 1944 hrs the German long range radar stations began passing information to the Fighter Control concerning British bombers only fifty miles out from Skegness on an east-north-easterly course. A few minutes later another group of aircraft was located by the enemy over Flamborough Head on a similar course: these were No 4 or 6 Group aircraft outward bound for Berlin having been airborne only a very short time. This was by no means extreme range for the German 'Korfu' detectors: they were capable of picking up a bomber over its own airfield in England — if the H2S was in operation. This particular equipment formed part of the German monitoring system after 1943 and from time to time various restrictions were placed on the use of the H2S in an attempt to conceal the approach of the bombers for as long as possible. Apart from 'Korfu' the powerful — and very accurate — Wasserman radars located on the coasts of Germany and Holland possessed a range of up to 150 miles and did not rely on H2S transmissions for identification. Thus, there was some merit in keeping low during the crossing of the North Sea providing the H2S was not switched on. Once near the enemy coast cover was 'blown' and the danger came from the airborne SN-2 radars carried by the Ju 88s and Me 110s of the enemy fighter groups.

The warning delivered at briefing concerning increased fighter activity over northern Germany was not lost on the crews. Evidence of the enemy's determination to defend Berlin had been displayed on each occasion the city had been under attack but repeated warnings lose some of their edge to crews already battle-weary: the shadow of Leipzig where seventy-eight bombers had been shot down — a loss of 9.5 per cent — hung over Harris's men. What odds could a few more fighters make? As for the ground defences — they were always part of the deal — but the constant flog, mile after long mile, in what has been described by Sir Arthur himself as 'appalling conditions' imposed a heavy strain accompanied by a sense of futility. In such circumstances morale may well be affected though there is little evidence of this.

Following Leipzig, the Commander-in-Chief switched the assault to what used to be believed less well defended areas, namely, southern Germany; and the seven operations which took place between Leipzig and the final attack on the enemy's capital brought some respite. Schweinfurt, Augsburg, Stuttgart and Frankfurt came under attack resulting in what were, by Bomber Command standards, relatively light losses. Nevertheless in the first three weeks of March the Command lost nigh on a hundred bombers over southern Germany and in the last three attacks of this short phase the losses began to swell — thirty-seven over Stuttgart on the 15th, twenty-two over Frankfurt on the 18th and thirty-three two nights later over the same target. It appeared from these figures the enemy was no longer content to retain the bulk of his defending fighters in the north but was willing to deploy them at increasing ranges from their home airfields using a greatly improved system of overall control. He was never short of fighters, both twin and single engined free-lances; a situation which did not change until, in the last months of the war, they were grounded for lack of fuel.

The series of heavy bombing attacks on Germany commencing in November 1943 ended at Nuremberg with ninety-five bombers missing. The Germans were fighting their own Battle of Berlin, as we had fought the Battle of Britain, but on a far greater scale. The numbers engaged in heavy bombers and opposing fighters — the long haul on the part of the attackers — the constant adverse weather in what was the worst winter ever for tactical deployment of bomber forces, and the terrible casualties forced upon us by the ferocity of the ground and air defence constitute a grievous chapter in the history of the Second World War — in terms of the sacrifice of the bomber crews. Men died by the thousand in the Battle of Berlin, often without seeing the enemy; the first indication of his presence being a stream of cannon shells ripping apart the heavily laden and ill defended bomber — ill defended because the elaborate turrets contained the equivalent of a pea-shooter when opposed to the quadruple cannon mounted in the nose of the attacking fighter. The Official History of the Bomber Offensive, describing the Battle, states:

'The heavy and medium bombers possessed neither the armament nor the performance seriously to damage the German Night Fighter force in the air. The best their gunners could do with their small calibre weapons was to provide some deterrent to the less skilled or the more unwary among the German pilots. Restricted to .303 calibre machine guns they were substantially outshot and completely outranged by their cannon-equipped enemies. Their armour plating was progressively removed, until little remained, to increase their bomb-lifting capacity. Belching flames from their exhausts as well as radar transmissions from their navigational and fighter warning apparatus made them all too apparent to those who hunted them. Once engaged in combat, they had little chance of victory and not much of escape, whilst the large quantities of petrol, incendiary bombs, high explosives and oxygen with which they were filled often gave spectacular evidence of their destruction. Out-paced, out-manoeuvred and outgunned by the German fighters and in a generally highly inflammable and explosive condition, these black monsters presented an ideal target . . .'

The Official Historian and co-author of these words wrote this paragraph with deep feeling, I believe; Dr Noble Frankland survived many sorties over enemy territory and none could put it better.

In the light of the above why was nothing done about it? Sir Arthur Harris *did* do something but there was little hope of any change in overall policy — it was far too late in the day. The Rose Brothers .5 turret was successful and a number of Lancasters were fitted up; and there it all stopped. Speed and manoeuvreability were more important factors than weight of armament if the bomber was to escape the fighter.

Removal of the heavy turrets would add another fifty or sixty mph to the bomber's performance: the aircraft would have been lighter and better streamlined in consequence whilst our casualties might well have been reduced. This is not hindsight — the matter came under scrutiny late in the war but nothing was done.

The men who sat in the turrets, frozen stiff for much of the time, rendered great service. Unassuming, cheerful and courageous, they

fought with inadequate weapons against a powerfully armed adversary
— and very occasionally destroyed him. Too often we took our
gunners for granted — unseen from take-off to return — apart from
the occasional check to ensure we were in contact; and yet in some
respects theirs was the worst task of all; the loneliness of the man at
the tail end staring into the darkness hour after hour could only be
appreciated by those who performed this duty. The captain,
navigator, flight enginer, bomb aimer and wireless operator were all
in touch with one another and free to move about the aircraft, but the
gunners knew only solitude; their lives were in the hands of the pilot
up forrard — his mistake could spell their demise.

From the coast of England to the rendezvous point low strato-
cumulus cloud lay on the sea with few breaks. There was no moon
and overhead the stars shone with great brilliance. In the clear air at
fifteen thousand feet visibility was good and assisted the gunners who
watched for anything unusual though at this stage of the operation it
was the odd Lancaster or Halifax steering a similar course which
might be too close for comfort. With the wind on the port beam
blowing strongly from the north some drift away from track became
evident as the navigators fixed position by means of the Gee co-
ordinates and corrections were made. The Eastern Gee Chain was
the favourite of all navigators since the signals were invariably strong
out to more than a hundred miles from the coast and continued to be
of service as long as the pulses could be seen. It would fade eventually
or suffer jamming by the enemy but while the dancing pulses
continued, position could be fixed with a degree of certainty that was
superior to any other form of navigation aid. On this night the
Eastern Chain was lost before reaching the rendezvous, but by then
the crews had become aware of a widening gap between the forecast
wind strength and that encountered as they pressed on to the Danish
Coast. The airborne radar with its big scanner below the belly of the
aircraft was not in use for reasons already given.

After leaving the RV point a marked rise in the wind velocity was
experienced; whereas the forecast had been 'strong north-westerly up
to 60 miles an hour' at 20,000 ft it was estimated to be nearer the 100
mark veering to the north. The result was to cause many bombers to
drift off track and interception of radar plots made by the enemy
showed a wide scatter to the south. Thus instead of making a landfall
at the island of Romo a high proportion of our aircraft were passing
below Sylt heading for the most sensitive area between Flensburg and
Kiel. Here the Germans took first blood and a number of bombers
were observed shot down in flames. There was much searchlight
activity and crews who escaped the trap reported flak, intense and
accurate, firing up to 20,000 ft. Combats between fighter and bomber
took place; two more aircraft were lost and several sightings were
made. Had it not been for the scatter caused by the hurricane wind it

is likely more casualties would have resulted: a compact bomber stream offered the prowling night fighter easy victims once he had nosed into the mass — picking up the slip-stream and certain of a kill. The accurate shooting by the flak batteries was the cause of much comment later: in general a strong wind at height made for poor shooting but on this particular night from this point onwards the flak gunners excelled, as we shall see.

The valiant Edwards was captain of No 7 Squadron's S — Sugar and this extract from his diary portrays the scene:

'The weather report indicated clear skies, and the old hands pursed their lips; no cloud meant searchlights; flak and fighters were lined up for a field day. And to rub it in we were told to expect much night-fighter activity. As we flew across the North Sea the visibility was so good we could pick out the coast fifty miles off and there was plenty of evidence as to the activity of the defences. Our route took us to the German-Danish border where we turned south east, not so far from Kiel where we saw vast skeins of searchlight beams — gigantic lattices — hundreds of them. As we got closer I observed great pyramids of light and at the apex glittered a silver fish — a Lancaster surrounded by flashes of orange and red light which winked and flashed as the shells exploded. Several aircraft were caught and as I watched, the glistening object suddenly dissolved into a brilliant red mushroom — like a child's rocket on Guy Fawkes night: then it blossomed out and fell as red rain. We knew it was a Lancaster with seven tons of bombs, two thousand gallons of high octane and a full crew on board — going down in fragments — a burning incandescence. As the final moments came, and a 'kill' registered, the beams would extinguish: then, a moment later, quiver into brilliance again having locked on to another quarry.'

Flight Lieutenant Edwards had travelled this road before: he was prepared for the worst, his mind attuned to all the possibilities: reaction would be instant, automatic — and resolute. Not so the new boys for whom the 'Big City' was little more than a name — though an ugly one. It was commonly said that the first five sorties were critical; after that one might work up to twenty . . . and if the luck held one might stagger on to thirty — and complete a tour — but few achieved this goal. The odds were too great. One Squadron Commander of my acquaintance, a strong character, excelling in the light touch, drew his men after him by sheer force of personality, having little regard for the rules where his men were concerned. At the height of the battle he faced up to the problem that no crew ever finished a tour of duty — casualties had been heavy and his customary cheerfulness made little impact. The young officers and

NCOs facing the dais were resigned — their faces dead pan as he wound up the briefing:

'There is a rumour going round this Squadron that no one ever finishes a tour?' Stony silence; then a growl from the back answered him, 'Too bloody right they don't.'

He knew the voice; 'Flight Sergeant Brown — how many sorties have you got under your belt?'

'Twenty-eight, sir.'

'Right — you're finished — you can fall out and take your leave. It's time someone finished a tour, and you are the lucky one.'

This broke the spell. The fortunate Flight Sergeant, grinning broadly, stuck his thumb up and left the briefing room with his crew behind him. This was a main force squadron; no better and no worse than many others.

As we have seen, the Command was turning over its complement during the Battle of Berlin. I quote from the Official History,

> 'The high and sustained casualty rate amounting in the whole battle to more than the average daily strength of the Command during the period, meant, obviously, that an increased proportion of the Bomber crews were inexperienced . . . new crews still sprang forward eagerly to take the places of those who had been lost . . .'

I have remarked on the youthfulness of these crews . . . I have a letter from a member of a crew who joined my Squadron in September 1943 — Sergeant R. F. Raymond, Flight Engineer and his captain was Flt Lieut Hyde. I saw all new crews on arrival and the Adjutant brought them in to see me:

> 'I remember you looking at me and saying "How old are you Sergeant?" I replied "Nineteen Sir" and you said "Good God!" What you didn't know Sir, was that my flying experience including the training unit was thirty-five hours . . . and that my first operation would double my night-flying hours.'

He appeared to be no more than a boy. His story is interesting . . . he went to Kassel — a bad night — I was flying myself and remember something of it. His next trip was Berlin — the opening attack of the Battle — and was briefed for another Berlin operation when the aircraft blew up on the dispersal pan — killing several people and injuring others. Sgt Raymond suffered 'minor injuries' as he put it. After a spell in hospital he rejoined the squadron in the following February and flew two Berlin trips, Leipzig and Nuremberg followed by a crash landing coming back from Munich on two engines and was finally shot down over Brunswick the following May, spending the next year as a PoW. A most honourable record: and there were thousands more like him.

Lancaster K — King which blew up on the hardstanding at Wyton, serial number JA 686 provides an example of men and a woman killed on active service doing a vital job which we all took for granted. The casualty list totalled five killed, two missing and four injured including Sergeant Raymond. The aircraft had been bombed up ready for the Berlin operation that night; an electrician entered the aircraft to make final adjustments to the flare chute mechanism which contained a live, and highly sensitive, magnesium flare — commonly termed the Photo-flash which was released with the bomb load to record the point of impact of the bombs. It was said afterwards that the photo-flash slipped from the launching tube and exploded immediately, setting off the 4000 lb bomb which atomised everything within range. Included in those missing was a popular WAAF Corporal who drove the tractor which pulled bomb trolleys. I saw her doing her job quite often, as I made my rounds, hauling the string of five or six big bombs, each on its separate trolley — turning into the hardstandings one by one where the armourers unhitched a trolley and wheeled it under the waiting bomb bay. Then off she would go to the next hardstanding to repeat the process. A pleasant girl with a cheery word for everyone and we were all very sad at her death. Her contribution and that of the ground airmen killed with her should not be forgotten.

The Controlling Officer on duty at Headquarters 2nd Fighter Division, responsible for the territory north and east of Hamburg, had ample warning of the approaching bombers. By the time the first wave of heavies reached the Danish and German coasts at soon after nine o'clock that evening he had positioned a complete wing — NJG 5 — armed with Ju 88s and Me 110s in the Sylt area; a total of more than a hundred night fighters. Having done so he then called two more formations NJG 2 and NJG 3 to augment the defences; bringing aircraft from as far away as Holland and northern France to block the return of the bombers between Berlin and the coast. As for the spoof raid of one hundred and fifty aircraft drawn from the Bomber Command training units making for the Paris area he chose to ignore them, recognising this move as a dummy designed to attract fighters away from Berlin where the alarm bells were already ringing and the flak batteries standing to. The moves of these formations were quickly established by our Signals Intelligence Service intercepting the enemy transmissions and details of their operating wavelengths were passed to Bomber Command and No 100 Gp; the latter responsible for counter-measures and the control of the Serrate Mosquitos, eleven in number, mingling with the bomber streams. Individual jamming was effected by bomber crews; the wireless operator sending out blasts of noise from a microphone conveniently placed in one of the engine nacelles.

By the spring of 1944 the Luftwaffe Fighter Arm posed a formidable threat to the bombers. Whereas the German bomber wings had declined steadily in importance the defending fighters had reached a peak of supremacy within the Luftwaffe proper. The ability of the factories to increase production of fighter aircraft month by month, the development of new and more powerful radars for tracking and intercepting our bombers, the arming of the fighters with twenty and thirty millimetre cannon, flown by experienced pilots meant the odds were heavily weighted against the slow bomber. The mauling visited upon the American daylight formations by the swift Me 109s and FW 190s was seen as a clear victory for General Galland and his men, however temporary: the recent successes enjoyed by the Ju 88s and Me 110s in earlier attacks, including Leipzig, made by Bomber Command during the current series instilled a high degree of confidence: to which we may add a dedication to the task of saving Berlin from the kind of devastation which had flattened Hamburg. High scores were common among the night fighter pilots though it is a matter for debate whether they were 'victories' meriting the 'Sieg Heil' war cry. Fighter versus fighter is another matter: in that situation 'like meets like' but the stalking of a lumbering unescorted bomber armed with pea-shooters, blowing him out of the sky before he is aware of his destroyer is hardly a 'victory'. That the bomber must be destroyed is both legitimate and necessary for the protection of the city though some would argue it was not much to write home about. Sour grapes? — perhaps — who would wish to be a bomber pilot sitting upon seven tons of dynamite?

There was no moon on this night. Under a starlit sky with the jet stream blowing from the Arctic Circle at a temperature of minus forty degrees Centigrade the gunners kept watch, staring into the darkness — awaiting the expected onslaught. The tail gunner had little freedom of movement; the clear vision panels had been removed the better to see what was coming and he relied exclusively on the fine heater wires threaded into his padded Taylor suit, his face exposed above the oxygen mask, his hands always on the gun controls. Back at Command Headquarters some alarm was experienced over the wind values transmitted by selected crews and an adjustment was made to the final broadcast winds for use by the main force. In the event these proved in error by a margin of some thirty miles an hour; an error which was to have grave consequences once the bomber force began the return from Berlin to the North Sea coast. Even so, the timing of the attack was advanced by five minutes in view of the greatly increased groundspeed, and the message went out in code by W/T on the Group frequencies. Part of the main force received this message and there are remarks in the operational summaries such as

'Not understood — no action taken' and 'Came too late to be effective', 'Not interpreted correctly'. One crew reported receiving it on the 2200 hr Group broadcast by which time the bomber force was nearing the turning point north of Rostock. Once on this south easterly heading with the wind exceeding 100 mph (one crew estimated it to be 150 mph) nothing could alter the fact that the leading wave was well ahead of the planned time and must take its chance of overtaking the Pathfinders! Which is what took place.

There is no evidence among the documents — Operational Summaries, Tactical Reports, Intelligence Summaries and the like — as to whether the marking force ever received this order. It well may be that as the early Blind Illuminators, twenty-five in number, were booked to be on the job between Z−5 and Zero hour the Command Ops Staff decided to leave well alone. Indeed, Bennett's somewhat dry comment in the Pathfinder Provisional Analysis No 131 — Night of 24/25 March 1944 — as to the success or otherwise of the attack confirms this:

> 'This is even more difficult to assess than similar types of attack on this target. The bringing forward of the Zero hour by five minutes for the main force resulted in a great number of the main force being in the target area when the original Blind Markers arrived.'

He was not amused by this effort to patch up a carefully planned sequence which had got out of step, though it is extremely doubtful whether it made the slightest difference: the onward rush of eight hundred bombers was ordained by the elements. But . . . the Pathfinder Force conformed exactly to the agreed pattern: they too were affected by the jet stream but contrived to dog-leg sufficiently to lose those important minutes, observing Bennett's iron-bound law that the marking must, regardless of circumstance, commence at the appointed time.

At Rostock those bombers flying south of track received a hot reception from the ground batteries defending that city. In clear skies they were picked up by the searchlights and subjected to intense and accurate AA fire which destroyed at least two of their number. At 2202 and 2110 hrs aircraft were observed coned in searchlights at 20,000 ft and falling in flames. Fighters were active in the area releasing yellow flares to indicate their presence to the ground batteries which ceased firing to permit the fighters to shoot down the bombers trapped in the cones. On the final leg to the target the leading Pathfinders observed numerous aircraft shot down. Forms 'Z' for both 3 and 8 (PFF) Groups contain many entries; thirty-three in the former case and forty-three in the latter. This document is a mine of information, being compiled by Groups, following the operation, and whilst there must be some duplication it presents a depressing picture. Though few combats are recorded on the outward journey — relatively few — the score mounts rapidly once Berlin was left behind.

All crews reported an increase in cloud as they drew near the city. Squadron Leader Keith Cresswell, No 35 Sqdn PFF — one of the twenty-five Blind Marker Illuminators opening the attack gave this brief account on return to Gravely:

'Weather 9/10ths cloud, tops 8 to 10,000 ft; released marker flares at $2227^{1/2}$ from 18,000 ft, course 222 magnetic — A/S 155 knots indicated. Identified and bombed on H2S. Two markers seen on arrival. Attack very scattered at first improving in later stages with better concentration of markers. Attack seemed to be a terrific overshoot. A large bunch of reds and greens seen about ten miles south west of target on way out. Remainder of load brought back as conditions did not permit visual marking.'

This is a crisp statement with no trimmings. Cresswell was among the best of Bennett's Flight Commanders. His assessment was correct.

Whilst the Pathfinder Narrative describes the Berlin defences as less than expected not all shared this point of view. The cloud layer did much to keep down the searchlights but there were still gaps and plenty of heavy AA fire:

'Some distance ahead of us the first target markers were falling to open the attack and the ground defences redoubled their efforts to knock down the Pathfinders responsible. Searchlights swept upwards and red flashes from exploding flak shells engulfed the aircraft. Untouched by these horrors we rode through it and released our bombs; then we were on the far side of the city congratulating ourselves on a merciful escape when it happened . . . Suddenly, from below sprang a quivering beam of intense light which transfixed S — 'Sugar'; a single Master beam had picked us out and in a split second we became the centre of a web of blinding searchlights. Our turn had come — we were well and truly 'coned'! The first reaction was one of being robbed of all vision and sense of direction: the white light penetrated every chink and the perspex Astro dome became a shimmering hemisphere, intensifying the glare. The first salvoes of high explosive arrived with a shattering roar, bracketing the Lancaster which bucked and shuddered in the shock waves. There was nothing to be gained by looking outside; the only course was that of lowering my seat and starting the evasive action with eyes glued to the instrument panel — ignoring the maelstrom of fury surrounding us — and hope for the best. I twisted and turned diving and climbing as salvo after salvo came up from below until there came a tremendous bang right in front of the nose and instantly all was darkness on the flight deck — as if a great canopy had been flung over the Lancaster, shutting out all light. It was bewildering and I wondered what diabolical trick had been played. The sudden exchange from dazzling light to utter darkness was frightening and the mid-upper gunner called to say his turret was blanketed with a black substance. Here was a fine situation! We were at 18,000 ft harried by flak and blind as a bat. Then the rear gunner called me to say he could see and I took directions from him to avoid the flak bursts, "Down port — hold it — sharp starboard — keep diving . . ." and eventually the bursting shells were left behind. All this time I was flying on instruments and wondering that the hell had happened — but as we discovered later the explanation was simple enough; the main hydraulic feed to the nose turret had been shattered by the burst under the nose and high pressure oil had been released . . . covering everything. Fierce and bitterly cold draughts came through the jagged holes in the fuselage and a fire was burning in the lower end behind the oxygen storage and main spar. Flames were belching from the port inner engine and the exhaust stubs had been blown off — the smell of cordite was strong — but all four engines were running sweetly. Though we did not know it at the time the fuel jettisoning pipe had been blown from its housing in the mainplane and was dangling in the slip stream with a small but steady leak from the outer tank. The oil still lay thick on the windscreen; the fire in the fuselage was out and with freezing blasts from the torn nose panels we set a course for the North Sea coast. There were hundreds of miles to go before we would reach it and fuel was draining away: the loss of the hydraulics did not worry me; with any luck the undercarriage could be blown down by air pressure from the emergency bottle but the thought of all that water and the prospect of a ditching was uppermost in my mind. She was not handling too well but I was determined to get her back to Oakington again. My crew never seemed to doubt we could do it but it was a long flog. We were picked up again by searchlights but no flak arrived, and I assumed they were co-operating with night fighters so we kept the sharpest look out every inch of the way, but I was still virtually blind up front and flying by the instrument panel. The film of oil covered the side windows being very sticky and not likely to clear without external help so I knew the landing might be tricky, but put this problem to the back of my mind for the time being.

At long last the Dutch coast came up but the fuel was getting low in the tanks; we called up Woodbridge, the emergency strip, and I believed we would make it, but most of all I wanted to get her home. She was our own own S — Sugar and I did not want to abandon her on a strange airfield; she had carried us safely over many miles of Occupied Europe and was the best of all Lancasters. Well, we got her there — to Oakington — and put her down gently at 4 o'clock in the morning — bursting a tyre as we touched down causing a swerve to port which sent us careering toward the Flying Control Tower and she came to a shuddering stop right in front. I cut the engines and silence descended — it was uncanny after the racket of the past eight and a half hours. We were home. I remember getting up and wandering into the Mess Ante Room in time to hear the one o'clock news next day . . . "A strong force of Lancasters were out over Germany last night. Berlin was the target which was heavily attacked . . . causing many large fires . . . 72 of our aircraft are missing."

Happily, Flight Lieutenant Edwards was to survive the war; it had been a 'close call'; only superb airmanship brought him and his crew back to Oakington that night.

'The attack opened punctually at the planned zero hour by the Blind Marker Illuminators and eleven of those detailed had marked the target, and in the majority of cases, released sky markers over the target by $Z-1$. Cloud conditions prevented visual identification, and as a result the attack was purely Parramatta and Wanganui (code names for blind ground and sky marking). Only four visual markers were able to drop target indicators visually, and as a result the ground marking between zero and $Z+7$ was thin. At $Z+7$ the Blind Backers Up came into play and from then until the end of the attack a good continuity of ground marking was attained.'

This was the Pathfinder assessment after careful piecing together of the evidence; and it is borne out by individual reports from main force crews. Pilot Officer Ollson of No 426 RCAF Sqdn, Linton-on-Ouse made this report on landing,

'Marking was punctual at 2230 hrs with red and green TIs . . . with some red and yellow flares. The concentration was fair but results difficult to assess owing to cloud. Bombed at 2233 from 22,000 ft — defences normal. Not much heavy flak and S/Ls obscured by cloud five to seven-tenths cover. Good breaks occasionally permitting glimpses of buildings on fire . . . some overshooting, possibly due to strong winds . . . flak activity was considerable at all defended areas, especially south of Magdeburg.'

Flight Sergeant Reinelt, captain of Halifax Q — Queenie of No 433 RCAF Squadron, Skipton:

> 'Sky markers were scattered but a good concentration of markers seen on ground through broken cloud. The Master of Ceremonies was more a moral help than tactical. Heavy flak up to 18,000 ft and light flak to 15,000 — searchlights numerous but ineffective. At Flensburg, Rostock, Magdeburg and Hanover flak and S/Ls very active.'

Master Bombers could do little or nothing to help: their efforts were acknowledged though not all were gracious: one crew recommending the idea be dropped as the orders of the Master Bomber interfered with crew communications. Some crews overshot Berlin altogether — blown south — but stoutly returned and tried again — though by the time they got back into position the rest of the party had beaten it for home. This was commendable — since they were virtually alone over Berlin providing an easy target.

Flight Lieutenant Sherriff No 10 Sqdn, captain of P — Peter, was over Berlin at Zero hour:

> 'Very little cloud or haze over target. PFF marking very unsatisfactory . . . bombed on mixed red and green TIs accompanied by release point flares red with yellow stars. Five minutes later we saw still further red and green TIs. Both groups were bombed. Incendiaries were dropped all over the place. There was little flak over target but intense S/L activity. Extensive decoy oil sites with decoy red markers (short burning) active to north of target. Winds thirty miles per hour faster than forecast. Many aircraft strayed south on way in arousing defences as far off track as Kiel. Over Denmark defences very hot.'

And more in the same vein, from No 4 Group, Flight Lieut Stevens of No 466 Sqdn, Lissett:

> '6/10s thin low cloud, ground and sky markers very scarce and scattered, bombed concentration of fires mixed with red and green markers. Master Bomber was pleading with PFF crews to achieve a better concentration. Bombed at 2231. Many fighter flares seen on leg out of target, low down and not in lanes. Winds stronger by 30 mph than forecast. Coming home we passed uncomfortably close to the Ruhr defences.'

Warrant Officer Porter — 10 Sqdn — stationed at Melbourne:

'At 2227 the glow of fires ahead indicated our approach to
target. Red TI seen to cascade followed by others. Sky markers
already burning. 5/10ths cloud with tops at 5,000 ft — mass of
searchlights and many cones forming. Heard Master Bomber
exhorting crews. Got south of track leaving Berlin — touched
north of Ruhr — 4 bombers seen shot down between Dortmund
and Duisburg. Glow of Berlin fire seen 140 miles away.'

And Wg Cdr Lane, No 405 Sqdn — one of the two Master
Bombers:

'9/10ths thin stratus at 7000 ft. Released from 24,000 ft on
green TIs. Not enough to judge concentration . . . no ground
details seen. Initial marking bad . . . at 2235 gap in marking 4–5
minutes. Sky Markers concentrated at 2246 . . . lots of incendiaries overshooting as far as turning point. Raid possibly to SW
of town.'

There was no shortage of enemy fighters over Berlin. The early
Pathfinders identified some twenty single and twin engined aircraft of
which the majority attempted an engagement and were evaded whilst
two are claimed as destroyed. One of the latter was shot down by the
crew of B Baker, No 35 Sqdn captained by S/L Cresswell. Sgt
Rhodes, mid-upper gunner in the Halifax recalls the incident,

'The pyrotechnic display was a sight never to be forgotten —
the ack-ack shells exploding, the fiery red and green trails of the
target indicators, bombs exploding below, bombers blazing from
end to end all served to make the night skies over Berlin almost
as light as day. The enemy fighters sat up high out of range of the
flak where they could see bombers silhouetted against the
general conflagration. I searched the sky diligently — saw the
brief reflection from a propellor — and wasted not an
instant . . . "Fighter — Fighter — corkscrew port . . ." but S/L
Cresswell had already dropped the nose and wing as the enemy
opened fire making a large hole in the tail plane. The red and
green tracer shells streaked past no more than a foot from my
head; a fraction of a second delay on the part of the pilot and I
would have caught it. Then the fighter pilot made a fatal error;
instead of breaking away below where we could not possibly
have hit him he pulled up the nose exposing his underside to our
combined guns at close range. I saw the puny .303s bounce off
without doing any obvious damage, but this was not the case for
he levelled off above us, his undercarriage dropped and he began

diving down into the blazing city. If we had had .5 guns we could have ripped him apart. I confess I acted more from instinct than from certainty but upon such things rested our survival: a split second's indecision could have resulted in sudden death.

Sgt Randolph Rhodes — later Warrant Officer — was shot down in September of 1944 and became a Prisoner of War. He had then completed more than thirty trips of his Pathfinder tour of duty. The incident related above took place on his fourth sortie.

Somewhere in the melee of bombers, fighters, searchlights and flak were the Mosquitos of No 100 Group. Their brief was to make right hand orbits round Berlin for at least twenty-five minutes 'to intercept enemy fighters which might still be in the area'. Originally there were eleven of them from 169, 141 and 239 Sqdns, but two went home early with mechanical defects. Of that number one was lost and another destroyed an enemy fighter. This was F/Lt Kelsey with F/O Smith as his navigator and radar operator. The task set the 'Serrate' Mosquitos was one of the most difficult of any fighter pilot during the whole of the war . . . 'to identify the *enemy fighter* — to follow and destroy'. In the hugger-mugger of the bomber stream, including the area under attack, these crews attempted to contact the enemy using his own radar transmissions by which he was seeking out *our own* bombers: then pursue him until within range of their cannon. It was complex, and fraught always with the possibility of ramming one of our own aircraft: one marvelled at the persistence of Wing Commander Bob Braham and his men. The job was infinitely more difficult than that of the night fighter charged with destroying the lumbering bomber and yet Braham knocked down three enemy fighters in a single sortie on one occasion. And that was in a Beaufighter which was slower than the Mosquito. Here is Kelsey's report after landing,

'Crossed enemy coast 2139 hrs. Recrossed 0120 hrs. A number of very weak Serrate contacts to starboard on the way in were ignored. At 2245 hrs, when in the Brandenburg area, a strong Serrate contact was obtained astern and to port. After five minutes chase without AI the enemy aircraft switched off. In the target area, at 2303 hrs, an AI contact was chased and finally lost in a dive. This was followed immediately by another AI contact which, after chasing the jinking target for twenty-five minutes to the east, resulted in a visual on a fuselage with lights underneath. The visual was lost in a diving turn to port, but AI contact was maintained and the chase continued. The target was weaving hard and this enabled the Mosquito to fly straight and cut off vectors by allowing the contact to go from side to side of the tube until the visual was regained, and the enemy aircraft identified as a FW 190. After three bursts of cannon at 400 yards range, closing to 200 yards, the enemy aircraft exploded in the air and is claimed as destroyed. The remainder of the flight was uneventful.'

This was the only success that night; sheer persistence brought it off. The missing Mosquito was flown by F/Lt Armstrong with F/O Mold as his radar operator. Much credit devolves upon No 100 Group: Serrate was but a small corner of that remarkable organisation whose radar and radio countermeasures saved many a bomber crew. These penny packets of Serrate Mosquitos represented a brave effort to help the bombers, but it was too late in the day. We needed a couple of hundred to make any real impact whilst the tactical handling of such a force would have presented problems.

On leaving the target area the bombers continued south for thirty miles, turning on to a westerly course for the North Sea coast some four hundred miles distant. A further increase in the strength of the wind drove many of them south towards Halle: here a concentration of one hundred and twenty searchlights set up huge columns of white light for the benefit of the heavy gun batteries and a number of aircraft were seen to fall in flames. From Magdeburg to Leipzig the searchlights formed an unbroken line to trap the bombers struggling against a headwind which reduced the ground speed to a crawl, providing the predictor crews with ample time to gauge precisely the height and speed; the resulting salvo bracketing the target with deadly effect. At ten degrees East many bombers were so far south of track that the planned alteration of course — which was calculated to take them between Osnabruck and Bremen — brought them over the strong defences of the former city with disastrous consequences: others drifted on to Kassel and the northern tip of the Ruhr whilst a few, many miles south, tracked between Munster and Dortmund. No less than fourteen separate plots were registered by the German Fighter Control in this area between 2338 and 2358. Thus, the bulk of the retreating bomber force was spread over a hundred mile front, with isolated aircraft actually skirting the southern edge of the Ruhr and passing between Bonn and Cologne.

There was no slackening of the hurricane wind as the bombers clawed their way back to the Dutch coast. Crews nursing a battle-damaged Lancaster or Halifax had little prospect of bringing off a successful ditching with waves twenty feet high, and the terrors of a ditching in total darkness need no emphasis. If they were fortunate to descend to the surface of the sea without breaking up and succeeded in getting into the rubber dinghy this was but a prelude to a severe test of human endurance. In winter, death from exposure was never long delayed. A wounded man presented a problem and there are cases on record of getting him out, only to die later. We had great faith in the launch crews of the Air/Sea Rescue Service. Once a position had been given — even a very approximate 'fix' — the launches went out regardless of weather or distance in an effort to pull our men from the sea, and I take this opportunity to record our admiration for a 'silent' Service which received little or no publicity yet made a valuable contribution to our safety.

With the last bomber limping home to a Yorkshire airfield the long night came to an end. The cost had been high. Out of the eight hundred odd bombers dispatched to the 'Big City' seventy-two Lancasters and Halifaxes, plus one Mosquito from the tiny Serrate force, failed to return. Another seventy-seven were damaged either by flak or fighter attack. This was the equivalent to a loss of four and a half squadrons totalling approximately 500 officers and NCOs and another four and a half squadrons out of commission. It will be recalled that earlier in the conflict Sir Winston Churchill had minuted the Secretary of State for Air . . . 'You don't have to fight the weather as well as the enemy' but on this occasion indeed for the majority of the attacks against the German capital Bomber Command had done just that.

Table 3.   Summary of Bomber Command Casualties — 24 March 1944.

Casualties

No 1 Bomber Group	— 19 Lancasters
No 3 ” ”	— 7 ”
No 4 ” ”	— 15 Halifaxes
No 5 ” ”	— 11 Lancasters
No 6 ” ”	— 13 Halifaxes
No 8 Pathfinder Group	— 7 Lancasters
No 100 Group Fighter Support	— 1 Mosquito

Total   73 Missing.

Crashed Aircraft:

No 4 Group	1 Halifax of 78 Sqdn, crashed at Cranfield all crew killed
	1 Halifax crashed on beach near Cromer. all crew killed (included in 4 Gp total)
No 1659 Conversion Unit	1 Halifax crashed near Uxbridge, four crew baled out, Pilot killed

Time was running out for Sir Arthur Harris. In the near future Bomber Command was to come under the direction of the Supreme Allied Commander for the launching of Overlord — the invasion of Europe — and there was a need to conserve the force. Losses of the order of nine per cent could not be sustained and there was a sense of futility about the Berlin battle. An eminent writer, discussing our losses asked me if Berlin had been laid on again the following night what might have been the reaction of the crews? I answered him:

'They would have gone without question.'

Such was Sir Arthur's authority and grip on the fifty-odd squadrons stuck out on the bleak airfields of East Anglia, Lincolnshire and Yorkshire. There was no breaking point. A few days later they got off the transports to stumble through the snow to the waiting aircraft for the climax of the winter offensive — the bloodbath of Nuremberg — where the casualties exceeded all previous records and nigh on a hundred bombers would fail to return.

Chapter 10
Headquarters Bomber Command Reports and Assessments

Of the hundreds of night photographs taken at the time of release of the bomb loads relatively few show much ground detail. The evidence as to where the bulk of the attack fell is overwhelming: the greatest concentration of bombing took place between five and six miles down wind of the aiming point — the centre of Berlin. The familiar 'creep-back' — a common feature in all area attacks — is conspicuous by its absence, though this may be due to aiming at sky markers as opposed to ground markers. Nevertheless the bombing was scattered over many miles. Like the earlier attacks in the series this, the final assault, had failed in its objective. Considerable damage was done in the outlying suburbs, some of which fell on industrial premises, as indicated in the detailed report issued after photographic reconnaissance, but the high degree of destruction calculated to break the morale of the Berliners had not been achieved; whilst the grievous loss of nine per cent of the force did not pass without comment. Even before they returned to base the majority of the crews were in no doubt as to the success of the ground defences, which had scored so heavily. During interrogation all crews adverted to the multiplicity of searchlight cones and the intense flak fire, observing many bombers trapped and brought down over Magdeburg, Osnabruck and even as far off track as Leipzig — such was the southward thrust of the powerful jet stream as they battled their way to the safety of the North Sea. Pilot Officer McLean of 156 Sqdn suffered severe flak damage two minutes after releasing his bombs; the perspex nose of his Lancaster was blown off and the starboard inner engine put out of action yet he pressed on without charts or navigating equipment to land back at Warboys airfield. Pilot Officer Simpson was not so fortunate: Over the Dutch coast he called base saying his port and starboard outer engines were damaged and nothing more was heard until he was reported having crashed at the water's edge near Cromer — in a minefield. The aircraft blew up and all were killed. This was a Halifax of No 158 Squadron stationed at Lissett. Having nursed his crippled bomber back across the North Sea and succeeding in making a crash-landing on the beach this was a tragic end for a gallant crew.

I remember the morning after this particular raid; there was gloom in plenty around the Station, and an air of resignation. It was not unlikely a repeat performance might be ordered. With considerable relief I learned there would be no further call on the crews that night.

The Bomber Command Report on Night Operations for 24 March follows the customary form beginning with a short summary:

'811 aircraft were sent to Berlin. An exceptionally strong wind caused the Pathfinders to over shoot the aiming point and the bombing spread outside the southern suburbs. Considerable damage was, however, inflicted on the capital, the Siemens and seventy-three other factories were hit. 72 aircraft were lost (8.9 per cent), of which it is estimated that nearly three quarters were due to flak, the wind driving many bombers off their course over heavily defended areas. Mosquitos carried out a feint attack on Kiel, and precision raids at Munster, Duisburg and on airfields in the Low Countries. Other Mosquitos made intruder and Serrate patrols, destroying three enemy aircraft and damaging four others for the loss of one British fighter. A large diversionary sweep was carried out over France but this did not appear to distract the fighters.'

This somewhat bland statement does less that justice to the Pathfinder crews whose discipline and timing was in sharp contrast with many of the main force crews. The sky marker flares were released by means of the H2S radar and with a wind of 105 mph they were swept at a high speed to the south. This was the main cause of the marking going astray. Those main force aircraft bombing as much as twenty minutes early saw only the markers dropped by the Mosquitos; the real marking began punctually at the stipulated times but by then a great quantity of high explosive and thousands of incendiary bombs had been dropped creating a loose concentration five and six miles down wind of the aiming point. Squadron Leader Cresswell's immediate reaction was correct: 'The attack seemed to be a terrific overshoot'.

Examples of bombing well in advance of the corrected Zero hour (advanced by five minutes) are numerous . . . four aircraft of No 101 dropped at 2157, 2155, 2155, 2152; four aircraft of No 166 dropped at 2159, 2203, 2201, 2203; three aircraft of No 432 dropped at 2203, 2202, 2203 and there are others. These times are taken from the Operational Record Books. Bennett's frustration is understandable; his carefully planned marking schedule had gone adrift before the show even began and once this kind of situation, compounded by cloud and the violence of the air stream, had developed nothing could pull it back. As for the early bombers they had little choice; once over what they believed to be the city, and with evidence of some form of marking below, they released their loads though, as we have seen, there were exceptions with the odd crew making a second run and finishing up over Berlin practically alone.

Even under the best conditions a heavy bomber attack of this magnitude was never a cut-and-dried affair — it was never a neatly concentrated bomb pattern such as that obtained when bombing Krupps works with the aid of 'Oboe' — where the high flying Mosquitos dropped the target markers on the orders of a high precision radar equipment located in England — and where the relatively short distance to the target made for a tightly packed mass of bombers passing over the aiming point in conformity with a strict time bracket. Berlin lay deep in enemy territory: varying weather conditions en-route greatly affected track-keeping and timing: navigation errors, however small, accumulated over the distance and only experienced navigators succeeded in adjusting their track miles to meet the stipulated time-on-target. In this connection we have to remember that the high casualty rate guaranteed a sizeable proportion of raw crews as the Battle progressed; the young navigator flying his first Berlin sortie bore a heavy responsibility in getting his aircraft to the target. Bomber Command stood or fell by the skill of its navigators: theirs was an unenviable task, subjected to a constant barrage of noise, working in the worst possible conditions, interrupted occasionally by enemy action and 'nagged' not infrequently by requests for information; they were expected to remain oblivious to all external alarms.

The final breakdown by sorties and Night Photographic statistics are given in Tables 4 and 5.

Table 4.   Sortie Breakdown — Bomber Command Raid — Night 24 March 1944.

Sortie details	Totals	Per cent
Aircraft dispatched	811	100
Aircraft reporting attack on primary area	660	81.4
Aircraft reporting attack on an alternative area	26	3.2
Abortive sorties	53	6.5
Aircraft missing	72	8.9

Table 5.   Night Photographic Statistics — Bomber Command Raid — 24 March 1944.

Photographic Interpretation	Number	Max	Min
Aircraft plotted in target area	43		
(ground detail ..... 3)			
(fire tracks .... 40)			
Aircraft estimated to have bombed in target area		159	43
Aircraft estimated to have bombed within 3 miles		107	29
Aircraft plotted off target area			
(ground detail .... 4)			
(fire tracks .... 127)			

In his book, 'Bomber Offensive', Sir Arthur Harris stresses the great difficulty of determining the results of successive raids.

Time after time the reconnaissance Mosquitos flew over the city without success. However, between 25 March and 11 April photographs were secured

> 'showing fresh incidents of damage in Berlin as a result of the attack on 24 March and by attacks of the American 8th Air Force in daylight. The largest concentration of damage occurred in the South West district of Steglitz, where many fires were still burning on the morning of 25th March. The adjacent districts of Wilmersdorf, Schoneburg and Charlottenburg also suffered heavily. 74 factories were affected, including 10 engaged on high priority war work. The great Siemens branch at Siemenstadt was again badly hit, and damage caused to the A.E.G. at Wedding, Dutche Industrie Werke at Spandau, Schering A.G., Telefunken and the railway repair shops at Templehof. 4 Gasworks, a power station, markets, slaughter houses, barracks and hutted camps were among the other affected premises; and severe damage was caused to a large depot (probably Luftwaffe Signals) in Teltow, 10 miles South West of Berlin.'

Enemy Defences

Flak. At Berlin, the heavy guns fired a slight to moderate barrage from 17–22,000 ft with moderate to intense light flak up to 16,000 ft. Numerous searchlights illuminated the cloud base and formed cones through the gaps. As a result of the unexpectedly strong north wind many aircraft were engaged over defended areas off track, notably at Sylt, Magdeburg, Munster, Osnabruck, Kiel and Rostock; and at Leipzig, Kassel and the Ruhr. Not less than forty-five aircraft are estimated to have been lost to flak; seventeen on the outward route, seven over the target, and twenty-one on the way home. Seven were shot down over the Ruhr, six at Osnabruck, four at Flensburg and four at Magdeburg.

Fighters. A diversion to the west of Paris failed to distract the fighter controllers who concentrated forces at points in the Hamburg-Heligoland area as well as to the north-west of Berlin, and fed them into the bomber stream all the way from Sylt to the target. Others were held in readiness to follow the bombers once they had left the target. Actually, fighters achieved comparatively little success, because the strong wind that scattered the bomber stream proved unfavourable to consistent interception by fighters. They made thirty-six attacks . . . mostly over the target and claimed eighteen victims; six at Sylt, two at Flensburg, two at Rostock and Prenxlau, four over Berlin, one at Nordhausen, one over Osnabruck and two over Holland.

Own Fighter Operations

Ten Mosquitos of 100 Group were sent on Serrate patrols. Seven completed their sorties, one shooting down a FW 190 over Berlin. One Mosquito was lost without trace. At the same time seventeen Mosquitos from ADGB and two from No 2 Group carried out intruder patrols, destroying one Ju 88, one unidentified aircraft and damaging two Ju 88s, one He 129 and one unidentified aircraft. All these Mosquitos returned safely.' As always the fighter element was tiny when any question of bomber support by night arose and yet we were grateful for whatever was forthcoming. The clobbering of enemy airfields was a simple task and could be very effective with little attendant risk to the intruding Mosquitos of Fighter Command.

The tactical assessment of the operation contains nothing more than generalisations, pointing out 'the danger that flak can be to isolated aircraft . . .' and blaming the strong winds which scattered the force. All of which was well understood by the weary bomber crews. The weather forecasters did their best with the information available and no blame attaches to them. Had it been otherwise and no jet stream had been present to disrupt the operation the Flak/Fighter situation might well have been reversed and even heavier losses suffered at the hands of the Luftwaffe night fighter pilots. The long penetration of enemy territory by such a large force in the face of a strong fighter opposition virtually guaranteed an ascending casualty rate. This is well demonstrated by the two succeeding attacks on Essen and Nuremberg where only nine bombers were lost in the former instance and ten times that number in the latter. In the Official History we read:

> 'This temporary check to the fortunes of the German night fighter force was further and even more clearly illustrated by a highly successful return to Essen on the night of 26 March. On this operation 705 bombers were despatched and nine failed to return, but the Nuremberg action four nights later showed the extent to which Bomber Command's position was precarious.'

The Nuremberg disaster on 30 March marked the end of an era; the culmination of four long years during which time Bomber Command had carried the offensive by night to every corner of the German Reich alone and unaided. The winter battle for Berlin was without precedent: 'It was the greatest assault which had hitherto been launched against a single target. It involved the despatch of over nine thousand sorties, the overwhelming majority of which were carried out by four engined aircraft . . . considerable as the destruction was, Berlin was not "wrecked from end to end" nor did the operation cost Germany the war'. The campaign as a whole involved a further eleven thousand sorties flown against other leading cities. Neither the Battles of the Ruhr nor that of Hamburg ranked with Berlin where the sacrifice of the bomber crews was to become legendary. The destruction of Krupps factories in the Ruhr was a landmark: the advent of a single radar device made it possible and the degree of penetration of enemy territory was short. Hamburg, by virtue of its location was uniquely vulnerable to accurate marking since the land/water contrast reflected strongly on the airborne radar screens of the Pathfinders and was demolished in four swift attacks. Neither was a true 'curtain raiser' to the Big City save in terms of an expanding force embracing an ever-growing number of Lancasters — the biggest single factor in Sir Arthur's claim to wreck Berlin. That city lay at extreme range for the heavy bombers whose progress, mile by mile, was scrutinised and appropriate defensive measures put in hand — a running battle relieved on occasions by clever diversionary or 'spoof' attacks — in the face of winter weather conditions, barely predictable with certainty, and often hostile in the extreme. From a hundred fighter airfields spread between Sylt, Kiel, Hamburg and Rostock on the northern route to the city, along the well trodden path back to the Dutch coast via the concentrated ground and air defences of the North German Plain the enemy saw his opportunity. As the slow moving stream flowed out and back time was on the side of the opposition; the victims could neither defend themselves adequately nor run away. Evasive action was their best hope but a determined enemy was not thrown off easily.

The operation of 24 March represented the last of sixteen attacks on Berlin, and the 35th in the overall campaign commencing 18 November. Of the 20,224 sorties dispatched 1,047 bombers failed to return with 1,682 damaged. The figures for *Berlin alone* are as follows:

Total dispatched	9,111
Missing	492
Damaged	954
Write off	95

It has been remarked that Berlin was a defeat for Bomber Command. This is not so. Sir Arthur's crews stood ready to return to the enemy's capital if so ordered: the nine per cent losses of 24 March were quickly made good and there was no lack of men, willing and eager, to fill the gaps. It was Nuremberg which called a halt — a disaster attributed to 'bad luck and uncharacteristically bad and unimaginative operational planning' where the force, equal in strength to that sent to Berlin a few days earlier, suffered the highest loss rate of the whole Battle. In clear skies, with the moon at first quarter illuminating the unpredicted condensation trails behind the bombers, and the passage of the bomber stream close to radio beacons around which the enemy fighters were orbiting, the opposition 'had it made'. In the past the approach to Nuremberg had invariably taken advantage of French territory where interceptions on the inward journey were rare. On this occasion, 31 March 1944, the eight hundred bombers were routed north of Frankfurt before turning on to the final leg to Nuremberg. Heavy losses occurred on the way in, and in advance of the target area, whilst there were relatively few on the withdrawal via the southern route. This direct challenge to the Luftwaffe was met by hundreds of fighters in a running battle all the way to the target.

Liepzig, Berlin and Nuremberg cost us dear; such losses could not be sustained and, anyway, Bomber Command needed to conserve its strength for the coming invasion of Europe. This was the end of an epoch and the case for escort fighters was brought home, but the loss of more than a thousand bombers must be set against the disruption and havoc visited upon the enemy. The cost to Germany was enormous. In the overall Battle between November 1943 and March 1944 twelve great cities had suffered devastating attacks — apart from the sixteen major assaults on Berlin. In terms of manpower alone the necessity for maintaining both military and civil defence, for providing the essential services including transport, firefighting and water supplies, electric power and the raw materials for his factories drew heavily on the enemy's resources. Whatever the morale of the inhabitants their cities were crumbling and Germany was slowly grinding to a halt — as a direct consequence of the bomber offensive. There was little more to be gained in attacking Berlin or any similar objective.

The winter of 1943/44 — the bleak airfields of eastern England — the bitter cold — the problems of clearing the runways of snow and ice — the difficulty of hauling big bombs up the ice covered ramps from the dumps — the frustration stemming from a long struggle against both enemy and the grim weather conditions only to find the Big City hidden by its customary blanket of clouds . . . these were important factors to be considered when the question of morale arises. Boredom in a Nissen Hut with the gale blowing through the cracks was often the lot of the crews when not in the air, but it was infinitely preferable to life on an Arctic Convoy escort and few complained. As the casualties mounted most were philosophic and crew co-operation was at a peak: a crew was a team, one and indivisible: the life of the whole could depend on the reaction of a single member. With the bomber on fire and disintegrating the first duty was one of getting the wounded man on to his parachute and thrust out of the fuselage door. Many instances are recorded of the captain staying at the controls — holding the aircraft steady while the crew abandoned ship — only to lose his life in the process. Group

Captain 'Tiny' Evans-Evans knew he hadn't a hope of making it and went down with his Lancaster after every man had left. There are lighter notes . . . a Canadian crew — new to England — baled out on their way back and landed successfully. Following the correct drill they hid up all day and walked by night; as they peered out from the shelter of a convenient ditch the next morning a bus was observed coming towards them. As it rolled past they read the following: 'Kentish Bus Company. Maidstone'.

Appendix A

Order of Battle — 7 November 1941

No 1 Bomber Group
No 12 Sqdn — Binbrook, Wellingtons: 2 attacked.

Z 8407	W 5585	W 5611	W 5574
F/L D. T. Saville	P/O A Heyworth	P/O C. A. Barnes	P/O P. J. Oleinek
P/O J. C. Langley	P/O M. J. Garlick	P/O J. D. Seaman	Sgt J. M. Elliott
Sgt F. Weatherley	P/O H. J. Legge	Sgt P. R. Caldwell	Sgt E. D. Croxton
Sgt F. Chittenden	Sgt E. Long	Sgt C. W. Carson	Sgt L. A. Barham
Sgt D. Heap	Sgt K. Scholes	Sgt B. P. Lunn	Sgt R. P. Whiting
Sgt A. Page	P/O G. A. Merriman	Sgt F. J. Blute	Sgt F. Lockwood

W 5367
Sgt C. Voller
Sgt G. Yorke
Sgt E. Hill
Sgt W. Young
Sgt J. Wild
Sgt R. Driver

All crews experienced heavy icing in thick cloud which persisted as far as the target. Heyworth was forced to return short of fuel, Barnes' aircraft was iced up and Voller experienced oxygen failure. Saville and Oleinek attacked Berlin.

No 300 (Polish) Sqdn — Hemswell, Wellingtons: 3 attacked, 3 early returns.

B 1725	Q 1268	X 1220	K 1265
Sgt Kubacki	P/O Pankiewicz	P/O Kucmierz	P/O Klecha
Sgt Peczek	P/O Chorazy	Sgt Dusinski	Sgt Dzierzbicki
F/L Dukszto	P/O Idzikowski	F/O Wawerski	F/O Zurawski
Sgt Keryluk	Sgt Wysocki	Sgt Malecki	Sgt Wize
Sgt Dubiel	Sgt Kleniewski	Sgt Sierpina	Sgt Chanecki
Sgt Sikorski	Sgt Macierzynski	Sgt Mintakowski	Sgt Tomaszewski

L 1269
Sgt Leskiewicz
P/O Zelazinski
F/O Jakubowski
Sgt Kwiecinski
Sgt Niemczek
Sgt Czapski

D 1264
P/O Miszewski
Sgt Rokosz
P/O Tabaczynski
Sgt Tuliszka
Sgt Krenzel
Sgt Badelek

Kubacki, Pankiewicz, Klecha attacked others forced to return with icing and mechanical failures.

No 301 (Polish) Sqdn — Hemswell, Wellingtons: 6 detailed, 5 attacked, 1 failed to release.

R 1262	L 1520	T 1252	D 1685
F/O Wojcik	F/L Sliwinski	P/O Dobrominski	P/O Rzemyk
F/O Bernasinki	Sgt Kubiac	P/O Goldhaar	P/O Kolakowski
F/L Starewicz	F/O Wielcus	F/O Staerz	F/O Wybraniec
P/O Pantowski	Sgt Mucha	Sgt Piasecki	Sgt Twarkowski
Sgt Koc	Sgt Zewodny	Sgt Holc	Sgt Podgerski
Sgt Dolata	Sgt Blach	Sgt Lasocki	Sgt Radecki

A 1335
P/O Liszka
P/O Jaroszyk
F/O Kuzmicki
Sgt Janik
Sgt Sztwrc
Sgt Swlcwt

P/O Zygmuntowicz
Sgt Szal
S/L Przykorski
Sgt Wilmanski
Sgt Wojciechowski
Sgt Zuk

No 304 Sqdn (Polish) Sqdn — Lindholme, Wellingtons: 2 a/c detailed, 1 attacked Berlin.
1704
Sgt Obiorek
P/O Szczurowski
P/O Kurek
Sgt Kwicien
Sgt Sankowski
Sgt Ragouiski

No 305 Sqdn (Polish) Sqdn — Lindholme, Wellingtons: 3 detailed, 1 attacked, 2 abandoned.
8438
Sgt Dusza
F/O Rymkiewicz
P/O Ochalski
Sgt Laskowski
Sgt Frankowski
Sgt Szadkowski

No 3 Bomber Group

No 7 Sqdn — Oakington, Stirlings: 11 detailed, 4 primary*, 2 missing, remainder attacked alternatives or abandoned due to icing or mechanical failure.

N 3677 *Missing*	N 6087	N6091 *Missing*	N 6090
F/O D. B. VanBuskirk	F/L J. T. O'Brien*	Sgt J. W. Morris	F/O B. Parnall*
Sgt J. E. Chadwick	Sgt J. E. Rose	Sgt M. S. Jacobs	Sgt K. R. Taylor
P/O G. E. Sweeney	P/O Lopez	Sgt B. Wallwork	F/L Walker
Sgt D. H. Stronach	Sgt T. J. Ryder	Sgt P. Johnstone	Sgt R. Wheatley
Sgt D. G. Pack	Sgt P. Comroe	Sgt E. O. Brooks	Sgt T. P. Wright
Sgt J. S. Fenton	Sgt M. A. Sullivan	Sgt G. H. Chesman	Sgt R. G. Archer
Sgt C. Murch	Sgt J. Devlin	Sgt C. Walton	Sgt C. F. Simpson

W 7745	N 3669	N 6095	N 3668
F/S J. D. Hart	F/O W. N. Crebbin	Sgt K. R. Taylor*	F/S G. C. Bayley*
Sgt J. Davies	P/O W. R. Butterfield	Sgt F. K. Lister	P/O G. Gwilliam
Sgt W. Green	Sgt R. H. Cotton	P/O J. D. Waddell	F/O A. G. McLeod
Sgt F. L. Pool	Sgt T. Smith	Sgt R. A. Archer	Sgt R. E. Allen
Sgt E. C. Dowsett	Sgt C. F. Norman	Sgt F. J. Lloyd	Sgt J. M. Smith
Sgt L. C. Young	F/S J. Lowe	Sgt W. Mankelow	Sgt J. R. Brook
Sgt G. Rhodes	Sgt R. Ferguson	Sgt E. Blacklaw	Sgt L. K. Eagle

W 7746	W 7442
P/O H. G. Pilling	F/S S. G. Matkin
Sgt J. Lewis	Sgt W. J. Runciman
P/O W. L. Gillespie	P/O E. S. Baker
Sgt G. J. Kearns	F/S J. E. Button
Sgt W. H. Bracken	Sgt A. G. Coroon
Sgt P. C. Whitwell	Sgt E. E. Dejoux
Sgt J. Pellett	Sgt R. J. Surfleet

No 9 Sqdn — Honington, Wellingtons: 5 reached target area — none claim to have attacked primary due to cloud and severe icing conditions.

3289	3226	3352	3285	3281
S/L Inness	Sgt Roberts	Sgt Carter	Sgt Wilmot	Sgt Dalgleish
Sgt Doughty	Sgt Rogers	Sgt Runnacles	Sgt Silver	P/O Brooke
P/O Peel	Sgt Tarbitten	Sgt Cawdron	Sgt Welsh	Sgt Coulson
Sgt Poff	Sgt Atkins-	Sgt How	Sgt Hardy	Sgt Onions
Sgt Elgie	Tallentyre	Sgt Caldwell	Sgt Shepherd	Sgt Hutchinson
Sgt Welch	Sgt Skidmore	Sgt Vivian	F/S Webborn	Sgt Brown
	Sgt Dorrell			

No 15 Sqdn — Wyton, Stirlings: 4 reported bombing Primary on ETA 1 bombed Munster.

W 7450	N 3665	N 6044	N3671	N 3646
Sgt Barron	F/O Barr	F/O Boggis	F/O Conran	F/O Nicholson
Sgt Shepherd	Sgt Hayes	Sgt Higgins	P/O Flink	Sgt Southey
P/O Mulhall	P/O Young	P/O Ryan	F/O Bouney	P/O Rampton
Sgt Styles	Sgt Briggs	P/O Donati	F/S Munns	Sgt Carruthers
Sgt Spalding	Sgt Collins	Sgt Mounteney	Sgt Ward	Sgt Phillips
Sgt Coen	Sgt Davis	Sgt Wilson	Sgt McMahon	Sgt McCallum
Sgt Jackson	Sgt Pepper	Sgt Watson	Sgt Spicer	Sgt Tuck
Sgt Cunningham	Sgt Greenwood	Sgt Gould	Sgt Butcher	

No 57 Sqdn — Feltwell, Wellingtons: 6 detailed, 4 attacked, 2 early returns with mechanical failure.

Z 8893	X 9748	T2961	Z 1073
S/L Warfield	P/O Tong	Sgt Price	Sgt Williams
Sgt Austin	F/L Phipps	Sgt Heald	Sgt Plunkett
P/O Tettenborn	Sgt Durham	P/O Elliot	Sgt Finley
P/O Blench	Sgt Maskall	Sgt Barraclough	Sgt Pintches
Sgt Ford	Sgt Nash	Sgt Aldous	Sgt Morgan
P/O Low	Sgt Harries	Sgt Towndrew	Sgt Watson

No 75 (New Zealand) Sqdn — Feltwell — Wellingtons: No 3 Gp Form 540 called for 9 Wellingtons to attack Berlin and 5 to attack Ostend. No 75 Squadron casualties for the night include two missing crews but in the Squadron battle order (F.541) they are not shown. Group Headquarters state both were lost on Berlin and they are added to the total of those attacking the German capital.*

Z 1083	X 9268	Z 1099	X9975
Sgt Climie	Sgt Bray	Sgt Tye	Sgt Slater
Sgt Shepherd	Sgt Jones	Sgt Giddens	Sgt Kaiser
P/O Henderson	P/O Clare	Sgt Dromgoole	Sgt Fletcher
Sgt Walsh	Sgt Sarginson	Sgt Hibberd	Sgt Wainwright
Sgt Ries	Sgt Partridge	Sgt McAroy	Sgt Orr
Sgt Archer	Sgt Monk	Sgt McLinden	Sgt Burridge

Z 9941	Z 1053	X 9976 *Missing**	X 9951 *Missing**
Sgt Ramsay	Sgt Nunn	Sgt J. W. Black	P/O W. R. Methven
Sgt Colville	Sgt Greenwood	Sgt T. H. Gray	Sgt J. C. M. Gibson
P/O Hodson	Sgt Dundas	P/O E. Lloyd	P/O D. A. Webster
Sgt Errington	Sgt Harrison	Sgt L. C. Green	Sgt A. B. Frisby
Sgt Watson	Sgt Elliot	Sgt J. D. Thompson	Sgt T. P. Duffy
Sgt McQueen	Sgt Massey	Sgt C. T. Black	Sgt R. Pattinson

Sgt Black was last heard transmitting on the Group frequency at 2236 — 'target not attacked' — and P/O Methven transmitted an SOS at 2228 hrs.

No 99 Sqdn — Newmarket, Wellingtons: 8 detailed, 3 missing, no crew succeeded in identifying Berlin owing to thick cloud and severe icing.

L 7873	T 2554 *Missing*	X 9739 *Missing*	X 9740
Sgt Youseman	F/L Dickenson	P/O Moore	F/L Gee
SGT Carter	Sgt Bell	P/O Henderson	Sgt Marks
F/S Dignan	F/O Searcy	F/L Goodwin	Sgt Cleveland
Sgt Hood	Sgt Martin	Sgt Mackenzie	Sgt Strachan
Sgt Norman	Sgt Featherstone	Sgt Bowen	Sgt Franks
F/S Green	Sgt Bowman	Sgt Dale	Sgt Gittens

T 2516 *Missing*	R 1519	N 2856	R 1472
P/O Gilmore	Sgt Thomas	P/O Grant	Sgt Maclean
Sgt Wiggs	P/O Pinion	P/O Fahnestock	Sgt Fawcett
Sgt Harrowby	Sgt Smith	F/O Hughes	Sgt Davies
Sgt Sanders	Sgt Colpitts	F/S Hatton	Sgt Grigor
Sgt Harrop	Sgt Hancock	Sgt Lawrence	Sgt Brown
Sgt Scofield	Sgt Froude	F/S Ware	Sgt Robertson

No 101 Sqdn — Oakington, Wellingtons: 3 attacked primary, 1 missing, 1 abandoned sortie.

R 1701 *Missing*	R 1801	X 9601	R 3295
P/O Hardie	Sgt Callender	Sgt Raybould	P/O Pelmore
Sgt Wrampling	Sgt Attwood	Sgt Wickens	Sgt Chapman
P/O Miller	P/O Doig	Sgt Spencer	Sgt Fowler
Sgt Buchan	F/S Hewitt	Sgt Bott	Sgt Johnstone
Sgt Watson	Sgt Young	F/S Woodgate	Sgt Williams
Sgt Berry	Sgt Wigham	Sgt Tracey	Sgt Edmond

P/O Hardie transmitted SOS at 1955 'Landing in the Sea'. A 'fix' was obtained on this signal and three motor torpedo boats left at 2220 for the position — 25 miles from Haamstede and seventy from the Norfolk coast. Aircraft eventually posted as missing. Sgt Callender attacked through 10/10 cloud at 2255 and aircraft was hit by heavy flak in the rear turret.

No 115 Sqdn — Marham, Wellingtons: 5 attacked through thick cloud, 2 attacked alternative targets unable to reach Berlin.

LX 9733*	HZ 8848*	ZZ 8399	BZ 1070
P/O French	S/L Coleman	Sgt Dutton	Sgt Runagall
Sgt Dunn	Sgt Hyde	Sgt Owen	Sgt Frecker
Sgt Burnett	Sgt Foster	Sgt Dew	Sgt Hosea
Sgt Highett	Sgt Jenkins	Sgt Newbury	Sgt Sevenson
Sgt Holmes	Sgt Ingmire	Sgt Knott	Sgt Chamberlain
Sgt McMullen	Sgt Gregory	Sgt Arthur	Sgt Runner

AZ 1084	JX 9875	GZ 8863	
P/O Wiley	Sgt Leslie	Sgt Bruce	
Sgt Williams	Sgt Harris	Sgt Taylor	
Sgt Herring	P/O Nicholson	Sgt O'Shea	
Sgt Churchill	Sgt Symons	Sgt Evans	
Sgt Liversuch	Sgt Green	Sgt Crosbie	
F/S Addersley	Sgt Jones	Sgt Lawrence	

*LX 9733 hit by flak — starboard engine lost propellor — bombed Rotterdam docks. S/L Coleman bombed Ruhr target — iced up and unable to reach Berlin.

No 149 Sqdn — Mildenhall, Wellingtons: 1* attacked primary, 3 abandoned owing to severe incing, 1 missing.

X 9878 *Missing*	X 9824	Z 8837	X 9758*	X 9832
Sgt Dane	Sgt Parker	Sgt Swain	P/O Barnes	F/L Fox
Sgt Leeman	Sgt Simmons	P/O Bain	Sgt Baker	Sgt Woodhouse
Sgt Davis	P/O White	Sgt White	Sgt Phillips	P/O Mansfield
Sgt Crowe	Sgt Macrae	Sgt Robson	Sgt Cook	F/S Batten
Sgt Pengelly	Sgt Buchanan	Sgt Mason	Sgt Collins	Sgt Kerr
Sgt Jenkinson	Sgt Ellis	Sgt Binder	Sgt Gallagher	Sgt Jones

No 214 (Federated Malay States) Sqdn — Stradishall, Wellingtons: 5 detailed, 1 bombed on ETA, 1 missing, 2 early return due to engine failure and the fifth failed to find Berlin owing to cloud.

X 3206	T 2850	Z 8373	Z 8900	X 9979
P/O Ercolani*	Sgt Hetterick	F/L Hilton	Sgt Ruoff	Sgt Wilson
Sgt Hamilton	Sgt Weavers	P/O Baker	P/O Frowde	P/O Leech
Sgt McLennan	P/O Moore	Sgt Dawes	Sgt Wheway	P/O Clarkson
Sgt Holdsworth	Sgt Cooling	Sgt Shotter	Sgt Harvey	Sgt Allin
Sgt Weller	Sgt Hull	Sgt Cole	Sgt Calver	Sgt Murray
Sgt Fry	Sgt Hudson	Sgt Erby	Sgt Williams	Sgt Trevillion

*P/O L. B. Ercolani's crew was first reporting missing. Three days later he turned up in the Isle of Wight, having come ashore in their rubber dinghy at Ventnor. The circumstances are interesting, apart from the gallant effort to stay alive in the worst sea conditions for years — strong winds and high waves and bitter cold. Their Wellington was hit by flak on crossing the enemy coast and one of his incendiary bombs was pierced — and set on fire. For a considerable time the aircraft was 'flaming round the sky' before Ercolani put it down in the sea. His SOS was heard but the subsequent search failed and they drifted for nigh on a hundred miles in the open sea to fetch up at Ventnor. The crew (complete) was exhausted but unhurt. A splendid performance in terrible conditions.

No 218 Sqdn (Gold Coast) — Marham, Wellingtons: 13 aircraft, all went the distance, none were successful in identifying the target and some bombed on ETA. No early returns — weather thick cloud and severe icing. All returned safely.

AZ 1103	BR 1346	DX 9679	HZ 8853	JZ 8431
F/L Williams	S/L Spence	P/O Livingston	Sgt Thompson	Sgt McGlashan
Sgt Millichamp	Sgt Griffiths	Sgt Boyd	P/O Cottier	Sgt Fraser
Sgt Coulson	Sgt Willimham	P/O Jacobsen	Sgt Fry	Sgt Bowater
Sgt George	Sgt Randall	Sgt Stanley	Sgt Oldham	Sgt Stewart
Sgt Scammel	Sgt Grant	P/O Siddall	Sgt Slatford	Sgt Dobson
F/S Weir	Sgt Fudge	Sgt Hodge	Sgt Fuller	Sgt Adams

RR 1496	MR 1436	SX 9787	NR 1135	OX 9785
Sgt Vezina	F/L Dunham	Sgt Webber	Sgt McPhail	Sgt Lamason
Sgt Gregg	Sgt Johnson	Sgt Lowrey	Sgt Deadman	Sgt Medus
P/O Brown	Sgt Hinwood	P/O Hunter	Sgt Parkes	Sgt Campbell
Sgt Willett	Sgt Wheeler	Sgt Sheppard	Sgt Dixon	Sgt Harris
Sgt Toynbee-Clark	Sgt Murray	Sgt St John	Sgt Bird	Sgt McDonough
Sgt Howes	Sgt Turner	Sgt Grewcock	Sgt Howes	Sgt Richardson

XZ 8437	ZZ 8375	LZ 8965
F/L Humphreys	S/L Price	Sgt McKay
Sgt Fraser	Sgt Coggin	Sgt Crosswell
Sgt Cox	P/O Woodmason	P/O Grant
Sgt Hartley	Sgt Riley	Sgt Clark
P/O O'Callaghan	Sgt Giles	Sgt Smith
Sgt Taylor	Sgt Davidson	Sgt Fuller

No 311 (Czech) Sqdn — East Wretham, Wellingtons: 10 detailed, 7 claim attack on Berlin, 3 abandoned due to weather and engine failure*.

1167	9741	2971*	2553*
Sgt Ryba	Sgt Plecity	Sgt Svoboda	Sgt Siska
Sgt Hlobil	Sgt Para	Sgt Janek	Sgt Filler
F/O Palichleb	P/O Skorepa	F/L Naprstek	F/O Mohr
Sgt Prochazka	Sgt Rous	Sgt Masek	P/O Scerba
Sgt Dolezal	Sgt Nemecek	Sgt Svoboda-Sy	F/O Podstranecky
Sgt Kostelecky	Sgt Kral		

5711	9866	1451	1777
F/O Nejezchleba	F/O Pohlodek	Sgt Fina	Sgt Panek
Sgt Tomanek	Sgt Dostal	Sgt Bulis	Sgt Linka
P/O Divis	P/O Macenauer	P/O Krcha	P/O Nemec
F/S Tegel	P/O Simet	Sgt Osolsobe	Sgt Kincuriak
Sgt Sadil	Sgt Skutek	Sgt Kvet	Sgt Sestak
Sgt Tarantik	Sgt Muzik	W/O Kamarad	Sgt Hubicka

1458*	5682
Sgt Sebela	Sgt Knajel
Sgt Hradil	Sgt Jampot
P/O Rychnovsky	P/O Jelinek
Sgt Politzek	Sgt Fornusek
Sgt Sobotka	Sgt Vaverka
Sgt Husman	Sgt Jelinek

No 4 Bomber Group
No 10 Sqdn — Leeming, Whitleys: 5 detailed, 2 reached Berlin area and bombed, 3 bombed alternative targets owing to thick cloud up to 18,000 ft and severe icing.

Z9119
P/O Hacking
Sgt Walmsley
Sgt Turner
Sgt Hyde
Sgt Porritt

The attack was made from 14,000 ft over thick cloud with intense heavy flak — aircraft holed and struck by lightning. Whitley airborne 10 hours.

Z 9149
Sgt Whyte
Sgt Allen
Sgt Corke
Sgt Charlton
Sgt Reid

Attacked alternative.

Z9166
F/L Clapperton
P/O Clothier
Sgt Allport
Sgt Howick
Sgt Walker

Attacked alternative — Rostock — encountering storms and high winds with 10/10 cloud. 'Most trying conditions encountered on the return' — an understatement!

Z 9188

Sgt Wieland	Unable to reach Berlin — high petrol consumption. Attacked
P/O Drake	Rostock. Conditions similar to above.
Sgt Westland	
Sgt Glanville	
Sgt Darwin	

Z 9161

Sgt Boothright	Bombed Berlin area on ded. reckoning. No results seen. Flak
P/O Elliott	intense and accurate. Aircraft damaged. Airborne ten and a half
P/O Davis	hours.
Sgt Carlyle	
Sgt Richardson	

No 35 Sqdn — Linton-on-Ouse, Halifax: 4? detailed, 4 attacked, none missing.

L 9569	L 9671	L 9606	L 9600
P/O R. A. Norman	Sgt Bradshaw	P/O Cresswell	Sgt Williams
Sgt Brunskill	P/O Frew	P/O McIntyre	P/O R. G. Lane
P/O R. G. Baker	Sgt Fuce	Sgt Henry	Sgt Sykes
Sgt Long	Sgt Burry	Sgt Turner	Sgt Thorpe
Sgt Izzard	Sgt Hampton	Sgt Hezelton	Sgt Flint
Sgt Olsen	Sgt Tyler	Sgt Carrington	Sgt Martin
Sgt Butchart	Sgt Higgs	Sgt Hunt	Sgt Crowther

No 51 Sqdn — Dishforth, Whitleys: 5 attacked primary*, 1 alternative, 2 missing.

Z 6879*	Z 9130 *Missing*	Z 6389 *Missing*	Z 9133*
Sgt Brown	S/L Dickenson	Sgt MacMurray	P/O Monro
P/O Hanlon	Sgt Walley	Sgt Robotten	Sgt Bray
Sgt Kay	P/O Simpson	Sgt Kelly	Sgt Camp
Sgt Cocker	Sgt Carpenter	Sgt Telfer	Sgt Bradshaw
Sgt Cattle	Sgt Chambers	Sgt Wilkins	Sgt Chisholm

Z 6554*	Z 9146*	Z 9165*	Z 9164
P/O Potter	Sgt Abercassis	Sgt Pohe	Sgt Edwards
Sgt Oliver	Sgt Harris	Sgt Grut	P/O Austin
P/O Smith	P/O Grierson-Jackson	P/O Lambert	F/O Gallaher
Sgt McLaren	Sgt Keen	Sgt Daft	Sgt Miller
Sgt Bydwell	Sgt Prince	Sgt Cox	Sgt Craven

No 58 Sqdn — Linton-on-Ouse, Whitleys: 8 detailed, 3 attacked primary, 2 missing, 3* attacked alternative targets.

Z 6580	Z 9210	Z 9153	Z 6972 *Missing*
P/O Pestridge	P/O Stoney	P/O Earp	P/O Tuckfield
Sgt Alcock	P/O Mason	Sgt Parsons	Sgt Rowley-Blake
P/O Trickett	Sgt Hodges	Sgt Stone	P/O Lane
Sgt Taylor	Sgt Styles	F/O Harris	Sgt Scott
Sgt McHugh	Sgt Hennessy	Sgt Cameron	Sgt Stentiford

Z 9205 *Missing*	Z 6841*	Z 9211*	Z 6506*
P/O Brown	P/O Mandeno	Sgt Jones	Sgt Meredith
Sgt Gresham	P/O Wilson	P/O Hammersley	P/O Johnstone
Sgt Monk	Sgt Paine	Sgt Mott	Sgt Hill
Sgt Fenton	Sgt Evans	Sgt Jarvis	Sgt Foster
Sgt Atkin	Sgt Yarnell	Sgt Fraser	Sgt Key

P/O Mandeno's Whitley was hit by heavy flak over Emden; port engine caught fire and fuselage was damaged. He contrived to return safely.

No 76 Sqdn — Middleton St George, Halifax: 5 detailed, 2* attacked, 3 abandoned.

L 6911	L 9611	L 9523	L 9583*	L 9604*
S/L Hillary	Sgt Borsberry	S/L Bouwens	P/O Calder	Sgt Herbert
P/O Perry	P/O Bowsher	P/O Anderson	Sgt Gates	Sgt Bingham
Sgt Thompson	Sgt Gillespie	Sgt Fairclough	Sgt Becker	Sgt Roberts
Sgt Linton	Sgt Pearce	Sgt Cook	Sgt Blair	Sgt Fanning
Sgt Barnett	Sgt Carrad	Sgt Roche	Sgt Toski	Sgt Fulton
Sgt Sprigge	Sgt Taylor	Sgt Rouse	Sgt Randall	Sgt Glover
P/O Higgins	F/S Salisbury	Sgt Wallace	Sgt Greenway	Sgt Hall

Form 541 for this operation records:

'Bad weather was encountered by all aircraft and as a result of the extreme cold Air Speed Indicators and Compasses were rendered unserviceable.

S/L Hillary and Sgt Borsberry both abandoned sorties, the former because his port outer engine ran continuously on rich mixture and the latter because his instruments were frozen up. S/L Bouwens abandoned his primary target and bombed Flensburg . . . P/O Calder and Sgt Herbert reached Berlin and bombed . . . from 15,000 ft. No results were observed owing to cloud.'

No 77 Sqdn — Leeming, Whitleys: 8 took off, 4 attacked Berlin, 3 abandoned and 1* attacked Sylt before returning.

Z 6943	Z 6628	Z 6952	Z 9225
W/C Young	P/O Ogier	F/L Parkin	P/O Havelock
Sgt Bootsma	Sgt Silva	Sgt Cox	Sgt Huggard
Sgt Cooper	Sgt Grundy	Sgt Darby	F/S Hancock
Sgt Matthews	Sgt Hutton	Sgt Gilfoy	Sgt Boucher
Sgt Waddell	Sgt Clark	Sgt Lewis	Sgt Rees

Z 6822*
P/O Scott-Martin
Sgt Vose
Sgt Clark
Sgt Thompson
Sgt Cormack

Wg Cdr Young, P/O Ogier, F/L Parkin and P/O Havelock were all ten hours in the air.

No 78 Sqdn — Middleton St George, Whitleys: 6 detailed, 3 attacked primary target, 2 missing, 1 attacked Kiel as an alternative.

Z 9129	Z 6490	???? *Missing*	Z 9151 *Missing*
P/O Knox	P/O Woodroffe	Sgt Bell	Sgt Sargent
Sgt Stevens	Sgt Hewell	P/O McCombe	Sgt Penn
P/O Davidson	Sgt LeBeau	Sgt Webb	P/O Saunders
Sgt Kerry	Sgt Lyndon	Sgt Cameron	Sgt Patterson
Sgt Thorn	Sgt Springham	Sgt Boucher	Sgt Hall
			Sgt Freeman

Z 9214	Z 9300
Sgt Lloyd-Jones	P/O Leyland
Sgt Connolly	Sgt Williams
Sgt Wilson	P/O Geddes
Sgt Beaton	Sgt Pugsley
Sgt Cragg	Sgt Brooks

No 102 Sqdn — Topcliffe, Whitleys: 9 dispatched, 3 attacked primary*, 3 missing, 2 early returns, 1 bombed alternative target.

Z 6820 *Missing*	Z 6796 *Missing*	Z 6747	Z 6940
P/O B. B. P. Roy	Sgt R. C. Matthews	Sgt E. P. Pike*	Sgt H. W. Wickham*
Sgt D. R. Pritchard	Sgr R. O. Bryant	Sgt J. B. Robinson	Sgt H. E. Batchelder
Sgt K. Harwood-Smith	Sgt E. M. Leftley	P/O S. R. Whipple	P/O N. L. Shove
Sgt S. Thomson	Sgt R. Brown	Sgt R. C. Perriam	Sgt E. R. Smith
Sgt P. H. Stanton	Sgt M. Miller	Sgt J. Rivers	Sgt D. K. Breary

Z 9282	Z 9128 *Missing*	Z 6974
P/O W. J. J. Welch*	Sgt T. H. Thorley	Sgt G. F. J. Hoben
S/L G. M. Lindeman	P/O J. C. A. Allchin	Sgt H. J. Marchalleck
Sgt F. H. Mylrea	Sgt D. L. Brown	Sgt D. L. Boyd
Sgt A. E. M. Moon	Sgt J. A. Steeves	Sgt F. A. Ringham
Sgt J. B. T. Teasdale- Smith	Sgt W. Clarke	Sgt D. Boddy

No 405 (RCAF) Sqdn — Pocklington, Wellington IIs: 10 detailed, *6 attacked primary area, 1 missing, 3 bombed targets of opportunity. No aircraft numbers given.

'L'*	'Q'*	'P'*	'T'
F/L McCormack	Sgt Sutherland	Sgt McLennan	Sgt McKay
Sgt Mather	Sgt Lloyd	Sgt McKinley	Sgt Higginson
F/O Fetherston	Sgt Curtis	Sgt Baldwin	P/O McEwen
Sgt Almond	Sgt Newenham	Sgt Dodds	Sgt Evans
Sgt McGill	Sgt Nutt	Sgt Paige	Sgt Brown
Sgt Clark	Sgt Cole	Sgt Forster	Sgt Morrison

'U'	'G'*	'K'	'R'*
P/O Robson	Sgt Suggitt	Sgt Williams	Sgt Frost
P/O Thiele	Sgt Lefurgey	P/O Wilson	Sgt Knight
Sgt Leith	Sgt Scharf	Sgt Donkin	Sgt Gardner
F/S Mallett	Sgt Oneson	Sgt James	Sgt Evans
Sgt Turnbull	Sgt Robertson	Sgt Langhorne	Sgt Hillmer
Sgt Piers	Sgt Smith	Sgt Bourgeau	Sgt Mann

'D'* *Missing*	'B'
Sgt Hassan	F/L Fauquier
P/O Solheim	Sgt Scott
Sgt Killin	P/O Gibson
Sgt Hynam	Sgt Tatro
Sgt Bell	Sgt Robson
Sgt McLeod	Sgt Andrew

Sgt Hassan signalled 'Mission completed' but did not return. Sgt McLennan was hit by flak — front turret, tailplane and starboard engine. F/L Fauquier was heavily damaged by flak but succeeded in returning to a crash landing.

Appendix B

Order of Battle — 24 March 1944

A record, by Groups, Squadrons, Aircraft and Crews, of those who took part in the raid on Berlin by 800 aircraft of Bomber Command on the night of 24 March 1944.

No 1 Bomber Group

No 12 Sqdn — Wickenby, 9 reported attack, 4 missing, 2 early returns.

ND 562	JB 748	ND 699	JB 405
F/L A. J. Cook	S/L J. G. Woollatt	P/O L. H. Blake	F/S J. D. Carter
W/O E. K. Mouchet	F/S R. Potter	Sgt R. Ellaway	F/O R. J. Ward
W/O B. Salt	F/S L. Black	Sgt F. D. Nelmes	Sgt G. Long
W/O R. Timperley	F/S W. Mann	Sgt P. Siegfried	Sgt K. N. Read
Sgt K. L. Summerscale	Sgt P. Frith	Sgt L. Lockwood	Sgt S. Hayhurst
Sgt J. E. McInnes	F/S Bayley	Sgt D. J. Collins	Sgt A. P. Simpson
F/S R. F. Bailey	F/S R. Hooper	Sgt P. Kelly	Sgt S. Johnson

JB 462	ND 441	ND 627	ND 679
F/L D. M. Carey	F/O P. G. Maxwell	P/O S. J. Black	F/S S. J. Carroll
Sgt J. Prior	F/O S. G. Garlick	F/S R. Holding	F/O G. W. Swann
Sgt W. Aikman	Sgt H. Lloyd	Sgt E. Goddard	Sgt G. W. Laurence
P/O C. W. Kruger	Sgt. H. F. O'Hara	F/O G. F. Carruthers	Sgt W. G. Blackburn
SGT P. H. Lambert	Sgt J. Crighton	Sgt J. Norris	Sgt D. Barker
Sgt F. W. Peppiatt	Sgt J. Davidson	P/O F. Bailey	Sgt M. D. Garlick
Sgt W. S. Smedmore	Sgt E. T. Townsend	Sgt Q. Woodruff	Sgt K. Appleyard

ND 528	JB 359 *Missing*	ND 710 *Missing*	ND 439 *Missing*
F/S A. F. L'Estrange	F/L J. Bracewell	F/O C. D. De Marigny	F/S C. J. Bates
F/O A. Leather	F/O D. A. Colombo	F/S R. G. W. Beer	F/S J. A. Brammall
Sgt R. W. Dee	F/O R. H. Stevens	Sgt S. J. Bentley	Sgt R. Plant
F/S R. N. Stark	F/O A. B. Hunter	Sgt P. Holland	Sgt H. F. McPherson
Sgt L. Hopwood	F/L F. J. King	Sgt J. S. Wright	Sgt P. Hendon
Sgt W. Lee	Sgt H. W. Norton	Sgt G. W. Henson	Sgt P. C. Emms
Sgt A. Davenport	Sgt C. W. Hicks	Sgt E. A. Anthony	Sgt D. Brown

ND 650 *Missing*
F/O F. C. Hentch
F/O C. Rudyk
Sgt E. Birch
Sgt A. V. Keveren
Sgt R. M. Cringle
Sgt A. C. Summers
F/O D. Wimlett

No 100 Sqdn — Grimsby, 14 attacked, 1 missing.

ND 644	JB 614	ME 670	ND 413
F/L P. Sherriff	F/S L. Holden	S/L H. H. Grant-Dalton	F/O J. K. Hamilton
Sgt J. D. Gray	Sgt A. Davison	SGT R. P. Anderson	Sgt W. F. Bloomfield
F/O Calloway	F/O T. G. Davies	F/O G. Robertson	W/O J. D. Hudson
F/O R. M. Girvan	F/S R. Pinkett	P/O H. L. Hamblin	Sgt D. H. Chapman
Sgt T. A. Hammill	Sgt F. E. Parry	P/O K. R. Rogers	Sgt D. F. H. Lacey
Sgt G. R. Dixon	Sgt J. Lethbridge	Sgt E. D. Molesworth	F/S J. Hesp
Sgt G. H. Warren	Sgt F. E. Bowler	F/S H. C. Prime	W/O R. J. Booth

ND 456	ND 458	ME 677	JB 603
F/L D. F. Gillam	Sgt E. Walton	F/S A. R. Oxenham	F/S J. Littlewood
Sgt K. Talbot	Sgt R. T. Rutter	Sgt D. J. Fuller	Sgt C. McCartney
F/S K. Drury	F/S J. O'Loughlin	Sgt E. Blackburn	F/S D. A. Tovell
Sgt D. C. Gemmell	Sgt T. E. Sanders	Sgt H. Goodall	Sgt J. G. Hughes
Sgt W. Moffett	Sgt L. Whitewood	Sgt G. F. Pearse	Sgt R. W. Gilbey
Sgt H. R. Crompton	Sgt J. R. Logan	Sgt J. Barber	Sgt S. C. Smith
F/S T. R. Jones	Sgt J. R. Taylor	Sgt D. A. Coggin	Sgt J. Taylor

ND 594	ND 675	ND 326	LM 321
F/S P. V. T. Ribbins	P/O A. J. T. Armon	F/S D. W. Sutton	F/O E. L. Eames
Sgt W. R. Hughes	Sgt B. V. Cox	Sgt D. J. Tait	Sgt R. W. Price
F/S P. L. Bloodworth	F/O R. F. Weedon	F/S S. Hampson	F/S D. S. Kirkwood
Sgt A. P. Fricker	Sgt P. R. Boxall	Sgt A. F. Bradshaw	F/O J. Spector
Sgt A. B. Phipps	Sgt D. Jones	Sgt. J. W. Cameron	Sgt A. J. Alcott
Sgt J. O. Beagley	Sgt L. V. Bowden	Sgt A. B. Reid	Sgt C. Bird
Sgt G. Edmund	F/S M. Robertson	Sgt R. L. Cross	Sgt E. T. Duckett
JB 289	ME 648	ND 642 *Missing*	
F/S D. Fairbairn	F/L J. H. Inns	F/O A. F. Jenkins	
Sgt H. R. Tufton	Sgt C. C. Davies	Sgt W. T. Moore	
P/O F. Tovery	Sgt E. Usher	F/S G. A. Saunders	
P/O J. M. Wilder	F/O S. Tincler	Sgt G. Pearson	
Sgt L. Gibbons	Sgt K. Pearton	Sgt. R. Ross	
Sgt S. Tunstall	F/O F. J. Blute	Sgt D. G. Harris	
F/S C. L. Foster	Sgt H. Flint	Sgt F. A. Farr	

No 101 Sqdn — Ludford Magna, 19? attacked primary, 2 attacked secondary, 2 early returns.

ME 617	ME 616	DV 276	DV 292
F/S L. F. Bateman	F/S K. D. Corkill	P/O J. Batten-Smith	F/L B. N. Dickenson
Sgt A. Fazackerly	Sgt E. A. F. Cole	Sgt R. Armstrong	Sgt L. Holden
W/O W. E. Buie	F/S K. G. Thompson	Sgt G. N. Williams	F/O R. S. Rocheleau
F/S E. Crook	Sgt C. Manser	Sgt R. R. Roberts	F/S J. E. Peyton-Lander
F/O F. G. Brooks	F/S R. M. Gundy	F/S A. M. Ross	F/O R. L. French
W/O J. J. Byrne	Sgt L. P. Swales	Sgt H. F. McClenaghan	Sgt R. A. J. Collier
Sgt H. A. Jamieson	Sgt G. G. Welsh	F/S A. Haynes	Sgt J. V. Bramhall
Sgt H. Dockerty	Sgt P. N. D. Skingley	W/O C. G. Woellfle	F/S G. E. H. Schultz
LL 779	ME 564	DV 302	LM 474
F/L D. H. Todd	S/L C. B. Morton	P/O E. T. Holland	F/O R. J. Goeres
Sgt S. Powell	Sgt J. Butterfield	Sgt T. Haycock	Sgt A. G. Moore
S/L R. G. Rosevear	F/O A. H. Bird	F/S H. Scott	W/O R. W. Code
F/O V. G. Viggers	F/O C. W. Chalmers	F/S A. P. Farquharson	Sgt D. K. Ball
Sgt K. H. Bardell	F/L D. K. Bradley	F/S I. R. Smith	F/S M. P. J. Roy
Sgt H. R. Whittle	W/O E. Cottrell	P/O J. P. Whymark	Sgt M. C. Carr
F/O C. R. S. Ricketts	W/O E. Friend	Sgt V. G. Smith	Sgt A. Smith
F/O P. J. W. Raine	F/S G. B. Scott	Sgt M. G. Smith	F/O R. Cooper
LL 774	DV 264	LL 773	ME 565
F/L F. C. Bertlesen	P/O W. I. Adamson	P/O A. F. Rowe	W/C R. I. Alexander
Sgt R. G. Lovegrove	Sgt A. M. Bowyer	Sgt A. S. Holland	Sgt J. Ormerod
F/O J. L. Ritchie	Sgt E. Kippen	Sgt P. A. Pearson	F/S A. Cowan
Sgt E. K. Slattery	P/O R. L. Luffman	Sgt R. M. Patmore	Sgt I. Arndell
F/O G. L. Scott	F/S A. G. Hall	F/S G. H. Cannon	F/S N. Westby
Sgt R. Mansbridge	Sgt D. Brinkhurst	Sgt I. I. Donovan	Sgt T. Dewsbury
F/S G. A. Clyne	Sgt J. A. Goodall	Sgt N. V. Creighton	Sgt H. S. Nunn
F/O E. H. Day	F/O N. Marrian	F/S P. S. W. Napier	Sgt E. H. Manners
LM 462	DV 245	LM 457	ME 619
F/S G. Tivey	F/O H. Davies	Sgt C. J. Harnish	F/O D. J. Irving
Sgt R. W. Farley	Sgt W. E. Lees	Sgt A. R. Luffman	Sgt F. Phillips
Sgt L. Lockwood	F/S H. Barlow	F/S G. W. Robertson	F/S S. G. R. King
Sgt B. M. Schofield	F/S E. Pritchard	F/S J. A. Marshall	F/S N. G. Muggett
F/S M. R. Butterworth	Sgt J. H. Kemp	W/O N. Baker	Sgt J. A. Noske
P/O L. Simpson	Sgt R. E. Stace	Sgt M. G. McGeer	F/S J. B. Newman
Sgt A. D. Dickson	Sgt T. Jones	Sgt D. V. McIntyre	F/S W. J. Adam
Sgt G. L. Preece	P/O J. S. Scott	P/O R. H. Cond	F/O R. P. Litchfield
LL 779	LM 463	DV 290	LL 833
F/O L. D. McKenna	F/S J. W. Lintott	F/S J. King	P/O K. E. Forsyth
Sgt E. R. Sawyer	Sgt J. McDonald	Sgt D. H. Perrett	Sgt T. G. Holt
F/S T. J. Butler	F/S J. D. Bradbury	F/O W. D. Manger	F/S A. E. Charman
Sgt B. B. Straw	Sgt J. Fulton	Sgt A. E. Wortts	P/O E. Copland
F/O N. M. Neale	Sgt G. W. Carey	F/O H. J. Moore	Sgt W. F. Bates
Sgt A. J. Williams	Sgt F. Eckersley	Sgt T. Bathgate	Sgt G. D. Dowdeswell
P/O W. C. H. Brown	Sgt E. Cheetham	F/S R. L. Williams	F/S C. T. Akers
Sgt J. F. Doyle	Sgt V. H. Harris	Sgt J. Childs	Sgt G. A. C. Eby

LM 479	DV 275	ME 592
F/S M. A. Carson	F/O G. Hall	P/O G. Baker
Sgt K. Dick	Sgt T. K. Nichol	Sgt D. H. Crow
W/O W. G. Wilson	F/O L. W. Stewart	Sgt G. D. Steward
Sgt J. G. Johnson	Sgt P. E. Tovey	F/S D. McNaught
F/O L. M. Joyner	F/S L. M. Taggart	Sgt D. H. Ainsworth
Sgt E. T. Chambers	Sgt L. C. Belinger	Sgt M. J. Hackett
Sgt D. R. Billson	Sgt A. Day	Sgt A. J. Ridgeway
Sgt R. Herscovitch	P/O H. H. King	P/O G. A. Blair

No 103 Sqn — Elsham Wolds, 16 attacked, 1 missing.

ME 674	JB 746	ME 673	JB 278
F/L G. M. Russell-Fry	F/L J. Hart	P/O E. T. Jones	P/O B. B. Lydon
Sgt D. H. Edwards	Sgt E. J. Kilminster	Sgt A. J. Pugh	Sgt J. R. Thomas
P/O I. H. Dobbin	F/S D. C. Jones	F/O E. N. Hooke	F/S T. C. Forster
F/O I. W. Saunders	P/O W. F. Langston	P/O J. R. Boyes	Sgt A. P. Collings
P/O D. J. C. Fleming	Sgt G. C. Mitchell	Sgt J. G. Johnson	F/S E. B. Benney
Sgt G. L. Hill	Sgt L. A. Bridges	F/S F. G. Smith	F/S S. J. Edwards
Sgt A. C. Sykes	Sgt C. H. Seldon	Sgt S. Willis	F/S S. F. Donnahey

ND 381	JB 555	ND 411	ND 402
F/L M. P. Floyd	F/O L. Young	Sgt K. W. Mitchell	F/S R. Whitley
P/O R. H. Mansfield	F/S A. J. Goodman	Sgt D. Howells	SGT D. W. C. Benstead
F/S J. Niven	W/O A. Shields	F/S W. Kelley	W/O J. A. Carter
Sgt C. Wood	F/S L. Clark	Sgt D. F. Pegrum	Sgt R. B. Webb
W/O J. H. Perrin	F/S B. G. Hathaway	Sgt R. Tapp	Sgt G. N. Crutchfield
Sgt C. Fuller	Sgt R. E. Gardner	Sgt C. E. Bish	Sgt K. M. Martin
F/S P. Wild	Sgt N. T. L. Storey	P/O T. K. Wright	Sgt J. W. Smith

ND 572	ME 655 *Missing*	JB 655	ND 629
F/S F. G. Brewings	S/L K. G. Bickers	F/O T. G. Leggett	F/O W. H. Way
Sgt A. Richardson	F/S J. Wadsworth	Sgt W. A. Edwards	Sgt E. Jennings
F/O R. Walker	F/O C. J. Plummer	F/O R. H. Beer	F/S Hollingsworth
Sgt K. G. B. Smart	F/S D. Cannon	P/O J. G. Apostolides	F/S L. W. Zingelman
F/O N. G. Barker	F/O P. A. C. Bell	P/O A. A. Wilkes	F/S J. D. Gallacher
Sgt J. R. Spark	F/S L. J. Comer	F/S A. Jones	Sgt R. H. Cooper
Sgt R. Thomas	F/O N. Tombs	F/O A. V. Jones	Sgt G. R. Jones

ND 624	JB 732	ME 674	JB 733
F/L D. Allwood	F/S J. W. Armstrong	W/O G. W. Chase	W/O J. J. Robchak
Sgt R. Pearce	F/S J. H. Beddis	Sgt H. C. Kidd	Sgt A. F. Carter
F/S J. R. Carroll	F/O A. W. Drage	F/S T. Wilcox	F/O D. H. Woodley
Sgt H. R. Freckleton	F/O M. F. Dillon	Sgt W. L. Hill	Sgt W. L. Churchill
Sgt F. J. Hutchings	Sgt A. J. McCauley	F/S F. Gwartney	Sgt M. C. Coulghan
Sgt H. Shaw	Sgt L. Fisher	Sgt D. Cunliffe	Sgt F. N. Bradley
Sgt J. Selwyn	Sgt R. P. Bowler	Sgt C. Greenwood	Sgt P. H. Crockett

460 Sqdn RAAF — Binbrook, Lancasters: 22 attacked, 2 missing.

ND 586	JB 598	ND 656	ND 364
F/O A. H. Probert	F/S R. Allen	P/O R. N. Mullins	F/S C. H. Hargreaves
Sgt B. G. Wiseman	Sgt D. Lord	Sgt W. Hendry	Sgt D. F. Siddall
Sgt A. H. Palfreyman	F/S K. P. Collett	Sgt E. Wilson	F/S W. H. Spargo
F/O R. B. McDougall	F/O W. M. Orr	F/O J. A. Duckworth	F/O J. E. Beaumont
Sgt D. E. Robbins	Sgt S. McSwinton	Sgt D. H. Cochrane	F/S G. D. Moody
F/S W. G. Hogg	Sgt J. S. Stewart	Sgt J. R. Espley	Sgt T. F. J. Waller
F/O K. F. Ryan	Sgt J. G. Bond	Sgt R. S. Pountney	Sgt G. Jones

ND 630	ND 634	JB 741	JB 613
F/S J. W. Smart	F/L D. E. Donaldson	F/O C. S. Fulloon	F/O R. R. Anderson
Sgt T. Oulton	Sgt R. Owen	Sgt J. W. Ranger	Sgt L. T. C. Gramson
F/S G. R. F. Warnock	F/S B. G. D. Dillon	Sgt B. Prout	F/O D. S. Wilkinson
F/S G. C. Barber	F/S J. G. Earl	F/S T. O. Stewart	P/O E. Noble
Sgt F. F. Naismith	F/S L. E. Weldon	F/S R. J. Guthrie	Sgt L. A. Barron
Sgt A. B. Moore	Sgt B. Wilson	Sgt L. Wintle	Sgt T. A. Hutchison
F/S E. F. Stannett	W/O J. K. McDonald	F/S L. J. Burrows	Sgt R. K. Gant

ND 361
P/O R. Burke
Sgt E. H. Stedman
F/S J. L. Brooks
F/S A. Henry
F/S P. S. Fleming
Sgt S. W. Cooper
F/S J. S. Hosier
F/S P. R. Anderson

JB 700
P/O J. R. E. Howell
Sgt C. Hewitt
F/S N. J. Lukies
P/O S. A. Moorhouse
F/S L. M. Field
Sgt A. C. Hill
Sgt W. C. Shaw

ME 640 *Missing*
F/L A. F. McKinnon
Sgt G. F. White
W/O J. I. Goodwin
F/O J. P. Bird
F/S A. Craven
P/O G. D. Fitzgerald
F/S J. D. West

ME 649
W/O R. H. White
Sgt P. P. James
Sgt J. Bailey
F/S A. C. Tweedie
Sgt H. F. Doleman
Sgt D. A. Goldstone
Sgt C. W. Foster

JB 662
F/L A. V. Willis
P/O I. J. Bowen
F/O R. C. Gordon
F/S B. H. Beaumont
F/O N. Ratten
F/O A. W. Delohery
W/O C. R. Anderson

ND 463 *Missing*
P/O M. J. Cusick
Sgt J. Foster
Sgt J. W. Clifton
F/S J. R. Martin
F/S P. A. Forrest
F/S G. N. Speering
F/S A. Bumpstead

JB 743
P/O P. A. Crosby
Sgt M. H. Bender
F/S C. Billett
F/O C. E. Suffren
F/S L. H. Chapman
F/O L. W. Robb
Sgt S. F. Hodge

JB 734
W/O C. B. Lynch
Sgt J. L. Petch
Sgt H. Simmonds
F/S H. H. Beattie
F/S G. Schofield
F/S A. G. Forbes
F/S N. A. Smith

ND 652
P/O R. N. T. Wade
Sgt H. G. Goulden
F/S V. A. Potter
F/S A. R. Hoyle
F/O C. C. Chapman
Sgt T. W. Mortimer
Sgt J. Eley

ND 674
W/O J. Proud
Sgt T. McKinstry
F/S D. H. Martin
F/O L. M. Ryan
F/S W. G. Boyce
Sgt S. Edwards
F/S E. Oberhardt

JA 683
F/L D. D. L. Lloyd
Sgt J. G. Turnbull
F/S D. R. Ridell
F/S R. H. Hobbs
F/S D. R. Barr
Sgt P. D. Fry
Sgt R. A. Johnson

ED 750
F/S S. O. Daley
Sgt D. J. Thomas
F/S Englart
F/O J. F. O'B. Young
F/S R. H. Loader
Sgt R. J. Thompson
F/O L. W. Bown

DV 193
F/S J. McCleery
Sgt W. A. Law
F/S H. J. Long
F/S W. H. Betts
F/S V. Widdup
Sgt A. F. Hamilton
F/S D. J. Dyson

ME 663
F/O L. Petney
Sgt M. Wood
F/S A. J. Mildred
F/S A. G. King
F/S D. M. Falconer
Sgt F. J. Mills
F/S D. T. Baldwin

ND 615
F/S V. H. Neal
Sgt R. E. Holder
Sgt G. R. Beard
F/S W. A. Gourlay
Sgt R. Robinson
Sgt J. D. Colbert
Sgt C. W. Ebbage

ND 658
F/L E. G. D. Jarman
Sgt D. G. Champkin
F/O F. G. Jackson
F/O M. W. Carroll
F/O H. R. Harrison
P/O R. L. Neal
P/O T. J. Lynch

ND 738
F/O B. D. Burnell
Sgt H. Pole
F/O R. B. Bestwick
Sgt R. H. Knight
SGT R. D. Taylor
Sgt T. W. Bailey
Sgt E. A. Milliner

No 166 Sqdn — Kirmington, 16 attacked, 4 missing, 2 early returns.

JB 142
P/O P. J. Wilson
Sgt V. D. Edwards
F/O A. J. N. Noble
W/O W. G. Knowles
Sgt P. J. Hardiman
Sgt B. Wilkinson
Sgt A. O. Manuel

LM 386
S/L R. A. Mackie
F/O Fleming
Sgt F. Reed
F/S G. T. A. Dunn
F/O J. B. Stent
F/S J. W. Clarke
Sgt G. L. Nordbye
F/S J. Douglas

LL 743
F/L S. J. Arnfield
Sgt S. L. Cole
F/S W. J. C. Barber
F/S R. Boursnell
Sgt J. McLuskie
F/S W. R. Bedford
F/S O. E. Bryant

ME 624
F/S R. B. Fennell
Sgt W. Pettis
F/S W. J. C. Keigwin
F/S J. Smyth
Sgt A. C. Trotter
F/S A. P. Jones
Sgt W. Harris

LM 388
F/S R. B. Ridley
Sgt J. J. Eaton
F/O R. E. A. Phillips
F/O A. C. Piggott
Sgt L. Cotton
Sgt L. Clarke
Sgt A. M. Weir

ME 627
F/S A. J. Owen
Sgt D. Hawkins
F/O R. C. J. Conrad
W/O C. D. Burrows
Sgt J. R. Woolf
W/O F. Edmunds
Sgt T. L. Raeburn

ME 647
F/S J. Boles
Sgt A. Harding
F/S G. E. Pinfold
Sgt J. Hughes
F/S A. Madden
Sgt A. G. Seaman
Sgt W. J. Bradley

ND 579
F/S A. I. Wiggins
Sgt V. A. Stapley
Sgt E. Pilley
F/S J. P. Sparkes
Sgt P. C. M. King
Sgt D. Fraser

ND 651
P/O G. D. Jones
Sgt H. T. Gregory
F/O C. G. Neville
F/O R. D. Crone
Sgt J. Maguire
Sgt B. T. Williams
Sgt C. E. Mayne

ND 707
F/L F. Taylor
Sgt J. A. Hargreaves
F/S W. Watson
F/S L. F. McCarney
Sgt S. N. Whitlock
Sgt F. A. Thrower
P/O H. A. Standen

EE 200
F/S J. H. Booth
Sgt J. Robinson
Sgt J. Macgregor
F/O A. L. Hill
Sgt D. G. Bicknell
Sgt J. Terry
Sgt J. Moffett

ND 620 *Missing*
F/L W. R. Jackson
Sgt R. V. Keen
F/O B. C. Jones
F/O C. C. Reed
Sgt E. Fountains
F/S K. G. Mitchell
Sgt P. O. Fenner

ND ???
F/S R. V. G. Frandsen
Sgt K. L. Pile
Sgt R. G. Leevers
Sgt K. W. Latham
Sgt L. V. Randall
Sgt. H. V. Reed
Sgt W. V. Francis

ND 621
P/O J. M. Bridges
Sgt E. N. Whitfield
F/O D. G. Wood
P/O J. L. Atherton
Sgt J. Buncher
Sgt J. Weatherell
Sgt J. Opie

LL 749
F/S V. L. Perry
Sgt J. J. McInroy
Sgt A. G. Coney
F/S L. V. Woodfield
F/S M. D. H. Williams
Sgt S. P. P. Neeves
Sgt P. G. Robins

ND 625
F/S P. J. Dunston
Sgt F. G. Shields
Sgt T. R. Dunlop
W/O J. M. McCullum
Sgt K. Clough
Sgt H. W. Pound
Sgt C. E. Dyckhoff

ND 401 *Missing*
F/O J. L. McGill
Sgt J. Mowbray
F/O C. M. Torgat
F/O E. J. Underhill
Sgt R. Tugman
Sgt O. S. Roberts
Sgt E. F. Pates

ED 371 *Missing*
F/O T. L. Teasdale
Sgt W. Dawson
F/O J. B. Auld
F/S F. E. Johnson
Sgt L. Gammage
Sgt D. E. Hunt
W/O J. Skeel

ME 635 *Missing*
F/S E. Brown
Sgt J. E. Scruton
Sgt R. Royde
F/S W. Mitchison
Sgt J. Flavell
Sgt W. H. Burnell
Sgt W. C. Mason

ED 905
F/S J. A. Sanderson
Sgt F. L. Solomon
Sgt C. Farley
Sgt R. G. Marks
Sgt W. T. Viollett
Sgt J. Cockburn
Sgt J. A. Bodsworth

No 550 Sqdn — Grimsby, Lancasters: 15 attacked, 1 attacked alternative in Berlin area, 1 early return.

LM 319
Sgt W. N. H. Brawn
Sgt R. Paxton
F/S C. H. Sowden
Sgt P. Pindar
Sgt E. K. G. Smith
Sgt R. A. Caley
Sgt W. J. Jones

ND 425
F/S C. G. Foster
F/O D. F. Neilson
Sgt J. McGhie
Sgt J. C. Garratt
Sgt R. Johnson
Sgt E. W. Wash
Sgt W. Barratt
F/O D. W. Morgan

ME 581
F/L R. W. Picton
Sgt T. H. Guest
F/O J. J. Logan
F/O J. E. Potter
Sgt K. P. C. Williams
P/O W. H. Keen
Sgt J. W. Porteous

ME 556
W/O D. McCrae
Sgt R. A. Drury
F/O M. Shapiro
F/S F. G. Lebano
Sgt A. G. Hall
Sgt C. A. Bonner
Sgt A. H. Brown

LL 826
P/O A. J. Grain
Sgt J. E. Legg
F/O M. R. Oliver
F/O E. C. Jones
F/O H. W. Batt
Sgt K. R. Dye
Sgt J. Ellis

LL 834
P/O V. J. Bouchard
Sgt R. Binney
W/O D. H. Knight
F/S J. M. Knor
Sgt A. T. Paget
Sgt C. A. Rann
Sgt J. W. Galvin

LL 747
F/O J. O. Richards
Sgt A. G. Day
W/O T. E. Boyle
F/S R. W. Scott
Sgt J. G. Hill
Sgt W. J. Carthew
Sgt T. J. Conaghan

LL 850
F/S A. H. Jeffries
Sgt E. G. W. Bull
Sgt H. Simpson
F/L A. D. McConnell
Sgt S. A. Kierle
Sgt W. G. Upton
Sgt D. W. Whitley

LL 837
P/O N. S. Rogers
Sgt R. H. J. Pearce
F/O H. T. A. Evans
Sgt N. C. Jenkins
Sgt D. M. Salmon
F/S M. E. Mills
Sgt J. H. Marshall

LM 460
F/L A. B. Craig
Sgt L. C. Woodcock
F/S E. M. England
W/O G. C. Notman
F/O L. W. Denton
Sgt R. S. Pilson
F/S S. H. Brasher

DV 309
F/S G. W. Hinds
Sgt T. L. J. Whittick
Sgt D. Hughes
Sgt G. C. Sharland
Sgt D. R. M. Davies
Sgt E. C. Beacham
Sgt W. A. J. Young

LM 455
S/L G. D. Graham
F/S A. B. Frost
F/O J. R. Harding
Sgt H. Jennings
F/S B. G. Winzar
Sgt E. Brennan
Sgt J. W. Nash

LL 831
F/O E. V. Sage
Sgt H. P. Robinson
F/O O. L. Albutt
Sgt W. G. Taylor
F/O D. A. Goulden
Sgt W. W. Hopper
Sgt E. G. R. Pepper

ME 687
W/O R. A. Rember
Sgt L. Whybrow
F/O E. E. Radcliffe
Sgt E. W. Smalley
Sgt K. Hibbert
Sgt A. H. Bowers
Sgt D. H. Phillips

LL 851
F/S P. Maxwell
Sgt R. W. Willey
F/S F. Fowkes
F/S S. J. Oalund
Sgt P. R. Greenhalf
Sgt C. Whittles
Sgt R. Greathead

From Sqdn Record . . . 'Soon after leaving Berlin Lancaster 'D' — ME 581 — Captain Flight Lieutenant Picton — was engaged by a Fokker Wulf and both the Mid-Upper gunner, Sergeant Keen, and the rear gunner, Sergeant Porteous, were seriously injured by cannon fire . . . After the action the wireless operator, Sgt Williams, went to the rear gunner whose oxygen tube was severed and gave him his own mask whilst assisting him out of the turret. Earlier, Sgt Williams had taken position in the astro hatch where he continued to give advice and evasive instructions to his captain. Sgt Williams prompt action combined with the pilot's skilful handling of his aircraft undoubtedly prevented the enemy fighter from making a more effective attack.

No 625 Sqdn — Kelstern, Lancasters: 14 attacked, 3 missing, 1 early return.

LM 426	ND 641 *Missing*	ND 639	ND 619
F/L E. S. Ellis, CGM	W/O J. D. Owen	P/O D. M. Blackmore	W/O R. W. D. Price
P/O W. M. Knowles	Sgt W. H. Broadmore	Sgt D. North	Sgt L. A. Knowles
Sgt A. W. Fairclough	W/O F. B. Magee	Sgt G. Yates	P/O Conley
Sgt J. A. Lloyd	Sgt J. C. Lavender	P/O C. H. Bancroft	P/O D. E. Ball
P/O A. G. Boud	Sgt P. H. Simpkins	Sgt D. K. Lewis	Sgt J. H. G. Harris
Sgt B. Richardson	Sgt H. W. Nixon	Sgt K. C. Webb	Sgt H. W. Powter
Sgt M. J. Wallen	Sgt W. Clark	Sgt E. B. Thomas	Sgt F. Sutton
P/O R. J. Coxhead		F/O G. G. Smith	

ND 407	ND 459	ND 742	ND 636
P/O C. K. Bradshaw	W/O B. P. Goldman	P/O C. L. Mims	F/S N. McA. McGaw
Sgt A. H. Brakes	Sgt P. H. Miller	Sgt L. Jenkins	Sgt K. Garner
Sgt D. J. Gunn	F/O J. F. Dunn	F/O W. H. Johnson	F/O D. Moriarty
P/O J. E. Goldsmith	F/O L. M. Bowen	W/O G. R. Mills	Sgt F. C. Clarke
Sgt R. F. Wright	Sgt S. Baldridge	F/S W. J. Lawrence	Sgt R. J. Tailby
Sgt J. R. Cavanagh	Sgt F. E. Brimecombe	P/O R. C. J. Waters	Sgt R. W. Andrews
Sgt J. Sutcliffe	Sgt S. Harrison	F/O J. L. Ware	Sgt T. C. White

ME 682	ME 684 *Missing*	ED 317 *Missing*	ED 988
Sgt J. H. Marks	F/L M. Clark	F/S R. D. W. Jamieson	F/S T. H. Burford
Sgt N. R. Truman	Sgt D. S. Beckwith	Sgt E. B. Tones	Sgt P. H. Yarwood
F/O W. S. Telford	F/O A. D. Bull	Sgt E. G. Waller	F/O J. D. Lines
F/S A. E. Tomkinson	F/O G. Brand	F/O B. Rogers	W/O C. Douglas-
Sgt G. Cooke	F/O R. C. T. Armytage	Sgt J. I. Scott	Brown
Sgt J. G. Ritch	Sgt J. B. Remington	Sgt J. F. Etheridge	Sgt R. R. Lawrence
Sgt F. N. Larard	Sgt J. Munro	Sgt J. R. Honey	Sgt C. E. Callas
			Sgt E. W. Gilbert

ED 594	ED 940	ED 814	W 5009
P/O B. R. Pengilley	1st Lieut M. E. Dowden	W/O J. P. Cosgrove	P/O R. E. Beadle
Sgt E. Dagger	(USAAF)	Sgt A. Bennett	Sgt A. L. Dix
F/O A. H. Grange	Sgt F. H. Moody	Sgt G. Jeeves	Sgt H. R. Lawson
F/O D. R. Anderson	Sgt A. W. Brickenden	F/S R. A. Mercer	F/O W. R. Merrall
Sgt D. Holden	F/O D. J. Weepers	Sgt C. Williams	Sgt E. Wilkinson
Sgt A. E. Scott	Sgt R. E. Reeves	Sgt C. J. Page	Sgt J. Potter
Sgt T. C. Davies	Sgt R. Margerison	Sgt D. H. Beechey	F/S N. McDonough
	Sgt G. F. J. McElroy		

N0 576 Sqdn — Elsham Wolds, Lancasters: 16 attacked, 2 missing, 1 early return.

LL 749	LM 439	ME 586	LL 799
P/O A. J. Bodger	F/L G. S. Morgan	W/O R. Whalley	F/L S. Slater
Sgt R. P. Lloyd	Sgt J. R. Mearns	Sgt C. VandeVelde	Sgt C. C. Rudland
Sgt S. P. Barnes	P/O N. A. Lambell	Sgt J. Parrs	F/S J. Pasley
Sgt W. Scott	F/O E. M. Graham	Sgt J. D. Ward	Sgt D. Waterhouse
Sgt K. Watkins	Sgt J. R. O'Hanlan	Sgt F. Burgess	Sgt P. Harris
Sgt P. W. Roberts	Sgt S. S. Greenwood	Sgt J. McCool	Sgt R. E. Rogers
Sgt J. A. Russell	Sgt C. E. Shilling	Sgt L. Scott	Sgt M. A. Frost

LL 796	ME 583	LM 438	LL 830
P/O H. M. C. Thomas	P/O A. C. Blackie	F/L J. M. Shearer	F/O F. S. Barnsdale
Sgt D. Arlott	Sgt G. Nicol	Sgt C. N. G. Drew	Sgt A. W. Knapp
Sgt A. E. Danslow	F/O H. Gerus	Sgt J. A. Ford	Sgt E. C. Edwards
P/O A. E. Elliot	F/S J. A. Cooper	W/O A. H. Biltoft	F/S A. G. Campbell
Sgt C. L. Radbone	Sgt H. Williams	Sgt C. V. Fox	Sgt K. J. Willett
Sgt E. G. Page	Sgt H. E. Gray	Sgt J. W. McLeod	Sgt C. Clamp
Sgt L. Mulholland	Sgt A. J. Newman	Sgt A. R. Jackson	Sgt G. N. Morris

LL 800
P/O R. R. Reed
Sgt A. Taylor
F/S M. A. Saruk
F/O G. Hallows
F/O W. Murphy
Sgt A. A. H. Hodson
Sgt W. J. McIntosh

DV 365
F/O G. A. J. Wood
Sgt H. Catling
Sgt R. E. Williams
F/O A. R. Marsh
Sgt W. Bird
Sgt H. Lillicrap
Sgt E. Conner

JA 715
F/S W. A. Scheerboom
Sgt H. R. Piper
F/S R. J. Tinsley
F/O W. Woodfine
Sgt C. E. Harris
Sgt L. Hannah
Sgt J. G. Delamothe

DG 386 *Missing*
F/O P. H. Brooke
Sgt E. A. Lodge
T/Sgt S. H. Chidester
    (USAAF)
F/O N. R. G. Pronger
Sgt A. E. Evans
Sgt A. H. Daines
Sgt N. V. Burgess

ND 385
F/S A. H. Young
Sgt D. G. F. Smith
F/O J. L. Ray
W/O S. B. Pennington
Sgt B. J. Hudson
Sgt C. E. Fox
Sgt A. C. Perkins

LM 471 *Missing*
F/S L. J. Collis
Sgt E. Smith
F/O A. C. Harper
Sgt R. J. Roper
Sgt K. MacDougal
Sgt B. Warren
Sgt E. Robinson

ED 767
F/S C. G. Wearmouth
Sgt L. R. Willis
Sgt J. W. Carter
F/O H. T. Wilson
Sgt A. MacDonald
Sgt J. Graham
Sgt S. J. Bott

JB 460
P/O V. P. Tomlin
Sgt A. E. Palmer
Sgt J. L. McTernaghan
Sgt G. Maiden
Sgt G. F. Fitzgerald
Sgt F. A. Dowling
Sgt F. M. Emerey

ED 748
F/S D. W. McIvor
Sgt S. Mee
F/O H. A. Rolph
F/O H. J. Riviere
Sgt N. C. Stafford
Sgt J. Armstrong
Sgt J. S. McGinn

LL 836
F/L C. A. Davison
Sgt L. E. Martin
F/O R. C. Rice
W/O A. Selman
Sgt B. G. Davies
Sgt C. Gregory
Sgt J. P. Duns

Flight Lieutenant Shearer was shot up both by flak and a night fighter: he flew back on two engines and a third engine cut out as he was about to land — crash-landing safely with no crew injuries. This Squadron reported intense opposition.

No 626 Sqdn — Wickenby, Lancasters: 13 attacked, 2 missing, 1 early return.

W 4990
F/S G. Smith
F/O L. E. Jackson
Sgt D. Biggs
Sgt P. Lane
Sgt R. Dorling
Sgt S. A. Lambert
Sgt P. T. Gallagher

JB 646
P/O J. T. Torrance
F/S H. Tabony
Sgt J. A. B. Hicks
F/S G. W. Fox
Sgt A. E. Beckett
Sgt J. M. Smith
Sgt F. A. Taylor

EE 623
F/S D. B. Laidlaw
F/O K. W. Gordon
Sgt G. Burrows
Sgt C. R. Todd
Sgt D. S. Lockett
Sgt H. W. Parsons
F/S R. Drummond

ME 587
P/O D. S. Jackson
F/S H. A. Riddle
F/S R. H. Watts
F/S J. Liebscher
Sgt J. A. Sutton
Sgt A. G. Brooks
Sgt R. McFarlane

LM 393 *Missing*
Sgt K. H. Margetts
P/O H. L. Shortliffe
Sgt G. T. Probert
Sgt D. F. Brooker
Sgt R. W. Chandler
Sgt R. C. Waters
Sgt C. J. C. Bateman

EE 148
F/S T. E. Newton
F/O W. G. Lafferty
Sgt J. M. Davies
F/O T. Dempster
Sgt P. H. Scott
Sgt D. Watt
Sgt D. J. Fowkes

LL 829
F/S D. H. Manson
F/O J. W. Stapleton
Sgt A. Fretwell
F/O E. A. Saloma
Sgt J. Geeves
Sgt D. Eggleston
Sgt E. J. Fancy

HK 539 *Missing*
W/C Q. W. A. Ross
W/O J. Gibson
F/S C. C. Christie
F/S C. Nathanson
Sgt H. Watts
Sgt T. W. Bint
F/S S. W. Jones

LL 797
W/O R. J. Lone
F/S Abrams
F/S S. J. Nosworthy
F/S M. H. Hawkins
Sgt A. J. H. Cockerill
Sgt K. S. W. Rees
Sgt R. R. Begley

LL 835
F/L A. J. H. Wright
F/S S. M. Hicks
Sgt H. Hatchard
F/S T. W. Carr
Sgt F. D. Glen
F/O A. G. W. Wade
F/S G. R. Hardy

W 4967
F/S R. S. Bennett
F/O K. W. Lofts
Sgt E. S. Cooper
Sgt L. E. Paradise
Sgt J. Slattery
Sgt J. Rippingale
Sgt J. M. Reid

JB 559
P/O A. H. Rew
F/S P. W. Lynn
W/O J. S. Sinnott
F/S G. W. Annesley
Sgt B. E. G. Soper
Sgt W. Redding
Sgt F. C. Boyd

LM 472
P/O J. F. V. Butcher
F/S R. M. Mogg
F/S E. A. Wise
F/O G. L. Wilson
Sgt L. O'Byrne
Sgt J. F. Francis
Sgt J. T. Legge

No 3 Bomber Group

No 15 Sqdn — Mildenhall, Lancasters: 14 attacked, 2 missing, 2 early returns.

L 7527	LL 781	LM 468	R 5904
P/O T. Marsh	F/L R. Purry	F/S A. Jarvis	F/L A. Amies
F/S M. Spice	F/O J. Weir	F/S E. Spriggs	P/O A. Hayden
Sgt A. Newell	F/S N. Goodridge	Sgt W. Scott	Sgt S. Watson
F/S V. Lewis	Sgt E. Gilleade	F/S D. McCrae	F/O E. Jones
Sgt E. Bland	Sgt T. Nixon	Sgt D. Parker	F/S V. Reid
Sgt B. Brophey	Sgt C. Cantwell	Sgt R. Grant	F/S E. Orchard
Sgt W. Dean	Sgt W. Sneddon	Sgt K. Hollinrake	Sgt R. Hearne

ED 473	LL 801	LM 490 *Missing*	ED 310
S/L P. Lamason	F/L L. Miller	F/S L. Wheeler	F/L S. Soper
F/O K. Chapman	Sgt J. Eastman	Sgt R. McIntosh	F/O R. Gibson
F/O L. George	Sgt A. Matthews	Sgt F. Wells	Sgt W. Heward
F/O G. Musgrove	F/S G. Mead	Sgt A. Smith	Sgt S. Lee
W/O R. Aitken	Sgt W. Culley	F/S E. McCullum	Sgt G. King
F/O T. Dunk	Sgt P. Slater	Sgt J. Briggs	Sgt D. Wood
F/L J. Marpole	Sgt A. Beasley-Long	Sgt H. Longworth	Sgt B. Watts

LL 827	LM 473	W 4181	LL 854
P/O O. Brooks	F/L J. Funnell	P/O G. Claydon	F/L H. Lee-Warner
Sgt K. Pincott	P/O G. Heathcote	F/S R. Sargeant	F/O F. Good
Sgt L. Barnes	Sgt H. Dolby	Sgt R. Child	F/S H. Wilson
W/O R. Gerrard	F/O D. Minns	F/S Wood-House	F/S J. Court
Sgt R. Wilson	F/S A. Jordan	F/S M. Melnyck	W/O R. Gibson
F/S H. Marr	F/S M. Brown	F/S J. Adams	Sgt M. Kieff
Sgt C. Chandler	F/S J. Bowen	Sgt M. Peto	Sgt J. Holdcroft

LM 441 *Missing*	LM 465
F/L W. Grove	F/S C. Thompson
Sgt A. Jackson	W/O R. McMillan
P/O J. Sills	Sgt J. Trend
F/S F. Holland	F/S R. Lemky
F/S A. Thompson	Sgt T. Stubbs
P/O I. Tvrdeich	Sgt M. Pelham
Sgt J. Johnson	

No 115 Sqdn — Witchford, Lancasters: 16 attacked, 4 missing, 2 alternative target.

DS 682	DS 728	LL 667	*Missing*
W/O L. Hammond	F/S H. Taylor	P/O R. Moon	F/S I. Williams
Sgt W. Groom	F/S P. Carter	F/S H. Durham	Sgt M. Ward
Sgt H. Howie	Sgt W. Lawrence	F/S D. McRae	Sgt J. Kearley
Sgt A. Stoneman	Sgt I. Witton	Sgt J. Swan	Sgt E. Meikle
Sgt J. McCue	Sgt E. Ashley	F/S F. Kanarens	Sgt T. Watson
Sgt J. Carter	Sgt E. Banham	Sgt W. Fraser	Sgt R. Howells
Sgt K. Haddow	Sgt S. Gibbs	Sgt G. Sharpe	Sgt J. Morris

LL 704	DS 620	DS 781	LL 666
P/O R. Anderson	P/O G. G. Hammond	W/O G. Treasure	F/S C. Campbell
Sgt L. Wilkinson	F/O R. E. Hawkins	F/S R. Gould	Sgt S. Guiver
Sgt H. Noon	Sgt E. Beer	Sgt A. Hollinrake	Sgt Parry
F/S P. Cameron	F/O F. A. Baggaley	P/O L. W. Scott	F/S J. Campbell
Sgt E. Redhead	Sgt P. Kennedy	Sgt W. Dawson	Sgt King
F/S W. Moulden	Sgt R. Chaplin	Sgt A. Caseley	Sgt F. McLean
Sgt H. Jones	Sgt D. Cooke	Sgt F. Holland	Sgt T. Tweedie

LL 726	LL 624	DS 678 *Missing*	LL 694 *Missing*
F/L G. D. L. Seddon	F/S D. Cameron	P/O L. M. McCann	P/O T. Vipond
F/O R. Sullivan	Sgt R. Townsend	W/O H. Gray	F/S J. Duffy
P/O R. Chappell	Sgt C. Body	Sgt W. Bowey	Sgt J. Hammond
F/O T. Sweeting	Sgt G. Attwood	Sgt D. Geach	F/O E. J. Deemer
W/O J. Chabot	Sgt K. Gallimore	Sgt D. Keeley	Sgt A. Hull
F/S P. Rock	Sgt G. McDonald	Sgt V. Watson	Sgt R. Coulter
Sgt J. Anderson	Sgt W. Jones	Sgt J. Burke	Sgt A. Diggle

LL 652
P/O E. Gibson
F/O J. Stock
F/S H. Maskell
Sgt Jones
Sgt W. Dawson
Sgt W. Andrews
Sgt J. Saunders

LL 641
P/O R. Milgate
Sgt H. Griffin
Sgt R. Hulse
F/S S. Banks
Sgt G. Chapman
Sgt R. Richardson
Sgt J. Zipfel

LL 646
F/S R. Chantler
P/O D. M. Drew
Sgt R. Francis
Sgt Farmer
Sgt W. Brown
Sgt Fielder
Sgt R. Nash

LL 622
S/L G. Y. Mackie
           DSO
Sgt R. Mather
Sgt R. Giles
P/O S. Atkin
Sgt J. Rafferty
Sgt L. Mehden
Sgt A. Dewar

LL 695
P/O McKechnie
F/O F. R. Leatherdale
Sgt B. Payne
Sgt K. Demly
Sgt Wilkin
T/S O. Koss (USAAF)
Sgt France

DS 664 *Missing*
F/S Newman
Sgt J. Cleary
Sgt Burwell
Sgt C. Hilder
Sgt N. Alkmade
Sgt J. McDonough
Sgt E. Warren

No 514 Sqdn — Waterbeach, Lancasters: 17 attacked, 1 missing, 1 early return.

LL 728
F/S E. A. Kingham
Sgt R. H. Hutt
F/O J. Peake
Sgt B. Bloom
Sgt F. N. Ansell
Sgt G. D. Davies
Sgt J. Black

LL 727
F/O L. Greenburgh
Sgt P. G. Butler
Sgt D. L. Bament
F/S G. H. Stromberg
Sgt F. J. Carey
F/S C. A. Drake
Sgt L. Weddle

LL 738
F/O G. S. Hughes
F/S L. S. Smith
F/S A. D. Hall
W/O G. J. Goddard
Sgt L. Moorhouse
Sgt G. H. Thornton
Sgt H. West

LL 687
F/S N. R. Wishart
F/S A. Gray
Sgt J. Thornber
Sgt N. J. Turner
Sgt T. J. Saint
Sgt F. Fairbrass
Sgt L. Cartwright

LL 733
F/L R. C. Chopping
F/O I. G. Barham
F/S H. J. Friend
Sgt J. Wilson
Sgt T. Combe
F/S P. J. Fox
Sgt D. C. Hughes
F/S C. J. Medland

LL 739
P/O D. A. Woods
F/O F. Longson
Sgt E. T. Shanks
Sgt K. R. Heron
Sgt W. C. Udell
Sgt H. L. Doherty
Sgt R. S. Cole

LL 683
F/L D. A. A. Gray
Sgt R. R. Brown
F/S E. W. R. Brazier
W/O H. G. Sharpe
F/S R. A. Hoddle-
           Wrigley
Sgt R. Helliwell
Sgt R. A. Hounsome

LL 731
P/O N. W. Thackeray
Sgt P. C. Davies
F/S J. R. Moulsdale
Sgt P. Hughes
F/S R. E. Bromley
F/S C. H. Henn
Sgt C. W. Banfield

DS 818
F/S F. C. V. Steed
Sgt A. Watts
F/S M. J. Bulled
F/S A. M. Robertson
Sgt W. H . Sweet
Sgt C. A. Forsythe
Sgt J. Cumming

LL 645
F/S A. B. Cunningham
F/O R. J. Ramsey
F/O R. E. Brailsford
Sgt J. W. Stone
Sgt B. L. Roberts
Sgt F. W. Brown
Sgt J. F. G. Hay

LL 625 *Missing*
F/O J. R. Laing
Sgt A. Vickers
F/S J. Knights
F/S G. E. Scott
F/S R. B. McAllister
Sgt C. A. Salt
Sgt P. C. K. Bennett

LL 691
F/S L. M., Petry
Sgt E. J. Reid
F/O F. J. Parker
Sgt H. T. Boal
Sgt R. A. Pitt
Sgt A. McClean
Sgt H. E. Chandler

LL 677
P/O A. Winstanley
F/S H. Tysoe
Sgt R. P. C. Scrase
Sgt N. Dixon
Sgt J. S. Johnson
F/S J. S. Everitt
Sgt G. S. Homer

LL 620
P/O H. Bilbrough
Sgt D. Kellock
W/O G. Metcalfe
Sgt L. L. Stanforth
Sgt C. R. W. Braithwaite
F/S R. M. Rogers
Sgt W. T. Barber

LL 732
F/L R. J. Curtis
F/O R. Davey
P/O D. Mcleod
P/O C. E. Baud
F/S R. H. Marshall
F/S W. J. Clubb
Sgt M. C. L. Bristowe

LL 670
P/O E. Protheroe
Sgt D. Kellock
F/S P. W. B. Sach
Sgt R. G. Law
Sgt S. W. Birse
Sgt R. M. Collins
Sgt S. Proctor

LL 698
F/S C. J. Johnson
Sgt P. Henser
Sgt E. Lush
Sgt T. Green
Sgt J. Poad
Sgt R. A. Dymott
Sgt P. Whitmore

LL 696
F/S J. D. Harrison
F/S R. N. Kirkpatrick
Sgt F. D. Nash
Sgt A. G. Buttling
Sgt R. S. Woosname
Sgt R. W. Norris

No 622 Sqdn — Mildenhall, Lancasters: 9 attacked, 1 early return.

ED 474	LM 511	ME 693	ED 619
F/S J. A. Harris	P/O Curling	F/L A. Jameson	F/S H. C. Struthers
W/O A. J. Kelly	F/S E. Featherston-	F/O N. J. Fairbairn	F/S D. Y. Andrews
Sgt D. B. White	haugh	Sgt J. Cochrane	Sgt P. Brooke
F/S D. C. Blackmore	F/S R. I. Smith	F/S R. S. Moore	F/S L. C. Hilford
Sgt A. Notley	F/S J. R. Short	Sgt A. MacLean	Sgt D. R. Guilt
F/S R. H. Campbell	Sgt H. Harris	F/S E. E. Lock	Sgt W. W. A. Joy
Sgt B. E. Wareham	Sgt H. P. R. Russell	Sgt W. C. Pearce	Sgt C. B. Dawkins
	Sgt J. K. Humphries		

R 5514	LL 793	LL 859	ED 808
F/S J. L. Walker	P/O J. Sutton	F/L D. L. Murgatroyd	P/O T. Hargreaves
F/S P. A. Atkinson	F/S J. A. McLean	F/O A. H. Musson	Sgt R. L. Urwin
Sgt E. Crowther	Sgt L. E. Read	Sgt C. Emmott	Sgt S. S. Crawford
Sgt H. Hodgson	W/O D. J. Laberge	F/O D. McCormac	F/S C. R. Burns
F/S P. J. Pearce	F/S E. F. Jarvis	Sgt J. H. W. Reid	Sgt H. Malpass
Sgt H. H. Herbert	Sgt P. Newman	Sgt R. S. Howe	Sgt F. D. Glynn
	F/S J. F. Richardson	Sgt J. T. E. Hargreaves	Sgt. F. Williams

LL 872
S/L H. Tilson
F/O J. Pawlynshyn
P/O L. E. Chapman
P/O D. Smith
F/S G. A. Pidgen
W/O H. F. Jones
P/O W. R. Birkett

No 4 Bomber Group
No 10 Sqdn — Melbourne, Halifaxes: 9 attacked, 1 overshot.

HX 295	LW 371	LV 867	HX 232
P/O R. Simmons	W/O J. Porter	P/O D. Evans	F/L R. LeCudenee
Sgt T. Arnold	Sgt E. Rowlands	Sgt S. Hamilton	Sgt N. Perella
F/S L. Chapman	F/S M. Rumbles	F/S J. S. Manson	P/O G. Jenkins
Sgt I. Laughlin	Sgt L. Making	Sgt J. Nicholas	Sgt R. W. Ryan
Sgt W. Farmer	Sgt A. Jepson	Sgt L. Duncan	Sgt K. Wood
Sgt J. Hendry	Sgt N. F. Jones	Sgt J. Morley	Sgt S. Roberts
F/S R. C. Corby	W/O G. Mould	Sgt H. J. Hull	F/S M. T. Barling

LV 825	LV 870	LV 858	LV 818
F/L R. Kennedy	P/O R. Taylor	F/O W. G. Barnes	F/S G. Lassey
F/O R. A. Rath	Sgt R. E. Lark	P/O M. Steel	Sgt D. Knowles
F/O R. Skinner	Sgt R. Haydon	F/O E. L. Pottier	Sgt J. Hartley
F/S J. Capstick	Sgt A. E. Andrews	F/S H. W. McNeice	Sgt J. Burton
Sgt N. Round	Sgt T. Welding	P/O W. Alliston	Sgt F. Lucas
Sgt F. N. Payne	Sgt T. L. Lees	Sgt G. Matthews	Sgt N. Miller
Sgt K. C. Beard	Sgt A. Polmear	Sgt G. Howell	F/S D. J. Setter

HX 326	HX 347		
F/O C. Allen	F/S G. Cartwright		
Sgt C. Hagerty	F/O J. Skolnik		
F/O A. G. Hendry	Sgt A. Andrews		
Sgt D. Cooper	Sgt N. Bennett		
Sgt D. Duerden	Sgt J. Witter		
Sgt S. Weare	Sgt J. H. Beech		
Sgt H. S. Jones	Sgt W. R. Booker		

No 51 Sqdn — Snaith, Halifaxes: 14 attacked, 2 missing.

LW 544	LW 496	LW 538	LW 480
F/S H. H. Wastell	F/S R. J. Feaver	F/S H. Hall	P/O L. Rothwell
Sgt M. E. McCarney	Sgt A. J. Howson	F/O F. G. Kirkwood	Sgt S. G. Peacock
Sgt R. Kelly	F/S R. L. O'Neill	F/O C. T. Hartley	F/S W. G. Clark
Sgt R. J. Bellinger	Sgt E. Millett	F/S J. Osborne	F/S S. Buckingham
Sgt R. D. Payne	Sgt Stocker	Sgt G. Peck	Sgt J. McQuater
Sgt S. V. Pearce	Sgt C. Grainger	Sgt B. W. Hegarty	Sgt E. Boyles
Sgt G. C. Booth	Sgt C. M. Smith	F/S M. Fairclough	Sgt J. E. Sinclair

HK 350
F/L J. G. Rees
F/O G. S. Henderson
F/O Rubery
F/O J. Binham
Sgt D. M. Keith
Sgt A. J. Henshaw
Sgt T. E. G. Parson
Sgt L. W. J. Tostevin

LV 777
W/C R. C. Ayling
F/O A. G. Striowski
F/S G. C. Buglade
F/O L. Watts
Sgt K. Clough
F/O R. E. Cook
Sgt P. J. Parker

LW 522
W/O A. H. Hayes
F/S H. R. Cooper
Sgt J. M. Vassiere
Sgt M. W. R. Ramsey
Sgt F. W. Sweet
Sgt M. M. Hamilton
Sgt F. S. Brightwell

LW 462
Sgt M. J. O'Loughlin
Sgt J. M. McCoss
F/S I. C. Carib
Sgt W. W. Grant
Sgt W. Morrish
Sgt A. G. Goulding
Sgt P. Bailey

LW 537
F/S M. Stembridge
Sgt E. Parker
F/S D. Stewart
Sgt D. A. Smith
Sgt F. Clinton
Sgt D. A. Nicholson
Sgt J. D. Goskirk

LW 504
P/O J. Brooks
Sgt G. R. Hyndman
F/S D. P. McCormack
F/O W. C. A. Harris
F/S G. W. West
SGT T. S. Connell
F/S D. A. Churchill
F/S D. Glass

LW 461
F/S L. R. Norton
Sgt E. Perry
Sgt S. K. Smith
Sgt W. J. Sweetapple
Sgt E. G. Bullock
Sgt R. Hope
Sgt J. Cran

LW 478
F/S A. Duckworth
Sgt J. D. Heddon
F/S J. Muir
Sgt A. W. Lunn
Sgt A. W. Newton
Sgt K. A. Booth
Sgt E. W. Stanton

LW 541
F/S A. Sarjantson
F/O W. G. Meeson
Sgt R. S. Scheffler
Sgt H. D. Nash
Sgt M. C. McCarthy
Sgt S. G. Myers
Sgt J. A. Smith

LW 578
Sgt L. J. Melling
F/O R. F. Watkins
F/S L. Bell
F/S H. R. S. Sullivan
Sgt J. E. Blyth
Sgt E. G. Ostime
Sgt A. Hitchcock

LW 539 *Missing*
F/O G. M. McPherson
F/O W. B. Gillespie
F/O R. J. H. Nelson
Sgt D. F. Bowthorpe
Sgt C. D. Herbert
Sgt T. Clouter
Sgt K. Davies

MZ 507 *Missing*
F/L R. Curtis
Sgt W. V. Willson
F/S J. S. Scott
Sgt A. Sidebotham
Sgt R. Hepworth
Sgt J. L. Middleton
Sgt A. L. Taylor

No 76 Sqdn — Holme-on-Spalding Moor, Halifaxes: 15 attacked, 1 missing, 2 early returns.

LW 620
F/L R. G. West
F/S J. Johnson
F/O P. S. Milliken
F/S W. J. Lowe
Sgt L. J. Barnard
Sgt C. Clarke
Sgt T. Glen

LW 784
P/O H. M. George
Sgt O. Thomas
P/O J. R. Shrosbery
F/S L. W. Powis
Sgt J. Danes
Sgt W. Mays
F/O D. P. J. Smith

LK 783
F/S A. J. Innes
F/S J. O. Paige
F/S E. Bryan
Sgt E. Tonge
Sgt G. N. Glithero
Sgt J. W. Golder
Sgt G. R. Whittle

LW 627
S/L J. W. H. Harwood
F/O G. K. Mundle
P/O G. E. Brown
F/O S. W. Palmer
P/O G. H. P. Potter
Sgt D. J. Brown
F/S W. C. Connelly

LK 788
F/L R. J. Bolt
P/O C. W. Crathmell
P/O F. P. G. Hall
Sgt B. C. Josey
Sgt H. VanDenBos
P/O A. J. Bate
Sgt W. C. Cassidy
F/L Webb

LW 628
F/O L. Falgate
P/O F. S. Francis
P/O A. D. Wallis
Sgt F. W. D. Emery
F/S G. J. E. Jennings
P/O R. J. Dewey
F/S W. O. Day
F/S F. E. Fuery

LW 644
W/O A. L. Johnston
F/S F. G. Griffiths
F/S L. W. J-Wynch
Sgt C. J. Trott
Sgt A. S. Stokes
Sgt E. E. Lewis
Sgt A. Moult

LK 790 *Missing*
F/S L. Marshall
F/S T. Wilkinson
F/S F. Kinch
Sgt P. Cramp
Sgt W. Longhorn
Sgt W. Lawton
Sgt Albon

LW 648
S/L R. A. M. Lemmon
F/O J. G. Gunnell
P/O W. Booth
F/S E. Butcher
F/S J. W. Chapman
Sgt G. Griffiths
F/S D. Yuille

LW 363
F/O G. C. Greenacre
F/S A. S. Arneil
F/O A. Thorpe
Sgt J. A. Henthorn
P/O A. D. A. May
P/O A. Monk
P/O A. H. Death

LW 656
F/O P. E. Sinclair
F/S A. G. Rogers
F/O G. Watkins
Sgt W. Ray
Sgt P. Phillips
Sgt E. Neville
F/S A. Garcia

LW 695
F/L H. D. Coverley
F/S W. A. Blake
F/S K. A. H. Trott
Sgt P. G. Wilmhurst
Sgt D. N. J. Scott
Sgt D. E. Motts
Sgt D. M. S. Bauldie

LV 873
P/O F. W. Cole
F/S A. F. Rae
F/S A. Houghton
Sgt J. A. Reid
Sgt R. McCracken
Sgt T. Farnworth
F/S G. Gibson

LW 637
P/O D. R. Forsythe
Sgt J. H. Terry
F/S G. W. H. Uwins
F/O Wingate
P/O E. L. Anderson
Sgt J. H. Spooner
Sgt J. C. Owen
F/S E. R. Buck

??
2 Lt C. Larsen
F/S E. E. Willis
F/O M. S. Edmonds
Sgt H. W. Kirtland
Sgt M. Ransome
Sgt A. C. Wilson
Sgt A. Horn

LW 656
F/O P. E. Sinclair
F/S A. G. Rogers
F/O G. Watkins
Sgt W. Ray
Sgt P. Phillips
Sgt E. Neville
F/S A. Garcia

No 78 Sqdn — Holme-on Spalding Moor, Halifaxes: 19 attacked, 5 missing, 2 early returns, 1 crash-landed at Cranfield, all killed.

HX 241	LV 899	LV 872	LV 868
F/O F. Harris	F/S H. Wilkinson	P/O B. Downs	F/L D. Davies
Sgt J. Woodward	F/O A. Bell	F/S W. Hendry	P/O D. Spence
F/S L. Preece	Sgt D. Garraway	P/O J. Middlemiss	F/O J. McNabney
W/O W. Harvey	F/S F. Sampson	F/S F. Garget	Sgt W. Parton
Sgt J. Evans	Sgt J. Fell	Sgt G. Jupp	Sgt A. Cadman
Sgt E. Hamlyn	Sgt L. Dyment	W/O R. Dawson	Sgt H. Lillicoe
Sgt B. Carey-Wood	Sgt J. Bennett	F/S F. Joiner	Sgt J. Firth

LV 905	LW 520	LK 762	LV 820
F/S M. Lovatt	F/S R. Gill	F/S L. Tait	F/L J. Watson
F/O E. Sait	Sgt G. Flint	F/S F. Hawkins	P/O E. Burgess
Sgt J. Chisholm	F/S J. Sanders	F/S. L. Wetherby	F/S T. McKenzie
Sgt E. Roberts	Sgt T. Eakin	Sgt W. Keenan	P/O R. Harrington
Sgt W. Smith	Sgt R. Woodrow	Sgt W. Smith	P/O D. Clayton
Sgt F. Scholfield	Sgt F. Miller	Sgt R. Rudd	P/O A. Woodward
Sgt P. Cottrel	Sgt C. Duncan	Sgt R. Graham	Sgt L. Hannay

LL 510*	LV 815	LW 518 *Missing*	HX 355 *Missing*
F/O A. Wimberley	F/L R. Gordon-Davis	F/S K. Barden	F/L Everett
F/S W. Shields	Sgt P. Jones	F/O A. Lees	Sgt J. Stewart
F/O S. Kelly	Sgt C. Laws	F/S S. Davidson	F/O J. Green
Sgt J. Edge	Sgt K. Gillam	F/S W. Spencer	Sgt J. Johnson
Sgt H. Neal	Sgt J. Stark	Sgt F. Curtis	Sgt K. Jones
Sgt R. Nelson	Sgt C. Wanbon	Sgt P. Cleal	P/O A. Sinden
Sgt A. Brignell	Sgt E. Charles	Sgt J. Lincoln	Sgt J. Graham

LV 788	LW 515	LW 589 *Missing*	LV 903 *Missing*
F/L E. McGregor	F/S M. Buchanan	F/S H. Jackson	F/L D. Constable
P/O P. Snell	F/O D. Rayment	Sgt J. Dear	Sgt C. McCleod
P/O J. Kirner	Sgt A. McKenzie	Sgt J. Smith	Sgt T. Ratcliffe
Sgt W. Smither	Sgt J. Rice	Sgt T. Patchet	F/O A. Mace
F/S W. Pattison	Sgt W. Bailey	Sgt Crawford	Sgt D. Cash
F/O J. Palmer	Sgt J. Harmer	Sgt W. Baker	F/S T. Schioler
P/O A. Stark	Sgt J. McGannon	Sgt R. McNeil	Sgt F. Byford
			F/S G. Lovells

LK 749	LW 507 *Missing*		
F/L J. Hudson	Sgt E. Smith	F/L C. Bennett	*Crash-landed at
F/L A. Taylor	Sgt L. Edwards	P/O W. Gorley	Cranfield on return.
F/O W. Uyen	Sgt Middleton	F/O H. Officer	All crew killed.
Sgt A. Monks	Sgt S. Johnson	Sgt T. Wright	
Sgt J. Hillis	Sgt P. Willis	Sgt R. Hawthorne	
Sgt J. Morris	Sgt P. Finn	P/O A. Herbert	
F/S L. Nugent	Sgt L. Daniels	Sgt K. Bongard	

No 158 Sqdn — Lissett, Halifaxes: 13 attacked, 1 missing, 1 crash-landed.

HX 349	HX 340	LV 790	HX 334
F/S J. Hitchman	P/O R. A. Gray	P/O M. V. Lawrence	F/S B. D. Bancroft
F/O H. J. S. Harmar	Sgt F. Anderson	F/L A. F. Forsdike	F/S A. F. C. Fripp
Sgt A. O. Pearson	W/O I. A. Korman	F/O J. D. O'Hara	F/O E. A. Tansley
Sgt L. E. Fisher	Sgt T. Stonebank	Sgt R. Barnes	Sgt L. S. Dwan
Sgt R. B. Higgins	Sgt E. Salmon	Sgt W. J. Christie	Sgt K. L. G. Leheup
Sgt W. Tunstall	Sgt L. R. Harman	Sgt R. E. Stubbs	Sgt D. R. Arundel
Sgt A. E. Rice	Sgt W. J. Burns	Sgt R. P. Freeman	Sgt L. Cottrell

LV 917	HX 322	LW 568	LW 722
S/L W. J. Weller	P/O E. G. Strange	F/L J. N. Reynolds	F/S A. J. S. Wright
P/O A. E. Surridge	P/O T. R. Lister	F/S H. M. Catt	Sgt P. T. Heard
F/O H. V. Taylor	P/O R. G. Hales	P/O S. Dale	F/S D. P. McGorkle
P/O J. D. Koch	F/S T. W. Blain	F/S T. J. Lincoln	Sgt R. Ward
F/S K. A. Bray	Sgt R. R. Morris	P/O E. Grace	Sgt J. G. Divers
F/O L. A. Ingram	Sgt J. Mitchell	Sgt W. McLean	Sgt M. J. Tremayne
F/L C. C. Fox	Sgt K. L. Riddle	P/O D. R. Courage	Sgt F. W. Bird
		Sgt R. C. Diment	

LV 792	LW 635	LW 719	LW 634
F/S G. W. Johnson	F/S P. Kettles-Roy	F/S W. C. Read	F/S S. Hughes
Sgt F. C. Thompson	F/O P. G. Taylor	Sgt L. W. Tomlin	Sgt D. V. Simmonds
F/S H. Whittaker	Sgt G. McEwan	F/S J. J. Fernandez	Sgt A. Herring
Sgt L. A. W. Howes	F/S R. W. Wright	Sgt J. Squires	Sgt W. Jones
Sgt R. B. Benton	Sgt M. Madden	Sgt A. G. Thompson	Sgt F. Birtwell
Sgt G. Ochs	Sgt A. F. Kneller	F/S G. Titman	Sgt J. McDougall
Sgt J. A. Blackshaw	Sgt L. Sowden	Sgt L. M. Byrne	Sgt L. Robinson

LW 721 *Missing*	LW 718*
F/S A. R. Van Slyke	P/O K. S. Simpson
P/O J. McGillivray	F/O N. Hindley
F/S J. N. A. McDonagh	P/O D. J. Hemsley
Sgt H. Ball	F/S W. Suddaby
Sgt W. Grant	Sgt W. A. Buchan
Sgt M. Mowbray	F/S M. F. McKay
Sgt R. Whitelaw	Sgt T. J. Barnett

*A message was received from this aircraft over the Dutch coast at 2240 hrs stating that port and starboard engines were stopped. Pilot carried on with two remaining engines returning to England attempted a crash landing on the beach at Ingham in Norfolk where a minefield was laid. Aircraft blew up and all crew were killed.

No 466 Sqdn RAAF — Leconfield, Halifaxes: 10 attacked primary, 1 missing, 1 overshot target, 2 early returns.

LW 837	LV 936	LV 875	LV 900 *Missing*
F/S J. H. Cole	F/S E. H. Gaggin	F/L J. H. Stevens	F/S R. L. Robertson
F/S T. L. Vary	F/S P. W. Nicholls	F/O D. N. Rankin	F/S V. W. Bath
F/O J. McIsaacs	W/O L. J. Nichols	F/L R. H. S. Fryer	F/S H. F. Smith
F/S M. A. Rodger	F/S R. T. Craig	P/O D. D. G. Green	F/O E. Iveson
F/S J. W. Close	F/S D. A. Bowern	F/S L. F. Harris	F/S R. I. Cummings
F/S L. Milner	F/S N. E. Locklier	F/S L. A. Kemp	Sgt H. J. Hughes
Sgt J. H. Monk	Sgt H. Forbes	Sgt G. A. Rimmer	Sgt J. Strathern

HX 242	LV 791	LV 919	LV 883
F/S F. C. Pope	F/O B. J. McDermott	F/S G. A. Sargant	F/O C. N. Lamb
F/S C. S. Wilson	F/L C. O. Chapman	Sgt J. O'R. Sykes	F/S H. A. Jacob
W/O J. J. Downs	F/S L. T. Sanders	F/S J. G. Schroder	F/O S. M. Slatter
F/S T. A. Rowe	Sgt T. Evans	F/S H. E. Hunt	F/S R. S. Westerman
Sgt R. E. Catt	F/S W. V. Dodd	F/S H. A. Ward	F/S R. A. Ince
F/S C. R. Draper	Sgt W. S. Shoemaker	F/S P. J. Doyle	Sgt G. Harrison-
Sgt J. T. Barclay	Sgt N. McA. Brown	Sgt C. Walsh	Broadley
			Sgt A. S. Harman

HX 243	HX 266	LV 824	HX 343
F/S D. F. Grant	F/S J. C. Scott	F/S C. R. Wilson	P/O F. B. Black
F/S P. J. McCosker	F/S R. E. Tickell	F/S A. M. Stark	P/O E. E. M. Lilley
F/S I. Melville	Sgt D. V. Westley	F/S A. F. Baldick	Sgt M. Malins
F/S N. W. Barrie	F/S M. W. G. Pointon	F/S W. A. Turner	F/S L. E. Stockwell
F/S J. G. Thwaites	F/S K. S. Oakes	F/S W. F. Towler	F/S K. W. Mansell
Sgt J. R. Tremain	F/O T. C. Drake-	F/S R. J. Peggs	Sgt P. L. Wallace
Sgt R. Osthoff	Brookman	Sgt L. H. Cary	Sgt D. Blake
	Sgt W. K. Handley		

No 578 Sqdn — Burn, Halifaxes: 12 attacked, 3 missing, 3 early returns.

LW 474	LW 794	LW 478	LV 784
F/S J. Malvern	W/O V. Starkoff	F/S G. A. Marsden	F/L D. W. McGowan
F/S G. H. Morris	Sgt J. F. Fink	F/S R. L. Thomson	P/O L. E. Evans
F/S W. O. Ingleby	Sgt D. E. Morgan	F/S R. Black	F/O E. J. McConkey
Sgt W. F. Pountney	W/O L. H. Hopper	Sgt H. Rolls	Sgt W. Martin
Sgt K. Dyer	Sgt G. T. Nicholson	Sgt C. McBrearty	Sgt M. Banika
Sgt R. Murray	Sgt J. Clague	Sgt H. Furher	Sgt P. J. Garland
Sgt T. Taylor	Sgt H. C. Sloan	Sgt N. A. Farley	Sgt J. A. Waddia

LK 797
P/O C. J. Barton
Sgt J. Lambert
F/O G. Crate
P/O J. Kay
Sgt M. Trousdale
Sgt F. Brice
Sgt H. Wood

LW 469
Sgt P. Edwards
Sgt H. Kendall
Sgt H. T. Flindall
Sgt R. C. Young
Sgt G. Johnson
Sgt L. A. Perris
Sgt W. Harrison

LW 675
Sgt M. H. Clarke
F/O J. E. Bower-Binns
F/L F. Hart
Sgt D. Dickson
Sgt W. G. Richards
Sgt J. Scorer
Sgt L. Roberts

LW 475
Sgt G. M. Henderson
Sgt P. J. Smith
Sgt W. W. McDonald
Sgt N. S. Whitwell
Sgt R. G. Corker
Sgt W. J. Wilkinson
F/O P. J. Grey

LW 543
F/O A. T. Hope-
        Robertson
Sgt J. Smith
P/O K. C. Parsons
Sgt D. F. Jones
Sgt R. Johnson
Sgt T. R. Gunn
F/S G. H. Jones

LW 478 *Missing*
P/O J. M. Row
F/S V. R. Glaysher
F/O R. J. Hayhurst
F/S W. R. Crick
Sgt F. Eland
W/O R. V. Burch
W/O F. C. Wood
P/O G. A. Pope

NZ 512 *Missing*
Sgt R. G. Arthur
F/O K. J. Avant
F/S R. T. Middlemas
Sgt L. R. Morgan
Sgt N. B. Lowlett
Sgt P. J. Kinsella
Sgt Davidson

LW 508 *Missing*
P/O D. A. Lang
F/S H. Johnson
F/S R. E. Priest
Sgt H. Burkitt
Sgt L. K. Clack
F/S A. W. Snowden
F/S W. G. Chase

No 640 Sqn — Leconfield, Halifaxes: 13 attacked, 2 missing.

LW 463
F/L K. Cassels
Sgt W. Roddham
F/O J. Dowsett
F/S E. Malngren
Sgt T. Geary
Sgt S. Coleman
Sgt R. Asquith

LW 654
Sgt D. Johnson
P/O R. Lane
Sgt D. Hancock
Sgt J. Smith
Sgt C. Ellis
Sgt H. Webb
Sgt R. Mitchell

LW 464
F/O C. O'Brien
P/O R. Vanfleet
P/O R. Carleton
Sgt B. Wangler
Sgt E. Bake
Sgt T. McFadden
Sgt E. Martin

LW 640
Lt A. Kornegay
F/O G. Williams
F/O G. Prosser
Sgt K. Grantham
Sgt R. Chapman
Sgt H. Wilcox
Sgt A. Wooler

LW 555
W/O D. Burke
Sgt R. Eastman
F/O F. Woods
Sgt W. Hadden
Sgt W. Crory
Sgt M. Stilliard
Sgt A. Jamieson

LW 651
Sgt R. Axton
Sgt A. Jackson
F/O R. Dunlop
Sgt J. McNaughton
Sgt W. Phillips
Sgt J. Judd
Sgt H. Whitfield

LW 673
F/S H. Cotton
Sgt T. Lonsdale
P/O S. Kritzer
F/S D. Ottley
Sgt N. Jennings
F/S A. Neall
Sgt N. Kelly

LW 549
F/O J. Laidlaw
F/O M. Corcoran
F/S F. Shuttle
F/S J. Henderson
F/S M. Bush
F/O K. Austen
Sgt D. Ostler

LW 434
F/S J. Wisbey
Sgt J. Carey
Sgt G. Kerruish
Sgt E. Todd
Sgt E. Spink
Sgt S. Butcher
Sgt J. Kenrick

LW 544
F/S A. Forrester
F/O T. Johnston
F/S H. Wainwright
F/S G. Young
Sgt F. Butler
F/L D. Smith
Sgt W. Jones

LK 757
W/C D. Eayrs
F/S J. Hindle
F/O D. Jackson
W/O T. Doull
Sgt J. Cunningham
Sgt W. Pilling
Sgt W. Harris

MZ 510 *Missing*
F/O R. Hodgson
F/O A. Bunster
Sgt S. Rayner
Sgt R. Thorpe
Sgt E. Ayres
F/S R. Draffin
F/S F. Hursey

LW 422
F/S. R. Earnshaw
F/S J. Riordan
Sgt P. Sherburn
Sgt W. Mahon
Sgt W. Pullen
F/S J. Murphy
Sgt C. Hensey

LW 430 *Missing*
P/O W. McLeod
Sgt W. Wheeler
Sgt N. Cooper
Sgt J. Burdett
Sgt A. Turner
Sgt J. Boston
Sgt A. Webb

LW 502
F/S F. Ainsley
Sgt W. Houston
P/O J. Chapman
Sgt B. S. Simmins
Sgt J. Webster
Sgt C. Morritt
Sgt L. Robinson

No 5 Bomber Group
No 9 Sqdn — Bardney, Lancasters: 11 attacked Berlin, 1 attacked alternative.

DV 396
F/O N. Craig
Sgt C. E. Hansford
Sgt G. Freeman
Sgt K. Hughes
Sgt A. R. Marwood
Sgt S. G. May
Sgt A. V. Smith

W 4964
F/L H. R. Pooley
Sgt S. Bloom
Sgt C. L. Griffiths
F/O A. Manthorthe
Sgt J. A. Williams
Sgt N. Smith

EE 136
F/O R. W. Mathers
Sgt C. W. Howe
Sgt T. A. Cave
F/O D. A. Keeble
Sgt J. R. Donaldson
Sgt W. Wilson
F/S H. F. Robinson

LM 361
P/O J. A. Smith
Sgt R. Wilson
Sgt D. E. Moss
F/S C. H. T. Martin
F/O K. W. Light
F/S D. C. Bates
Sgt F. Heath

LM 432	LL 884	LL 845	JA 690
P/O H. Blow	P/O K. L. Porter	F/S W. R. Horne	P/O G. F. Maule
Sgt F. S. Colman	Sgt R. J. Baird	Sgt T. W. Powell	Sgt H. C. Dixey
P/O S. W. A. Hurrell	Sgt W. I. S. Richardson	F/S J. J. Shipley	P/O L. B. Connery
F/S F. H. Smith	F/S D. D. McLean	Sgt J. T. Johnson	F/S G. E. Riley
Sgt R. O. Smith	Sgt A. L. Pickering	Sgt R. A. Morton	Sgt J. M. Smith
Sgt R. Hartley	Sgt R. F. Hedicker	Sgt J. S. Parkes	Sgt H. Barney
F/S W. E. Miller	Sgt G. A. Sangster	Sgt T. Smith	Sgt G. Charlesworth

W 5006	LL 787	DV 395	LL 853
P/O J. G. R. Ling	P/O W. J. Sheppard	P/O H. Forrest	W/O C. A. Peak
Sgt C. Moss	Sgt R. Johnstone	Sgt A. W. Hutton	Sgt E. W. Kindred
Sgt H. Laws	F/O J. R. Glashan	Sgt S. Harwood	2nd Lt E. J. Wilkes
F/S T. Fletcher	F/S J. Mulhearn	F/S R. D. Hassall	Sgt W. V. Torbett
Sgt E. A. Gauld	Sgt W J. K. Toomey	Sgt D. Macauley	Sgt J. W. Nelson
F/S E. J. Rush	Sgt W. J. Harris	F/S B. T. Utting	Sgt J. Hogan
Sgt I. Prada	W/O B. S. Dean	Sgt D. B. Pinchin	Sgt T. W. Varey

No 44 (Rhodesia) Sqdn — Dunholme Lodge, Lancasters: 11 attacked, 3 missing.

ND 741	ME 634	ND 631	ND 565 *Missing*
S/L C. H. Hunter	F/L P. A. Dorehill	P/O F. Levy	P/O A. Evans
Sgt F. S. Cooper	Sgt R. H. Turrell	Sgt P. W. Groom	Sgt C. J. Evans
F/O A. Greenwood	Sgt C. H. Norman	F/O C. I. Fox	F/O G. F. Garland
F/O C. K. Willis	F/S P. A. Deacon	Sgt E. W. S. Peck	F/S F. J. Hatton
Sgt F. A. Salmon	F/S J. Gurr	Sgt G. M. McGuire	Sgt A. P. Myles
P/O A. P. Miles	Sgt K. Woolard	Sgt L. J. Evans	Sgt M. E. Burnard
P/O R. C. Alexander	F/L R. McCurdy	Sgt D. G. Thomas	Sgt K. V. Miller
			F/s A. G. Terrell

ND 751	ME 672 *Missing*	ND 517	ND 578
P/O R. H. Smith	P/O B. M. Hayes	P/O W. A. Stratis	P/O J. Chatterton
Sgt J. G. Bennett	Sgt J. M. Ellis	Sgt R. F. Haly	Sgt K. F. Letts
F/S E. B. Farren	Sgt R. Wellfare	F/O A. C. Greenfield	F/O D. J. Royland
F/O K. Dutton	Sgt M. Fedoruk	Sgt E. P. Hawkes	Sgt M. M. Scott
Sgt C. J. Hussey	Sgt W. K. Walker	F/S G. H. Knight	Sgt J. Michie
Sgt I. G. S. Prowse	Sgt K. I. Radcliffe	Sgt H. P. Page	Sgt W. H. Champion
Sgt H. Dack	Sgt H. G. Perrie	Sgt E. J. Roe	Sgt J. H. Davidson
			F/O T. S. Calder

ND 698	ME 629	ND 689	ND 573
P/O R. T. H. Manning	P/O C. A. Frost	P/O V. F. Hobbs	P/O G. A. Skinner
Sgt E. Wren	Sgt F. Stanton	Sgt A. G. Hall	Sgt A. Farmer
Sgt R. Woodward	F/S T. Ashton	Sgt T. P. Fenwick	F/S W. T. Freeman
F/S H. L. Roberts	F/O A. H. Devon	W/O M. M. Scott	Sgt D. Prewer
Sgt J. H. Davison	Sgt A. J. Johnson	Sgt J. E. Garnsey	Sgt T. D. Ward
Sgt E. Hedley	Sgt J. H. Carr	Sgt C. T. Wright	Sgt J. Y. Scott
F/S D. H. Murray	Sgt W. T. Bray	Sgt J. B. Ingram	Sgt W. B. Singfield
F/O N. J. Smith			

ND 552
W/O E. Barton
Sgt J. Thompson
F/O R. H. Maury
F/S F. Barnes
Sgt T. Willett
F/O A. Rimmer
P/O A. G. Clarke

No 49 Sqn — Fiskerton, Lancasters: 16 attacked, 1 early return.

ND 512	JB 466	JB 695	JB 679
F/L J. W. Adams	P/O C. Roantree	P/O J. Lett	F/L W. A. Healey
Sgt S. Seymour	Sgt E. Grimshaw	Sgt E. McDonald	Sgt P. Boardman
S/L J. H. Evans	Sgt K. Paddick	Sgt B. Andrew	F/O J. Bailes
Sgt R. A. Daines	Sgt H. J. Lawrie	Sgt P. Campbell	Sgt T. Jones
F/O W. J. Hamilton	Sgt R. Franks	Sgt Woods	Sgt D. Kirwan
F/O E. Lowans	Sgt J. A. Peaker	F/S C. Mackew	F/O J. Jones
F/S G. M. Weller	Sgt H. K. Nelson	Sgt D. Irving	Sgt G. J. Parkinson

JB 701
P/O T. Jones
Sgt E. Eyles
F/L C. Patchett
Sgt Knowles
Sgt A. L. Ford
Sgt A. B. Harbottle
Sgt J. T. Jennings

JB 399
P/O J. R. Dickinson
Sgt R. B. Hainsworth
F/S F. W. Wale
Sgt C. W. Sizer
Sgt E. Ellenor
F/S W. A. McKenzie
Sgt R. H. Hudson

JB 714
P/O R. H. Ewens
Sgt E. Tritton
F/S V. Pitcher
Sgt P. Griffiths
Sgt G. A. Rae
F/O R. D. Grainger
Sgt H. Laws

JB 421
P/O G. Montgomery
Sgt R. J. Boyce
F/S S. Smith
Sgt T. Parkin
Sgt R. J. Mitchell
F/S R. F. R. Cluff
Sgt C. Baker

ND 683
F/L J. Woodroffe
F/S A. McCracken
F/O A. Ryder
Sgt N. Harvey
W/O H. Lewis
Sgt R. R. Ormiston
Sgt N. D. Noell

JB 314
F/O W. A. Colhoun
Sgt A. W. Black
Sgt R. Prinn
Sgt K. Ellam
Sgt L. H. Board
F/S C. Underwood
Sgt W. A. Simmons

ND 676
P/O A. W. Shinn
Sgt N. C. Pettit
Sgt J. Hague
F/S N. J. Herd
Sgt A. B. Dicken
Sgt V. C. Cully
Sgt A. Armstrong

ND 647
P/O G. E. Ball
Sgt D. Wardman
Sgt C. Millar
Sgt C. Kernahan
Sgt E. Quick
Sgt G. Rae
Sgt A. Eeles

ND 473
P/O J. Jones
Sgt J. O. Barker
Sgt J. Owens
Sgt J. Bartle
Sgt C. Charlesworth
F/O Jack
F/S C. Morrisby

JD 180
F/L D. J. Bacon
Sgt P. J. Hennessy
P/O C. W. Coward
Sgt C. Monck
Sgt S. W. Weedon
F/O N. Melnick
Sgt E. Richard

ME 675
Lt J. P. Stevens
              (USAAF)
Sgt R. Smith
F/S D. Andrews
F/O J. Smeaton
Sgt W. A. Wanklin
F/O K. S. Stokoe
Sgt L. Pysden

ND 674
P/O F. Clark
Sgt F. Shaw
Sgt D. Rolfe
Sgt T. Connatty
Sgt F. J. Castle
Sgt D. Adams
Sgt N. Nichols

No 50 Sqdn — Skellingthorpe, Lancasters: 15 attacked, 1 early return.

LM 529
P/O D. A. Jennings
Sgt I. T. Stephen
Sgt T. R. D. Carrell
F/S G. W. Hughes
F/S D. W. Coopey
Sgt W. H. Turten
W/O A. G. Matthews

ED 588
P/O E. Berry
Sgt B. R. Holmes
F/S L. Howarth
Sgt P. M. N. Honywood
Sgt R. Hamilton
F/S W. Bull
Sgt R. Phillips

JA 899
F/O B. N. Botha
Sgt H. R. Sinten
F/O A. A. Bishton
Sgt N. Turner
Sgt A. N. Blenkarn
Sgt P. B. Thompson
Sgt A. Lewis

EE 174
F/S G. A. Waugh
Sgt G. Prince
Sgt D. D. Chaston
Sgt R. A. Dunn
Sgt D. L. Senlin
Sgt D. G. Lynch
F/S R. F. Thibedeau

LW 394
F/L M. U. Robinson
Sgt A. R. Morgan
F/S V. A. Sanderson
Sgt A. Horsfield
Sgt R. H. F. Ogborne
F/O T. W. Lavery
F/S J. M. Mooney

LM 480
F/Lt H. Blackham
Sgt C. R. E. Walton
P/O D. Jones
Sgt S. C. Wilkins
Sgt H. G. Ridd
Sgt S. J. Godfrey
Sgt Dixon

LL 840
F/L A. S. Keith
Sgt G. Mitchell
F/O J. C. D. Guthrie
W/O G. W. Morrey
Sgt J. Brown
P/O J. L. Bendix
F/S J. Rowcliffe

LM 438
S/L F. W. Chadwick
F/S W. J. Beesley
W/O J. Watt
F/O A. R. Verrier
F/S G. F. Graham
F/O H. A. Hughes
F/S A. M. MacDiarmid

LL 741
P/O D. J. Oram
Sgt R. P. Haywood
F/S F. R. Brand
Sgt G. A. Benton
P/O D. T. Watkins
F/S J. H. Cole
Sgt D. P. Peirson

LL 841
P/O L. Creed
Sgt S. G. Attwood
Sgt D. Groscop
Sgt G. A. Horn
Sgt H. P. S. Elder
Sgt L. C. Hogben
Sgt I. C. Evans

LL 842
P/O R. H. Lloyd
Sgt M. T. Avenell
F/S D. S. Richardson
F/S J. N. Hewson
SGT A. G. McCarthy
Sgt E. T. Dewhirst
F/S N. F. Bacon

W 4933
F/S G. C. Bucknell
Sgt L. Barlow
Sgt L. B. Daitz
Sgt G. C. Dyke
Sgt W. Patience
Sgt R. McAllister
Sgt L. Farmer

R 5503
F/O G. C. Startin
Sgt D. P. Duggan
F/O I. Evans
Sgt E. D. Rowlinson
Sgt W. E. McIlwaine
Sgt K. G. Lawrence
Sgt E. Hopkinson

LM 437
P/O D. J. Lundy
Sgt M. Stevens
F/S A. E. Jordan
F/S S. O. Smith
Sgt W. M. Rundle
F/O A. H. Bignell
Sgt D. R. Oliver
P/O Skillen

LL 744
F/L M. J. Beetham
F/L A. E. Adamson
F/O W. F. Swinyard
Sgt R. Payne
Sgt I. Higgins
F/S A. L. Bartlett
P/O J. R. Blott
Sgt A. Handley

No 57 Sqdn — East Kirkby, Lancasters: 16 attacked, 2 missing, 1 early return.

ME 579	ND 472	ND 622	JB 529
S/L M. I. Boyle	F/L R. V. Munday	F/L E. W. Tickler	F/L W. M. Walton
Sgt A. T. Cox	Sgt M. J. Stoneman	Sgt K. R. Marriott	Sgt J. G. Robson
W/O R. D. Waddell	P/O D. A. West	F/O R. H. Smart	P/O R. W. Cleary
F/S H. Dixon	F/O T. E. Evans	T/S W. E. Steeper	F/O J. Lavery
Sgt M. Webb	P/O D. Bracher	Sgt A. A. F. Goddard	Sgt F. Roberts
Sgt J. W. Higdon	Sgt S. Bradford	Sgt A. Ferguson	Sgt J. A. Robinson
Sgt M. P. Butler	W/O D. Lightfoot	Sgt R. E. Locke	F/S J. D. Haddington

JA 872	JB 723	ND 468	ND 547
F/L K. D. Smith	F/O F. A. Thomas	F/O A. Bayley	P/O I. S. Ross
Sgt F. E. Young	Sgt W. C. Adams	Sgt R. Heaseman	Sgt W. Walter
P/O H. Welland	F/O S. Bradley	F/O J. Maunsell	F/O T. C. O'Brien
F/O H. W. Honig	F/O C. Paton	Sgt A. Naysmith	Sgt E. G. Tilby
F/S J. A. Edwards	F/O M. Kingsley	F/S J. F. Beecher	Sgt K. H. Jenkinson
Sgt M. E. Harris	W/O R. Young	Sgt V. Marshall	Sgt C. T. King
Sgt N. G. Loads	Sgt A. G. Buckley	Sgt J. H. Donovan	Sgt A. F. McKellar

ND 506	JB 539 *Missing*	ND 405	ME 626
P/O R. A. Beaumont	P/O E. P. Cliburn	P/O R. E. Walker	P/O A. A. J.
F/S M. A. Clarke	Sgt T. J. Evans	Sgt E. Chung	Castagnola
F/S D. J. McCrudden	F/S A. Hamilton	F/O H. B. MacKinnon	Sgt S. J. Henderson
F/S T. H. Mayne	Sgt L. H. Green	F/O K. E. Bly	F/O F. J. Gorringe
Sgt F. P. Robinson	Sgt P. R. Oxley	Sgt A. Hammersley	Sgt N. Evans
Sgt R. I. Hudson	Sgt H. A. Spencer	Sgt W. W. J. Carver	Sgt W. T. Eaves
Sgt A. R. Muir	Sgt P. J. MacInnes	P/O T. Quayle	Sgt T. Craig
			Sgt J. K. Ronald

ND 671 *Missing*	ND 509	JB 370	JB 526
P/O G. Hampton	P/O J. C. Marland	F/S J. Lumsden	F/S K. B. Canever
Sgt F. S. Bodkin	Sgt D. C. Gallacher	Sgt R. Thomas	Sgt K. A. Hilton
Sgt R. E. Nuttall	Sgt W. Low	W/O S. W. Walters	F/S D. G. Twine
Sgt T. J. Adkison	F/O L. E. Mason	Sgt D. Preskett	Sgt T. E. J. Greary
Sgt J. Milfull	Sgt W. J. Norris	Sgt R. Odgers	Sgt D. R. Kenward
Sgt C. Strom	Sgt H. R. Bailey	Sgt J. Gauweloose	Sgt E. R. Armstrong
Sgt R. Youngs	F/S R. J. Nockolle	Sgt W. J. Thorne	Sgt J. V. B. Turner

No 61 Sqdn — Skellingthorpe, Lancasters: 16 attacked, 2 missing.

LL 777	EE 176	JB 636	DV 397
F/L B. C. Fitch	S/L S. J. Beard	F/L N. F. Turner	P/O D. Carbutt
Sgt J. Taylor	F/S K. Burnside	P/O G. A. Turnbull	Sgt J. McCreavy
F/O S. A. Jennings	F/L J. Anderson	P/O J. Barr	Sgt A. Fulker
F/O A. Lyons	W/C D. C. Davies	F/S J. S. Cook	F/O J. Palmer
F/S J. P. Kershaw	Sgt A. E. Wood	F/L G. L. P. Dunstone	Sgt A. Sherwood
F/S L. W. Cromarty	F/O J. C. Hodgkins	P/O G. A. Davey	Sgt A. Short
Sgt L. G. Whitehead	W/O J. Graham	F/O E. H. Walker	Sgt R. Cunningham

LM 493	R 5734	JB 129 *Missing*	DV 311
P/O E. W. Hallett	P/O G. A. Haste	F/O J. G. Cox	S/L E. H. Moss
F/L I. M. Pettigrew	Sgt H. J. Anthony	Sgt G. F. Lowe	Sgt L. S. Suddick
Sgt C. Iliffe	F/S J. R. Groves	Sgt E. G. Grundy	F/O A. D. Bull
F/S O. Olson	F/O R. A. Whitaker	F/O E. W. Mellander	F/O H. D. Glover
Sgt A. Brydges	Sgt W. N. James	Sgt E. Peacock	F/S T. Duff
Sgt A. Nicholson	Sgt P. W. Skelcher	Sgt K. Finch	Sgt W. M. Blake
Sgt H. Ellis	Sgt B. Nutley	Sgt W. Broderick	Sgt R. T. Wevill

LM 359	EE 186	LM 381	ME 596
P/O J. A. Forrest	F/L G. A. Berry	F/O R. J. Auckland	P/O H. H. Farmiloe
Sgt A. H. Davies	Sgt F. C. Astell	Sgt G. F. Crump	Sgt G. A. Jerry
F/S J. Wood	F/S A. G. Williams	F/O R. P. Kayser	F/O S. Halliwell
Sgt D. C. Newman	F/O R. T. Reid	F/S A. E. W. Ayre	F/S K. Vowe
Sgt L. Darben	Sgt E. F. Sutton	Sgt E. R. Kingman	Sgt E. A. Davidson
F/S H. W. Pronger	Sgt L. G. Brand	Sgt R. O. Willis	F/S A. E. Patchett
Sgt J. Macfie	Sgt R. W. Levett	F/S Middleton	Sgt R. Noble

ED 860	ME 596	LM 478	
P/O A. E. Stone	P/O D. Paul	P/O F. W. Burgess	
Sgt A. Dick	Sgt J. Bosworth	Sgt R. Cann	
F/S J. F. Mills	F/S R. Griffin	P/O G. W. Franklin	
Sgt W. J. Sinclair	F/S J. Millar	F/S G. P. Steedsman	
Sgt T. Francis	Sgt R. F. Brezzier	Sgt W. Dacre	
F/S G. E. Cunnington	Sgt S. Billington	Sgt C. Wilce	
Sgt A. Kane	Sgt P. McGibney	Sgt J. C. McQuillan	

No 106 Sqdn — Metheringham, Lancasters: 13 attacked, 1 early return.

JB 566	ND 331	ND 585	MD 339
F/O P. J. Richards	P/O E. F. Durrant	P/O W. C. Moxey	P/O D. W. Carey
Sgt J. Sydenham	Sgt F. R. Broad	Sgt E. M. Woods	Sgt L. W. Franks
Sgt R. Lawrenson	Sgt J. C. Pittaway	Sgt F. Thompson	F/S R. L. Kerr
F/S E. Clode	F/S A. C. Buchanan	Sgt C. A. Matthews	W/O D. H.
F/S R. Edwards	Sgt N. H. Jones	Sgt M. Richardson	MacLennan
Sgt J. R. MacFarlane	Sgt W. Martin	Sgt J. A. Harris	Sgt A. E. Young
F/S G. R. Carlile	Sgt K. N. Warwick	Sgt J. P. Mackilligin	Sgt L. A. Fowle
			F/S T. W. Price

ND 535	JB 641	JD 612	ND 332
P/O R. Starkey	F/O F. C. W. Clement	P/O C. A. Bartlett	F/O E. R. Penman
Sgt J. F. Harris	Sgt J. M. MacLachlan	Sgt B. D. West	Sgt R. N. Johnson
Sgt C. Roberts	F/O W. B. Wilkinson	Sgt R. A. F. Loretan	F/O E. L. Sharp
F/S W. M. Paris	F/O N. V. Cautschi	Sgt E. C. Fry	F/O E. O. Aaron
Sgt C. W. Walker	Sgt H. D. Potter	Sgt H. C. Pratt	Sgt S. R. Patti
Sgt Jamieson	Sgt J. Palmer	Sgt R. G. Williams	Sgt R. F. Stobelt
Sgt M. Ellick	Sgt J. Balmer	Sgt G. W. Wood	Sgt J. A. Roberts

JB 562	JB 292	JB 593	ME 669
F/O W. R. Lee	P/O J. O'Leary	F/O R. Hinkley	F/S J. Cunningham
Sgt A. P. Hebbes	Sgt E. L. Mortimer	Sgt R. H. Blythe	Sgt L. W. Lawlan
F/S A. Mackie	Sgt J. S. Williams	F/O J. Glazebrook	F/S W. A. Hovey
F/S G. Hoyland	Sgt R. A. Snowden	F/O A. Romano	Sgt W. O. Knight
F/S R. Richards	Sgt G. Mellor	F/S L. J. Llewellyn	Sgt J. M. Whitehead
F/s D. Pooley	Sgt A. E. Johnson	F/O C. B. Romigio	Sgt J. Van Stockum
Sgt R. Hunnisette	Sgt R. S. Miller	F/S J. E. Cooper	Sgt D. V. Whiting

ED 593
F/S T. W. J. Hall
Sgt C. M. Beston
F/S R. H. G. Parker
F/S J. T. Gill
Sgt R. D. Dack
Sgt C. A. Poole
Sgt C. S. Robertson

No 207 Sqdn — Spilsby, Lancasters: 18 attacked, 1 missing, 1 early return.

ND 570	ND 522	ME 688	DV 383
P/O G. Andrews	P/O V. G. Glann	P/O S. A. Edmunds	F/O J. F. Muir
F/O G. Furnis	Sgt G. V. Malon	F/O J. McPherson	P/O G. Buxton
Sgt E. J. Davidson	F/O R. W. Jew	Sgt S. R. Mills	Sgt D. N. Collins
F/S R. Edwards	Sgt S. W. Carter	F/O A. C. McLeod	Sgt D. A. Loveday
Sgt R. A. J. Capel	F/S J. A. Paterson	Sgt R. Duffy	W/O L. L. Inganni
Sgt H. G. Hall	Sgt K. E. Boone	Sgt C. R. Hanks	Sgt W. Upsall
Sgt H. A. Youngs	Sgt G. Littlemore	Sgt T. Heslop	Sgt G. S. Longmate

ND 566	EM 436	ME 685	LL 776
P/O D. M. Grant	P/O B. C. Riddle	W/O W. R. Birdling	F/L D. S. P. Smith
F/S Booth	Sgt G. F. Clulow	F/S L. B. Briggs	F/O H. L. McCarthy
P/O T. G. Muhl	Sgt F. Keightley	Sgt R. R. J. Ellis	Sgt H. Priestley
Sgt D. E. Clements	F/O J. L. Larson	Sgt K. W. Brudenell	F/S D. A. Dear
Sgt J. A. Baker	Sgt D. Anderson	F/S E. C. Williams	W/O E. A. G. Petts
Sgt G. Bryan	F/S J. W. J. Buckland	Sgt A. R. Baker	F/S C. B. Sutherland
Sgt D. Bryden	Sgt S. Jones	Sgt H. H. Slater	Sgt A. T. C. White

ND 521
P/O J. T. H. Giddens
Sgt E. Rashbrook
Sgt G. Walker
SGT L. J. Daniels
Sgt C. I. Hall
F/S H. F. James
Sgt K. A. Dobson

ND 575
Sgt C. Bell
F/S R. J. Cross
F/S R. E. Dance
F/O R. E. Casey
Sgt R. Barker
W/O S. Willis
Sgt S. Jones

ND 555
P/O N. Owen
F/S L. Levy
F/S G. M. Brown
Sgt P. A. Wildsmith
Sgt A. L. Sale
Sgt P. W. Corley
Sgt D. Smith

ME 683
W/O J. R. Senior
F/S S. W. Sayce
Sgt A. F. Wooley
F/S J. T. Read
F/S W. J. Waycott
F/S F. T. R. Bruce
Sgt H. Wilson

ME 680 *Missing*
P/O G. F. Polley
F/O G. C. Dunkley
Sgt S. Williams
F/S R. F. Thorpe
Sgt D. Smith
SGT R. G. Atkinson
Sgt B. Orr

DV 360
P/O K. McSweeney
F/O N. F. J. Holmwood
Sgt J. Lowery
F/O D. W. Major
F/S R. A. Austin
Sgt Pico
Sgt R. J. Johnstone

ME 678
F/O H. R. Briggs
F/O H. M. Murray
Sgt G. W. Boswell
F/O B. G. D. Bujac
Sgt J. A. Surridge
Sgt P. K. Skuce
Sgt M. T. Kelly

ME 667
F/L A. Hollings
F/O R. Y. Kenyon
P/O A. W. Hallam
P/O P. J. A. Redman
F/O F. W. Blake
Sgt J. M. Denton
F/O C. T. Harper

ND 564
P/O A. F. Heath
Sgt G. D. Hetherington
Sgt D. J. K. Churchouse
Sgt J. H. Myers
Sgt G. W. Bateson
Sgt G. E. Barker

ME 681
P/O D. L. Davies
Sgt A. H. Allison
Sgt C. Allsop
Sgt C. Gidman
F/S G. R. Scuffins
Sgt B. O. Hunt
F/S F. W. Logan

ND 567
P/O F. Collis
Sgt A. H. Atkin
F/S D. J. G. Griffiths
Sgt G. S. Fox
F/O R. K. Glossery
Sgt J. E. Topple
Sgt C. A. Skinner

No 467 RAAF Sqdn — Waddington, Lancasters: 17 attacked, 2 early returns.

DV 277
P/O D. L. Gibbs
Sgt K. Middlemast
P/O P. A. Sugg
Sgt S. L. Tong
P/O E. L. Green
W/O J. L. M. Giroux
Sgt L. W. Bird

LM 376
F/L A. B. Simpson
Sgt C. P. Curl
F/S K. W. Manson
P/O R. C. Watts
P/O G. G. Johnson
F/S C. A. Campbell
F/S H. Thompson

LL 789
F/L A. J. Colpus
Sgt K. Smith
F/S S. T. Bridgewater
F/O D. J. Stevens
Sgt P. MacDonald
Sgt M. E. Francis
Sgt E. A. Rutt

DV 372
P/O W. E. Felstead
Sgt C. Duthoit
F/S W. S. Hancock
Sgt J. Mellor
F/S B. G. Grasby
Sgt C. A. Nash
Sgt H. W. Ferguson

LM 338
P/O L. S. Ainsworth
Sgt J. W. Hillyer
P/O R. C. Iddon
P/O L. V. Connolly
F/S R. E. Peck
F/S O. J. Jones
F/S J. V. Jeffrey

LM 450
F/L D. T. Conway
Sgt A. R. Tanfield
F/S J. J. McDade
Sgt J. Wesley
Sgt J. R. Redman
Sgt J. Stone
Sgt R. M. Day

LM 475
S/L D. P. Smith
Sgt K. H. Tabor
F/S J. Parker
W/O R. W. Purcell
F/S A. D. Johnston
Sgt E. R. Hill
F/S G. F. Pate

LL 788
F/O M. F. Smith
Sgt R. A. Wilkins
F/O U. W. Kelleher
Sgt A. E. Williams
F/S A. J. Williams
F/S R. Troy
F/S K. W. Nicholas

LL 792
P/O N. R. McDonald
Sgt J. I. French
F/S R. J. Sawyer
F/S R. L. Davies
F/S E. C. Starr
Sgt G. T. Tipping
F/S S. R. Thomson

ND 732
P/O V. A. Baggott
F/S M. W. Hanley
F/O J. Cossens
Sgt R. H. A. Fasham
Sgt W. Wareham
Sgt G. A. MacGillivray
Sgt R. Sleigh

ND 729
P/O R. R. Cowan
Sgt H. K. Feltham
Sgt P. F. O'Connell
F/S A. L. West
F/S H. K. Brown
Sgt J. Sheffield
F/S A. A. Summers

LL 846
P/O C. B. Quarter-
   maine
Sgt J. F. Napier
F/S J. R. Spratt
F/O D. L. Harris
Sgt N. Corbett
Sgt C. Bewick
Sgt R. H. Botterill

EE 143
P/O R. E. Llewellyn
Sgt L. H. Dixon
F/O G. W. Venables
Sgt W. Prest
F/S K. Overy
Sgt F. Hammond
Sgt K. W. Ward

F 5485
P/O L. Hawes
Sgt E. J. Mortlock
F/O D. C. Nawell
F/S T. E. Pollard
F/S J. D. Tunnah
Sgt A. H. Miles
F/O B. T. B. Lendrum

DV 240
P/O W. Mackay
Sgt H. Levy
F/S K. G. Smith
F/O C. G. Abbott
F/S C. L. Chalk
F/O H. C. Bentley
Sgt T. MacFarlane

JA 901
P/O A. B. L.
   Tottenham
Sgt R. J. Taylor
Sgt S. Adams
Sgt J. G. Walsh
F/S H. A. Cummins
Sgt T. A. Stevens
Sgt G. G. Podosky

LM 440
P/O E. V. Dearnaley
Sgt D. Breedon
F/S R. M. Hill
F/S G. A. Acourt
Sgt J. E. Emmett
Sgt R. Trevethan
F/S R. J. Carlill

No 619 Sqdn — Coningsby, Lancasters: 17 attacked, 1 missing, 1 early return.

ND 730	ND 728	LL 783	LL 778
F/L F. E. Fuller	S/L W. N. Whamond	P/O F. G. Secker	W/C J. R. Jeudwine
Sgt R. C. Reid	Sgt A. Peets	Sgt J. W. Gillespie	Sgt R. C. Fryer
F/O C. K. Plunkett	F/O R. A. Marshall	Sgt W. J. C. Cave	F/S L. E. Gosling
F/O N. A. Loranger	F/L P. S. F. Walmsley	Sgt J. H. South	F/S E. Booth
Sgt J. Hill	F/O K. R. Makin	F/S W. H. Currie	Sgt A. S. Bates
Sgt J. Booth	F/S J. F. R. Tate	F/S D. Shortt	F/S L. J. Birch
Sgt L. Stevens	F/S J. Webster	F/S D. E. Hole	F/L J. A. Howard

JB 131	LM 484	LM 446	LL 784
P/O F. Griffiths	P/O P. Buttar	P/O R. W. Olsen	F/S J. Patterson
Sgt C. B. Prophet	Sgt G. G. Watt	Sgt H. T. Woodward	Sgt L. E. Lilley
F/S W. F. Asker	W/O R. W. Noble	P/O F. L. Chipperfield	F/S S. D. Rice
F/S G. J. O. Martin	F/O R. W. Wood	W/O F. J. Bogucki	Sgt F. H. Hall
Sgt J. Davis	Sgt W. J. Milligan	SGT A. Cameron	Sgt M. Rodger
Sgt R. Heslop	Sgt T. Fleetwood	Sgt R. A. Jones	Sgt E. Hunter
Sgt R. H. Mellard	Sgt R. A. Gibbons	F/S F. H. Bayntun	Sgt D. R. Butler
F/S Johnson			

JB 134	DV 328 *Missing*	W 4127	DV 326
P/O J. W. Aitken	P/O Thompson	P/O A. Whitley	F/S E. Whinfield
Sgt F. A. Towse	Sgt B. F. Gratwicke	Sgt D. H. Taylor	Sgt H. Goldgerg
Sgt S. Levy	Sgt I. I. G. Campbell	F/S D. S. Baker	F/S J. C. Horne
Sgt R. E. Hickling	F/O J. V. Leyland	Sgt A. L. Martin	F/S G. Langridge
Sgt J. Presland	Sgt J. D. Pedley	Sgt H. J. Kerrison	Sgt D. Chick
Sgt F. F. Dring	Sgt L. Minshull	Sgt F. Rawlinson	Sgt R. Watts
F/S L. Rhodes	F/S J. Hay	Sgt J. O. Hoey	Sgt W. Watson

LM 418	EE 116	EE 134	LM 420
Sgt J. Parker	F/S D. Schofield	P/O G. Gunzi	P/O L. Warner
Sgt N. Mc. Rice	Sgt I. F. Powell	Sgt D. J. Carter	Sgt A. M. McInulty
F/S G. A. Grigg	F/S R. Withinshaw	P/O N. Vlassie	F/S P. Lowen
F/S A. D. Aumell	F/S E. Brunt	F/S J. W. Mills	Sgt L. Aitken
Sgt W. A. Sharp	Sgt D. W. Golding	Sgt S. Pickstone	Sgt R. Waterson
Sgt A. Dickson	Sgt J. A. Durkin	F/S L. Feinndell	Sgt W. Hunt
Sgt J. H. Woodcock	Sgt J. Broll	Sgt L. Frank	Sgt M. Loosli

ME 568
P/O J. C. Dougherty
Sgt H. D. Campbell
F/S F. S. Garside
F/S L. Hope
Sgt G. F. Wilson
Sgt R. A. Wickham
Sgt A. J. Griffee

No 630 Sqdn — East Kirkby, Lancasters: 12 attacked, 3 missing.

JB 546	ND 554	ND 531	ND 335
P/O J. Kilgour	F/O F. Watts	P/O H. Rogers	P/O P. Nash
Sgt H. Owen	Sgt H. Luck	F/O C. Rodgers	Sgt J. Woods
F/S E. Doram	F/S C. Houseden	Sgt W. Cox	F/S R. Coates
Sgt J. Davison	F/S M. Mackay	F/S W. Irving	F/S D. Todd
Sgt S. Dougan	Sgt D. Cooper	F/S G. Weeden	Sgt J. Pulham
F/S J. Jones	Sgt R. Heggie	Sgt J. Credland	Sgt G. James
Sgt W. Jenkins	Sgt G. Matthews	Sgt R. Marshall	F/S E. Goehring
		F/S P. Gillespie	

LL 886 *Missing*	ED 944	JB 288	ND 537
W/O J. White	F/O J. Nall	P/O A. Johnson	F/L W. Kellaway
Sgt R. Southwood	Sgt J. Harrison	Sgt G. Watts	F/O G. Joblin
Sgt F. Elwood	F/S L. Grimshaw	F/S E. Farnell	P/O J. Whiting
Sgt R. Brydon	Sgt K. Coulbourn	Sgt F. Whitby	Sgt A. Lucas
F/S Y. Moor	F/S R. Lorimer	Sgt H. McGill	F/S S. Pinches
Sgt F. Settle	Sgt D. Dixon-Burt	Sgt W. Pearson	F/s J. Dawson
F/S F. Guy	Sgt C. Winter	F/S M. Dunbar	F/S F. Higgins
Sgt J. Jukes			F/S G. Cansell

ND 685	ND 688	ND 537	ND 788 *Missing*
P/O A. Wilson	S/L R. Calvert	F/L D. Roberts	F/S A. Perry
Sgt G. Bellman	F/O J. Langlands	F/S R. Clarke	Sgt D. Morrison
F/O J. Morschell	P/O W. Mooney	Sgt W. Brook	F/S G. Hather
Sgt F. Roche	F/O M. Beaudoin	F/S A. Jeffrey	F/S J. Duncombe
Sgt R. Wakely	F/S R. Hogg	Sgt G. Davies	Sgt J. Naisbitt
Sgt A. Henderson	F/O A. Connor	Sgt J. Tuck	Sgt M. Todd
Sgt J. Hanna	F/S D. Freeman	Sgt P. Christie	Sgt F. Giblin
	W/O G. Cruickshank	Sgt C. Walker	

ND 657 *Missing*	JB 556	ME 664
P/O C. Allen	P/O R. Bailey	F/L J. Weller
P/O K. Peacock	Sgt J. Allwright	F/S L. Rackley
F/S A. Leyva	F/S C. Richardson	Sgt A. Frame
F/S W. McMeekan	Sgt H. Henderson	Sgt D. Williamson
Sgt A. McCormack	F/O A. Truesdale	F/O A. Kuzma
Sgt J. Ingell	Sgt J. Lindsay	Sgt H. Edwards
Sgt R. Bourne	Sgt W. Murton	Sgt J. Smith
		Sgt H. Jones

No 6 Bomber Group (RCAF)
No 408 Sqdn (RCAF) — Linton-on-Ouse, Lancasters: 9 attacked, 3 early returns.

DS 727 *Abandoned*	LL 725	DS 692	DS 730
WO2 W. W. Kasper	F/L G. B. Latimer	F/S J. J. McCaffrey	WO1 C. McLeod
Sgt F. E. Elbourne	2 Lt A. Hanzenberger	WO2 R. Mitchell	F/S A. E. Bjarnson
F/S J. Nelligan	F/O Q. T. R. Grierson	P/O G. L. Crowe	Sgt A. N. Stock
WO2 R. G. Scott	WO1 J. Dingwall	WO1 A. F. Marsden	Sgt J. P. Plemel
Sgt J. L. Blais	P/O J. T. Guthrie	Sgt A. E. Candline	Sgt L. A. Silver
Sgt J. Moore	P/O F. C. McDougall	Sgt G. R. Harvey	Sgt J. P. Lawder
Sgt L. C. Newton	Sgt R. S. Westrope	Sgt E. Fearns	Sgt J. Innes

DS 726	DS 705	LL 633	LL 722
S/L H. T. Miles DFC	F/S W. G. Cooke	F/O S. R. Frankling	F/L J. F. Easton
F/O J. R. Marier	F/O N. G. Smith	F/O J. T. Dingwall	P/O B. D. J. Langtree
F/O D. B. Young	F/O B. C. Ferguson	Sgt M. Jakubiec	F/S J. H. Walker
F/O P. M. Hughes	Sgt L. M. Hogan	Sgt R. W. Brown	P/O R. S. Goddard
P/O S. C. Shepherd	Sgt G. C. Clark	Sgt J. A. V. Grondin	Sgt K. R. Adams
F/S E. J. Williams	Sgt E. J. Cunningham	Sgt R. Lennard	P/O E. W. Kneen
F/S T. R. Bailey	Sgt N. Bevan	Sgt E. A. Hayward	Sgt F. Scott
Sgt H. A. Nightinggale			

LL 723H	DS 768J
F/O A. A. Bryson	F/O D. T. Ryan
F/S P. E. Liwiski	WO2 R. D. Whitson
Sgt A. P. Trench	WO2 A. H. Durnin
WO1 R. J. Galloway	F/O G. Croucher
Sgt R. B. Redlin	Sgt H. E. Truscott
Sgt E. G. Bowles	Sgt J. A. Imrie
Sgt R. Moore	Sgt B. Scott

No 420 Sqdn (RCAF) —Tholthorpe, Halifaxes: 11 attacked, 1 missing, 1 early return.

LW 380	LW 783	LW 388	LW 674
F/S R. Coffey	F/S J. G. Ward	F/S F. K. Keegan	F/O H. Northern
Sgt M. M. Dingwall	Sgt P. E. Sisco	Sgt A. W. Springinotic	F/O P. G. Kelly
F/O R. J. Bayne	F/S J. R. Barclay	F/O F. W. Knox	F/O F. W. Morrison
W/O R. Rutherglen	Sgt G. R. Freeman	W/O P. J. Myers	F/S C. H. Lines
Sgt K. A. Hart	Sgt F. E. Beech	Sgt C. A. Hewson	Sgt W. H. Young
Sgt R. E. McWhirter	Sgt E. A. Bates	Sgt M. E. Meach	F/O A. H. B. Hall
Sgt W. Porter	Sgt F. T. Jones	Sgt R. W. Mills	Sgt L. J. Franklin
			P/O G. F. Wass

LW 421	LW 503	LW 389	LW 590 *Missing*
F/O E. J. Alberts	F/O A. Plumer	S/L G. C. Beal	P/O H. W. Rice
F/O J. R. Holland	P/O Kalle	F/O F. J. Robinson	F/S C. G. Fraser
W/O J. Nowazek	F/O Porterfield	F/O N. J. Andrews	F/O H. I. Altic
Sgt A. Knight	F/S R. F. Dunster	P/O D. W. Wooley	W/O C. Renwick
Sgt R. W. Wallace	Sgt J. E. Austin	Sgt W. T. Stainton	Lt J. H. Thomsen
Sgt G. Oxner	Sgt N. E. Price	P/O A. F. Goodall	Sgt J. B. Boire
Sgt H. Karred	Sgt D. Gallagher	Sgt W. Hicker	Sgt P. G. Bushell
	Sgt A. Pinder	F/O Campbell	

LW 392	LW 502	LW 676	
W/O J. M. Broadway	F/O F. C. Kruger	F/L R. C. Deegan	
F/O A. M. P. Harris	W/O K. E. Mills	F/S D. Anderson	
W/O L. J. O'Shell	F/O R. G. McInnis	F/S C. Axford	
Sgt S. Harle	F/S R. A. Moore	P/O J. A. Smith	
Sgt A. Johnston	Sgt E. W. Sneeling	Sgt M. J. Gibbs	
F/S A. Crawford	Sgt P. E. Menzies	F/S P. A. Dubois	
Sgt T. J. Ryalls	Sgt A. Brown	Sgt L. Corbeill	

No 424 Sqdn (RCAF) — Skipton-on-Swale, Halifaxes: 10 attacked, 1 missing, 1 early return.

HX 318	LW 435 *Missing*	LW 910	LW 416
W/O A. T. Mather	F/O W. E. Krampe	F/S D. R. Mackenzie	F/S B. Vanier
W/O A. Crain	F/O A. G. Fleming	F/O C. J. Combe	F/O W. Lawrence
F/S D. A. Corder	F/S W. G. Tillmann	F/O E. D. Cable	F/S R. Sirvage
Sgt G. Carey	Sgt L. G. Jewell	Sgt P. A. Bailey	Sgt R. Rogers
Sgt H. J. Catton	Sgt J. Mackintosh	Sgt J. D. Campbell	Sgt F. R. Jackson
Sgt C. A. Seeley	Sgt E. G. Evans	Sgt E. J. Parr	Sgt J. R. Adam
W/O C. T. Hayward	Sgt R. D. Wilson	Sgt F. H. Gibbs	Sgt J. Florence

LW 384	HX 314	HX 319	LW 462
F/S H. Kirby	F/O J. Doig	F/O D. A. Crosbie	F/S R. W. Burton
W/O T. Vanchuck	F/O J. R. Mason	F/S P. M. Moloney	F/S C. R. Thrasher
P/O C. Drummond-Hay	F/S A. H. Crosland	P/O J. E. Tinline	Sgt D. L. McMain
Sgt R. H. Parry	Sgt D. Stewart	Sgt R. W. Brown	W/O E. M. Crawford
Sgt F. S. Caine	Sgt J. S. Bolton	Sgt C. A. Phyall	Sgt J. M. McLeod
Sgt J. M. Cumbers	Sgt R. J. Atkins	Sgt L. Boudreau	Sgt E. G. Relf
Sgt F. A. Snider	Sgt T. J. Rogers	Sgt R. Z. Trudeau	Sgt C. L. McKay

LW 780	LV 879	HX 316	
S/L J. A. Westland	F/O W. B. Hill	F/O T. R. Millman	
F/O J. B. Hall	F/O T. S. Horswill	F/L H. T. Amy	
F/O J. W. Galvin	F/S J. A. Downer	W/O B. J. Starrup	
F/S S. W. Beer	Sgt I. E. Parsons	F/O L. R. Georgeson	
Sgt H. G. Davies	Sgt S. Nichols	Sgt J. Swarbrick	
Sgt R. H. Beilstein	Sgt D. M. Sweeney	P/O W. E. Marshall	
F/S W. S. Atkinson	Sgt W. A. Green	P/O F. N. Wilson	

No 425 Sqdn (RCAF) — Tholthorpe, Halifaxes: 8 attacked, 2 missing, 3 early returns.

LW 798	LW 387	LW 632	LW 672
P/O L. P. Dupuis	F/S L. B. Brochu	F/S J. A. Cote	F/O B. E. Wilmot
F/L G. D. Stevens	F/S J. P. Camire	F/O J. H. Demers	F/O J. H. Hudson
W/O B. Chene	W/O J. Racicot	Sgt D. Garrie	P/O W. E. Eaglestone
Sgt J. Longmuir	Sgt J. A. Bourasse	Sgt A. Hogue	Sgt T. E. Wiltse
W/O J. F. Benard	Sgt J. L. Sevigny	Sgt J. I. Gravel	P/O H. J. Powell
F/O S. Railton	Sgt H. J. Doust	Sgt J. C. Lacouffe	Sgt R. U. Furneaux
Sgt C. Hornsell	Sgt J. A. Audet	Sgt D. I. James	Sgt T. Holden

LW 394	LW 375	LW 424	LW 680
P/O J. R. Wells	F/O T. F. Rance	F/L L. H. Lecomte	Sgt C. D. Stark
F/S H. R. Mooney	Sgt N. Marshall	F/O W. H. C. Boyd	Sgt E. F. Pitken
Sgt W. G. Walker	W/O R. J. Whyte	Sgt E. Bright	W/O P. Davies
F/O B. Shutts	P/O G. Sveinson	F/S J. C. Cox	Sgt E. J. Pigeon
P/O S. G. Hunt	Sgt W. C. Osborne	Sgt L. B. Powell	Sgt J. E. Code
Sgt P. C. Draper	Sgt Q. J. McNab	W/O L. S. Lefoy	Sgt L. Snider
Sgt J. Q. Railton	Sgt H. V. Wall	Sgt J. T. Demiddelelaer	Sgt M. H. Waters
LW 428 *Missing*	LW 425 *Missing*		
P/O N. H. Jones	P/O L. A. Renaud		
P/O M. C. Laternell	P/O J. R. Brazeau		
P/O Laviolette	P/O R. A. Hanks		
P/O M. H. McLeod	Sgt J. J. Boyer		
P/O J. C. Teacey	Sgt J. J. Huot		
Sgt J. E. Bouchard	P/O C. S. Turner		
Sgt G. W. C. Mabbott	Sgt J. Hutman		

No 427 Sqdn (RCAF) — Leeming, Halifaxes: 12 attacked, 2 missing.

LW 938	LW 922	LV 830	LW 574 *Missing*
S/L J. M. Bissett	F/L J. G. Cribb	F/L W. A. Cory	W/O A. R. Yaworski
F/O R. J. White	F/O C. G. Tibbles	P/O P. Beaumont	Sgt A. I. Young
F/O F. R. Zulauf	F/O C. V. Biddulph	F/O J. E. Parkinson	Sgt J. J. L. Hamel
F/O J. G. Leclaire	P/O J. E. Wright	Sgt S. Welch	W/O H. R. Armstrong
Sgt W. C. Hall	F/S W. J. Brett	Sgt H. McCaffery	Sgt J. L. Jette
F/O R. A. Shannon	Sgt W. A. Fox	Sgt R. Beech	Sgt R. A. McBeath
Sgt B. F. Holloway	P/O J. E. Cartwright	Sgt T. Hume	Sgt T. J. Rigby
F/S R. Stevens			

LW 577	LW 576	LW 618	LW 883
F/S S. G. Dowdell	W/O A. J. King	W/O D. F. Foster	F/O W. M. Stephen
F/O G. I. MacKay	F/O W. A. Wilson	F/O G. M. Waddell	F/O J. I. Sanderson
F/O O. L. Jackson	Sgt W. Bailey	F/O T. W. Farr	F/S R. Bleich
Sgt M. C. Webb	Sgt R. S. Mowbray	Sgt E. Carter-Edwards	Sgt D. F. Walker
Sgt H. J. Halbert	Sgt S. K. Vallieres	Sgt C. W. Ford	W/O G. R. Pearce
Sgt L. J. Lozo	Sgt D. N. Cotton	Sgt M. Donnan	Sgt J. Sheldrake
Sgt J. Nesom	Sgt H. Morgan	Sgt G. W. Philliskirk	Sgt R. G. Bird

LV 831	LV 789	LV 923	LK 755
F/L F. N. Murray	F/L R. N. McCauley	F/O G. A. Weldon	W/O W. M. Patrick
F/O J. T. Head	F/O M. C. Utas	F/O D. R. Rand	F/O G. Clayton
Sgt G. C. Southcott	P/O R. F. Gruninger	F/S J. Heaton	F/S J. G. Robinson
F/S E. D. Cast	F/S J. Quinn	Sgt R. H. Franklin	Sgt L. Dring
Sgt D. Frayling	W/O J. I. P. Lahal	Sgt L. Litke	Sgt J. Wiebe
Sgt M. A. Larivee	Sgt N. Barlow	Sgt J. Hewitt	Sgt W. F. Smith
Sgt R. King	Sgt D. C. Jennings	Sgt A. E. Lowlett	Sgt D. Smith
	F/O W. N. McPhee		

LW 572	LV 821	LK 752 *Missing*	
W/O C. H. Coathup	F/O W. J. L. Weicker	W/O W. F. Magdalinski	
F/O G. H. Mills	F/O R. A. Pearson	F/O R. A. Parry	
F/S F. Dennis	F/O J. E. McDowell	Sgt J. Y. Roberts	
Sgt F. I. Edwards	F/O D. H. Brown	Sgt L. C. Glasser	
Sgt A. J. Whittaker	Sgt R. B. Nairn	Sgt M. C. Fugere	
Sgt E. Eppler	Sgt B. L. Martin	Sgt J. Papineau	
Sgt G. J. Patterson	Sgt K. A. Abbs	Sgt P. Guilder	

No 429 Sqdn (RCAF) — Leeming, Halifaxes: 9 attacked, 1 forced to return as a result of enemy action, 3 missing, 1 early return.

LW 713	LK	LK 805 *Missing*	LW
P/O T. Rawlinson	F/S P. C. Cadogan	P/O S. A. Wick	F/L W. B. Anderson
F/S G. L. Gaunt	Sgt R. C. Williams	W/O R. S. Glendenning	F/S A. Capusten
W/O A. J. Murphy	P/O G. A. McNamee	F/O J. H. Warkentin	Sgt L. S. O'Leary
Sgt A. Bates	Sgt J. Galloway	Sgt H. Hull	Sgt G. E. J. Steere
Sgt W. Bush	Sgt T. C. K. Woolf	W/O S. Bousteed	W/O J. D. J. Banning
P/O A. C. Shierlaw	Sgt J. D. Donaldson	Sgt R. L. Kift	Sgt J. Mangione
F/S J. R. H. Cochrane	Sgt D. Kitto	Sgt L. J. Keely	Sgt G. J. Ritchie
F/O D. G. Depew			

LW 688 *Missing*	LK 800	LW 684	LK 804
P/O E. A. Giles	P/O W. B. Dyers	P/O H. W. Mitchell	W/O L. L. Mitchell
F/S H. H. Nicholls	F/O D. W. Morison	P/O F. B. Fjeldstad	W/O E. Bannoff
F/O J. C. Rousseau	F/O R. J. Fawcett	W/O L. G. Churchill	F/S D. L. Thompson
Sgt R. M. Byrne	Sgt J. L. Moore	Sgt E. H. Stofer	Sgt W. Lawrence
F/S W. T. G. Peckham	Sgt R. W. Meredith	F/S R. Goatham	W/O G. S. James
Sgt W. G. Hampton	Sgt C. W. Holdgate	Sgt R. H. Fallon	Sgt C. F. Green
F/S A. W. Larochelle	W/O W. C. Patterson	F/L L. V. Pollard	Sgt C. E. Hunter
		F/O M. A. Sloski	
LK 792	LW 412	LV 914 *Missing*	LW 714
W/O M. A. Fernandez	F/O J. Atkins	S/L J. W. Bell	F/O A. MacDonald
F/O R. B. Rudd	F/O E. J. Haworth	F/O R. F. Conroy	F/O W. C. Shields
F/S L. M. Shetler	F/O J. L. Widdis	W/O O. D. McLean	F/S J. J. Mollison
F/S H. Dawson	Sgt J. Robson	F/L C. W. McIntyre	Sgt N. T. McCarthy
Sgt R. F. Christie	Sgt W. H. Griffiths	F/L A. P. Smith	F/S H. Guild
Sgt W. Stewart	Sgt A. R. Woolsey	Sgt L. C. P. Spencer	F/O J. R. Calderbank
Sgt K. H. Jackson	Sgt T. F. Barley	Sgt G. Wilton	Sgt T. B. Chapman

LK 806*
F/S N. L. Thompson
W/O C. E. Whitmore
F/O E. S. Coatsworth
Sgt S. Fisher
Sgt R. F. Budgen
Sgt C. Duglan
Sgt A. D. Fraser

*Aircraft suffered severe damage from heavy flak and fought off three enemy fighters. Wireless operated baled out during the action, but the Halifax returned safely to base.

No 432 Sqdn (RCAF) — Eastmore, Halifaxes: 8 attacked, 1 missing, 1 early return.

LW 592	LK 765	LW 686	
F/L M. W. Pettit	F/S E. A. Clarke	F/S C. R. Narum	F/S G. Millar
W/O A. Branch	W/O E. Bishop	F/S N. Goeson	F/O A. Holmes
F/O M. Gray	Sgt W. Brown	Sgt L. Pigeon	Sgt E. McCauley
W/O G. Keogh	Sgt H. Lewis	F/S J. Marini	Sgt W. MacPherson
W/O E. Bullivant	Sgt S. Burgess	Sgt R. Rathwell	Sgt G. Flather
Sgt D. Penny	Sgt J. Cook	Sgt S. Saprunoff	Sgt B. Harmsworth
Sgt A. Plummer	Sgt G. Bradshaw	Sgt R. Thompson	Sgt H. Ibbotson
LW 582	LW 614	MZ 506	LK 754
F/O E. K. Reid	F/S A. K. Clarke	F/O W. Smith	P/O S. A. Hawkins
F/O J. T. Smith	Sgt F. Cranch	F/O R. Plommer	F/O A. Raetzen
W/O V. McDonald	Sgt R. Hindmarsh	F/O C. Balsdon	Sgt M. O'Leary
Sgt G. Maguire	Sgt D. Bell	Sgt P. Clench	Sgt W. Parkinson
Sgt R. Clarkson	Sgt D. MacNeill	Sgt R. Pingle	Sgt G. Hand
Sgt J. Barr	Sgt E. Halliwell	Sgt J. Rudland	Sgt R. Banks
Sgt J. May	Sgt T. Woodard	Sgt E. Lestrange	Sgt J. McCart

LW 593 *Missing*
P/O J. McIntosh
F/O A. Small
P/O R. Elvin
P/O G. Schell
Sgt L. Randle
Sgt A. Dedauw
Sgt W. King

No 433 Sqdn (RCAF) — Skipton-on-Swale, Halifaxes: 10 attacked, 2 missing, 3 early returns.

HX 352	LV 840	HX 275	LW 368
P/O J. J. Major	W/O J. A. Bourgeault	F/O W. Canter	F/S F. R. Edmondson
F/O R. Bower	W/O W. D. Dennstedt	F/O A. Norris	F/S L. E. Jones
F/S F. Mose	F/S T. A. Miller	Sgt I. N. McCubbrey	Sgt M. C. Gorman
F/S J. J. Young	F/O J. W. Guignion	Sgt H. Boissevain	F/O A. H. Ellis
Sgt J. Greening	Sgt L. Plante	Sgt A. M. Camenzuli	F/O L. G. Hughes
Sgt A. Sumner	Sgt D. R. Bowerman	Sgt R. Calloway	Sgt A. Elliot
Sgt D. D. Skingle	Sgt R. Laframboise	Sgt H. C. Seedhouse	Sgt G. Ovington

HX 288
W/O J. E. Mitchell
F/O J. K. Shedden
W/O S. McDougall
F/O R. D. Wilson
W/O N. S. Brown
Sgt J. McDonough
Sgt J. R. Brown

LV 841 *Missing*
F/S R. W. Lossing
F/O D. A. Robinson
Sgt L. G. Davey
F/S G. A. Dancey
Sgt F. Osborne
Sgt O. Sporne
Sgt F. E. Simmons

LV 911
W/O W. H. Wright
F/O D. Townsend
F/S L. Gambold
W/O P. Groulx
Sgt D. Horton
Sgt H. K. Partridge
Sgt M. D. O'Reilly

HX 292
F/O E. B. Van Slyck
Sgt A. Phillips
F/S K. Shaw-Brown
F/S R. Blau
F/S R. H. Potentier
Sgt G. Rowland
W/O J. O. Weekes

HX 284 *Missing*
F/S W. F. Russell
F/O M. Topplin
Sgt W. Walmsley
F/O J. T. Shea
Sgt R. C. Cossar
Sgt P. McLuskie

HX 353
F/S R. C. Reinelt
F/S F. J. Devine
F/S A. Hardes
Sgt D. Williams
W/O D. F. Wilson
Sgt G. Dykes
Sgt J. Peppercorn
Sgt D. Carruthers

No 8 PFF Group
No 7 Sqdn — Oakington, Lancasters, 17 attacked, 1 alternative target, 2 missing, 1 early return.

ND 581 *Missing*
F/O J. M. Mee
P/O D. P. Bain
F/S D. N. Luxton
F/S D. Mortlock
F/S R. L. Grimes
F/L L. T. Berrigan
F/S R. A. Webb

ND 592
P/O J. M. Napier
F/S H. A. Wallis
W/O L. A. Brenton
F/S A. W. C. Darby
Sgt G. C. Spencer
F/S H. E. Martin
P/O J. D. Wyn-Evans

ME 623
P/O R. J. Sexton
F/L L. D. Goldinggay
F/S R. Clenahan
Sgt T. Tilley
Sgt T. C. Marchant
F/S G. N. Wright
F/S G. C. K. Platts

JB 722
F/L S. Evans
F/L A. Dickinson
F/S K. D. Matheson
F/S D. S. Heys
F/S R. E. Greenfield
F/S G. W. Brockway
F/S T. J. Hirst

JB 653
S/L J. M. Dennis
F/L S. E. Clark
F/L R. V. Cutts
W/O P. J. Aldridge
F/L D. N. Row
F/S A. Simpson
F/S. R. L. Jones
W/O C. S. Goodman

ND 590
F/O G. J. South
F/O C. C. Magee
F/O R. B. Hunt
W/O N. Kaye
F/O G. Inverarity
W/O C. M. Welsh
F/L E. G. Dawson
F/S J. G. Miles

JB 676
S/L K. A. H. Lawrence
P/O V. T. Fowler
F/S W. S. Baxter
F/S L. G. Gilmore
Sgt N. A. Bevans
F/S D. W. Johnson
F/S V. York

JB 313
F/S T. H. Strong
F/O P. A. T. Facer
Sgt E. B. Ede
F/S J. McCarron
Sgt F. F. H. Burnett
Sgt G. A. Walker
Sgt K. Monk

JA 964
F/O D. C. Davies
F/O H. H. Guy
F/L N. R. Anstey
F/O R. G. Moss
F/L E. E. Stocker
F/O J. Hatley
Sgt J. Beecroft

ND 350
F/L A. H. McGillivray
W/O L. S. Weir
F/O F. Bell
F/S C. A. McCarthy
Sgt T. Durbin
Sgt N. Twell
Sgt R. E. Smith

ND 443
S/L C. H. Wilson
Sgt J. Stevens
P/O J. S. Ferrier
Sgt K. G. Francis
Sgt W. Jenkins
Sgt T. B. Liddle
Sgt F. T. Fuller

ND 460
F/L R. Edwards
P/O H. B. Cooper
Sgt C. A. Thompson
W/O W. W. Bigoray
Sgt A. T. Cherry
Sgt L. Timmins
F/S H. G. Lawrence

ND 496
P/O L. Kidd
F/S E. J. Sanderson
F/S F. J. Stanton
F/S J. M. Cavender
F/S J. Hall
F/S T. Watt
F/S R. Wilson

JA 911
S/L A. H. C. Roberts
F/O D. E. Miller
F/O J. A. McCall
W/O N. L. Robertson
Sgt T. R. Gadsden
Sgt N. L. Humphries
F/O G. A. A. Howe

JA 968
S/L B. W. McMillan
F/L D. L. Gilson
F/O H. H. Michael
F/L F. Bell
Sgt L. E. Judd
F/S Long-Hartley
F/L J. D. Harris

ND 387
F/L A. O. Price
F/O T. H. C. Phelps
F/O C. W. G. Dpwse
Sgt F. L. Leach
Sgt W. N. Kennedy
Sgt C. W. Buffham
F/S S. N. Ettridge

JB 185
F/S B. F. Wallis
F/S H. R. Falloon
F/O W. A. F. Squibb
Sgt J. A. Sturgeon
Sgt H. W. Collins
Sgt G. Lyall
Sgt J. R. McGinn

JB 417
F/O K. H. Weir
F/S M. N. Walker
F/O J. F. Marks
F/S F. Mulholland
Sgt H. F. Maxwell
Sgt R. Brown
Sgt J. W. Clark

JB 345
F/S N. J. Tutt
Sgt H. Harris
Sgt R. H. Ames
Sgt R. F. Boots
F/S S. Parr
Sgt R. A. Tyrell
Sgt R. D. Pemble

JA 693
W/O P. G. McCarthy
Sgt A. Hargrave
Sgt H. W. Leyton-
        Smith
F/S F. C. Allford
Sgt J. G. Gay
F/S D. F. Blatchford
Sgt E. A. Batterbee

NZ 457 *Missing*
P/O T. B. Kyle
F/O W. Humphreys
F/S J. H. McDonnell
Sgt R. Hyde
Sgt F. H. Fowler
Sgt C. Butson
F/S G. Hughes

No 35 Sqdn — Lancasters: 12 attacked, 1 returned after flak damage, 1 missing.

ND 690	ND 692	ND 694	ND 703
P/O E. Holmes	F/L G. B. S. Honey	S/L L. M. Whetham	W/O F. G. Tropman
F/L M. G. Harris	P/O L. Roberts	Sgt R. McGuinness	F/S R. W. Bullen
P/O D. E. Coleman	P/O R. O. Tudberry	P/O C. H. Pettit	Sgt J. L. G. Marshall
F/O A. T. Maskell	F/S J. Brennan	F/S A. C. Aston	F/S N. W. Curtis
Sgt W. A. Hooper	W/O F. Hayward	Sgt K. J. Rees	F/S J. L. Stevens
F/S V. E. Bent	W/O D. A. Wagar	Sgt A. H. Wood	F/S M. E. Ladyman
P/O A. E. Waddicor	Sgt A. J. Dick	Sgt H. G. Smith	Sgt I. K. McGregor

ND 653	ND 697	ND 597 *Missing*	ND 648
P/O J. J. Osmond	F/L E. J. Chidgey	S/L R. T. Fitzgerald	S/L E. K. Cresswell
P/O R. W. E. Bennett	F/O D. A. Stoker	F/O J. F. Savage	P/O H. A. Millar
W/O R. M. Hilliard	Lt K. Stenwig	F/L W. S. Muego	S/L D. K. Allport
F/S M. Cochrane	P/O T. H. Warren	W/O R. A. Brewington	P/O A. C. Taylor
F/S G. A. Parry	F/S J. M. Colledge	F/S F. K. Smith	P/O C. Miller
P/O J. C. Black	T/Sgt F. W. Hall	F/S S. H. Boulton	Sgt R. Rhodes
Sgt J. K. Spedding	Sgt F. R. H. Smith	P/O C. J. Dineen	F/O W. J. Simpson
			Sgt A. J. White

ND 702	ND 693	ND 696	ND 701
F/O C. C. Price	F/O P. F. Jarvis	F/O H. C. Hoover	F/L G. F. Ingram
P/O E. T. Heard	F/O G. Hornsby	F/O P. R. Burt	P/O V. J. Murphy
P/O J. E. Sidnell	F/L A. W. Lister	F/O G. A. Goom	F/O G. W. Rushbrook
Sgt W. Steane	F/S G. King	F/O J. Mossop	Sgt S. Jackson
Sgt J. Carr	F/S A. W. Cox	F/S J. J. McKenzie	P/O D. A. Weatherall
Sgt A. E. Smith	F/S A. E. Huntley	F/S C. A. Hill	F/S W. S. Edmonton
F/S B. O. Baldwin		F/S G. W. Lloyd	Sgt D. B. Gerrard

ND 646	ME 620 (C)
P/O E. C. Gregory	P/O L. S. White
F/S C. Trott	P/O H. C. Wright
F/S D. W. Kermode	F/S R. C. Everest
Sgt R. Sadler	F/S R. Bull
F/S W. J. Stewart	F/S J. E. Levett
Sgt W. S. Nuttall	F/S A. E. Williams
Sgt J. Weaver	Sgt G. Smith

No 83 Sqdn — Wyton, Lancasters: 11 detailed, all attacked.

ND 649	ND 389	ND 494	JB 309
F/L E. Mirfin	W/O K. A. Lane	P/O A. C. Keeling	P/O A. J. Saunders
Sgt N. G. Whiteley	Sgt R. E. Raymond	Sgt J. G. Francis	Sgt D. M. Redding
F/S J. Pinkney	F/S J. A. Jones	Sgt G. K. Chapman	F/S J. F. Falconer
F/O J. Chadwick	W/O J. A. Aspinall	F/S D. L. Millar	Sgt T. A. Sheen
S/L Wilson	F/S D. E. Cope	F/O F. A. Harpham	P/O D. D. Govett
Sgt R. Griffiths	F/S H. J. Hall	Sgt G. H. Bateman	F/S K. G. Tennett
W/O A. Whitehouse	F/S. A. Davies	Sgt Gallagher	F/S D. M. Robinson

ND 395	JA 928	ND 333	ND 400
P/O C. McConnell	F/O G. M. Kennedy	P/O J. P. G. Pezero	P/O W. E. Siddle
Sgt T. Powell	P/O G. Robinson	Sgt E. S. Sowersby	Sgt A. R. Wilson
F/O A. J. S. Watts	Lt G. J. Van-Horn	Sgt A. W. Wade	F/S C. W. J. Lodge
Sgt W. Surgey	W/O P. J. Lynes	Sgt G. M. Tebbutt	F/S C. J. W. Culley
Sgt E. S. Vickers	Sgt O. J. Turner	F/S E. W. Greenwood	F/S N. Machin
Sgt G. H. Bradshaw	F/S A. W. Poyer	Sgt G. F. French	F/S J. C. Parker
Sgt W. J. Throsby	W/O A. Murray	F/S W. B. Baldwinson	W/O C. Moore

ND 551
F/O R. E. Walker
Sgt H. E. Holdsworth
P/O N. J. Cornell
F/S R. O. Bailey
F/O J. H. Wells
Sgt C. R. Taylor
Sgt D. R. Kelly

ND 529
F/L R. K. Eggins
W/O R. G. Goodwin
F/O D. W. Woolle
P/O J. W. Patterson
W/O Gray
S/L T. W. Blair
P/O G. J. Fursey
P/O G. J. Marden

ND 442
F/O A. P. Whitford
Sgt H. G. Millard
F/O W. T. Loftus
W/O N. J. Higgins
F/S R. J. Dobbyn
W/O D. Cross
F/S L. W. J. Arnold

No 97 Sqdn — Bourne, Lancasters: 12 attacked, 2 missing.

JB 708
F/L O. B. Hyde
F/S M. E. Putt
F/L E. H. Palmer
F/O J. Craig
F/S E. Hill
F/S Russell
P/O R. Taylor

ND 452
F/O R. D. Ellesmere
Sgt M. A. Johnson
P/O S. Carlyle
F/L N. G. Cooper
F/S L. F. Hughes
Sgt M. N. Duffy
P/O A. J. Newton

ND 572
W/C C. M. Dunnicliffe
S/L Bryan-Smith
S/L R. P. Ingalls
F/O H. W. Rieger
W/O J. K. Bell
F/O C. Chetham
F/O R. J. Weller

ND 600
F/L J. W. Comans
Sgt K. Randle
F/O D. Bowes
F/O H. H. Cook
Sgt R. Woolford
Sgt G. Widdis
F/S D. Bolland

ND 625
F/L C. D. Owen
Sgt D. E. Lacey
F/O O. W. Shires
F/S W. D. Knowles
F/S K. Florrest
W/O J. T. Stanton
F/S T. W. L. Leak

JB 346
P/O H. S. Van Raalte
Sgt M. Durn
Sgt D. Williams
F/S A. L. Lambert
Sgt E. H. Peace
Sgt R. G. Davies
Sgt C. Benfell

ND 500
S/L A. H. Lynch
Sgt C. O'Neill
F/O D. C. Armstrong
F/S T. H. James
F/S H. Abernethy
Sgt Errington
Sgt C. Denness

JB 683
F/O W. H. Benton
Sgt Rimmington
P/O J. I. Rogerson
F/O J. Skingley
F/S L. Hornsby
F/S F. Holbrook
F/S J. Fernandez

ND 643
F/O P. J. Drane
Sgt R. J. Bowen
F/S C. G. Trotman
F/S L. Wagner
Sgt J. Donald
F/S J. Henderson
F/S R. E. Buck

ND 495
P/O S. A. Edwards
Sgt D. H. Ryder
F/S R. Heap
F/S H. Grant
Sgt H. M. Kent
Sgt G. J. Hill
F/S J. Diggle

JB 671 *Missing*
P/O W. D. Coates
Sgt B. H. Nicholas
Sgt S. Nuttall
F/S J. M. Baldwin
Sgt W. Chapman
Sgt W. L. York
Sgt F. Thompson

MD 346
F/O W. M. Reid
Sgt Richards
F/O R. D. Parker
Sgt G. D. Moir
F/S B. Harthill
F/S D. P. Cannings
Sgt G. Brown

ND 440 *Missing*
F/O P. H. Todd
Sgt S. Robson
P/O C. T. Fuller
F/S J. R. Duvall
F/S W. Housley
Sgt S. McCloskey
Sgt J. Cartwright

ND 501
P/O W. T. Gee
Sgt P. R. Turner
Sgt S. F. Osbourne
F/S J. H. Maxwell
Sgt R. H. Utting
Sgt R. Moore
Sgt M. D. Inglis

No 156 Sqdn — Upwood, Lancasters: 18 aircraft attacked, 2 early returns, 1 missing.

ND 534
F/L D. O. Blamey
F/S G. H. Clements
F/S J. Dillon
Sgt K. Gilbert
F/L J. Booth
F/S G. W. Gracey
W/O W. Pedder

JB 228
F/S J. Cuthill
F/S G. Thorneycroft
F/S R. B. Tobin
Sgt D. R. Breeze
F/S R. Trotter
Sgt R. Smith
Sgt D. W. Aspinall

ND 406
F/L J. H. Hewitt
F/S H. L. Wilson
F/S V. B. Crosby
W/O D. Flynn
Sgt G. Cotterell
F/S A. Bouch
F/S W. Smith

EE 108
P/O R. McLean
F/L J. P. Flynn
Sgt M. Wenham
Sgt J. S. Burn
P/O F. H. Whybrow
F/S A. J. Duke
F/S J. S. Harrison

JB 230
F/O A. J. Hiscock
F/O J. A. Turk
Sgt J. S. Turner
Sgt T. Belcher
Sgt C. Wilson
P/O J. G. Cooper
Sgt E. W. C. Brackett

JB 239 E/R
P/O R. M. Etchells
P/O E. Williams
Sgt E. W. Hay
Sgt J. D. Gray
F/S A. J. C. Croome
Sgt J. F. Stearne
Sgt S. Freeden

ND 422
P/O N. D. Langford
Sgt J. E. Price
Sgt F. Urch
Sgt A. Swift
W/O H. W. Davy
Sgt E. B. Riley
Sgt G. A. Wilby

ND 492
F/O R. C. Wiseman
W/O J. H. Hudson
W/O D. D. Jackson
Sgt N. J. Loader
F/O L. H. Lawton
F/S L. C. R. Gilman
F/S K. K. Muir

ND 714
W/O J. A. Higgs
F/S D. J. Chase
F/S E. W. Parissien
Sgt M. Fowler
Sgt R. Keating
Sgt G. F. Woodhead
Sgt W. A. Webb

ND 349
W/O W. B. Marshall
F/S J. Hay
Sgt A. Ovenfield
Sgt D. H. Wheatley
F/S T. Duffy
F/S H. C. Geddes
Sgt J. S. Coward

ND 348
P/O G. D. Smith
F/S G. O. Paton
F/O L. H. Chester
Sgt A. J. Doswell
F/S G. P. Todd
F/S J. A. Taylor
F/S H. D. Jorgensen

JA 673
F/S W. J. Ward
Sgt E. Roberts
Sgt R. W. Watts
Sgt S. G. Smith
F/S A. E. Thomas
Sgt J. McCaffery
Sgt W. J. Lanktree

ND 502
F/S F. B. Gipson
F/S H. G. Stevenson
F/S J. M. Walker
Sgt J. R. Randall
F/S J. P. Gregory
F/S W. R. Hodges
Sgt J. S. Robertson

ND 409
F/O J. H. Gilmore
F/S E. F. Hearn
P/O J. R. Dodds
P/O F. Wadsworth
F/O K. G. Franklin
F/O G. H. Musgrove
F/O R. G. Sharland

ND 348
F/L G. S. Hopton
P/O T. W. Kennedy
F/L J. C. Eade
P/O P. J. Moyes
Sgt L. E. Gibbs
F/L R. B. Leigh
W/O A. R. Larkins
Sgt I. Campbell

ND 466
Capt F. Johnsen
F/S W. T. H. O'Neill
Sgt K. Gardiner
Sgt S. McConnell
P/O G. S. Leatherdale
Sgt H. M. Donnelly
Sgt R. Karsman

ND 737
S/L D. M. Walbourn
S/L L. Glasspool
F/L W. S. Walker
Sgt G. F. Felstead
F/O S. H. Jonson
W/O A. J. Irwin
F/L C. A. Kidd

JB 667 *Missing*
F/L R. Richmond
Sgt H. L. Bird
Sgt J. A. Green
Sgt G. P. Rae
F/O R. Kearney
Sgt R. J. Faulkner
Sgt K. A. Ward

ND 618
P/O E. J. Trotter
S/L B. M. Mathers
Sgt J. T. Broad
Sgt J. Rawcliffe
F/S R. A. Pullin
Sgt W. R. C. Parfitt
Sgt K. Archibald

ND 477
F/O J. A. Cameron
Sgt R. V. Dickeson
F/O H. C. Cavenagh
Sgt A. J. Walker
F/O J. E. Scrivener
F/S C. R. Alcock
Sgt G. R. Green

ND 577
P/O L. Lindley
F/O J. W. Henry
Sgt J. E. Bates
Sgt R. T. Harper
Sgt B. Vivour
Sgt N. T. Edmundson
Sgt D. B. Bloomfield

No 405 Sqdn —Gransden Lodge, Lancasters: 15 attacked.

'G'
F/L L. L. Mackinnon
F/L W. D. Renton
P/O V. E. Bowden
F/S G. Connell
F/S J. S. Rennie
F/O T. R. N. Duff
Sgt E. W. Chappell

'B'
P/O R. D. Borrowes
F/L J. Mitchell
F/O A. Hinecliffe
W/O R. J. Montgomery
W/O G. D. Spearman
W/O B. F. Pothier
P/O R. L. Squires

'M'
F/O A. J. G. Van Rassal
F/O G. W. Gillespie
Sgt W. Howard
W/O F. D. Billingsley
Sgt J. C. T. Bergeron
F/O E. G. Gray
Sgt G. O. Bondman

'D'
F/L W. M. Chase
F/L. G. W.
F/L W. Sinclair
Sgt J. T. Gill
Sgt C. M. Sylvah
Sgt R. D. Daniels
F/S J. M. Buckley

'O'
F/O G. P. A. Yates
F/O N. S. Ross
W/O A. J. Wilcock
W/O E. Hartley
Sgt W. G. Patten
Sgt B. L. Allard
Sgt K. Gunthrope

'A'
F/L H. A. Morrison
F/O L. W. Queale
F/O R. A. Smarts
F/S C. J. Darcy
Sgt G. A. Lajambe
F/S W. Embink
Sgt R. Matchim

'J'
Capt L. B. Copenhaven
F/O J. F. Lewis
F/S A. B. Leslie
F/L H. M. Shearer
Sgt J. W. Carter
F/O K. A. Nordheimer
Sgt W. E. Vine

'K'
P/O R. W. Long
F/S R. Brook
Sgt G. J. Edwards
Sgt W. D. Leavesley
Sgt A. W. Goudey
Sgt H. A. Stroud
Sgt R. I. York

'S'
F/L W. H. Spafford
P/O K. R. Himmel
F/O W. J. Campbell
P/O F. J. Perron
Sgt P. H. Gingres
P/O E. W. Bishop
P/O A. E. Parmenter

'H'
F/L P. Mains-Smith
F/O F. A. Sutherland
Sgt D. E. King
F/O H. F. Watson
Sgt J. Raiks
Sgt R. Bembo
Sgt E. Hilton

'W'
W/O A. E. Barlow
W/O C. A. Lorimer
P/O L. A. Nethery
Sgt A. Burrell
Sgt T. E. Utton
F/S D. J. Copeland
Sgt P. W. Richards

'T'
F/S E. O'Connor
P/O J. W. C. Nairn
F/S S. Manierka
Sgt J. R. Bristow
F/S J. Foulds
F/S S. Farr
Sgt J. Henderson

'U'	'Z'	'C'
P/O C. R. De Maria	W/C R. J. Lane	W/C J. E. Millward
W/O W. H. Pearson	S/L G. B. Ellwood	F/L E. W. Culpin
F/O M. G. Simpson	F/S A. D. N. Kamrens	P/O R. D. Milne
W/O A. R. Haddleton	P/O D. J. Langley	P/O R. C. Taylor
Sgt L. Strapps	F/L R. G. Wood	W/O G. D. Hirschfeld
Sgt J. Dickenson	W/O J. Scammell	S/L N. H. Coull
Sgt A. Hamilton	Sgt A. W. Bishop	Sgt G. D. Stewart
		S/L J. Baker

No 635 Sqdn — Downham Market, Lancasters: 11 attacked, 1 missing.

ND 924	ND 809	ND 735	ND 453
S/L R. B. Roache	P/O Beveridge	S/L J. R. Wood	F/O K. A. Petch
F/L H. J. L. Webb	F/O M. I. Massey	P/O H. P. Laskoski	F/O C. B. Potter
F/L G. A. Stocks	F/O J. G. Irwin	F/L G. D. Linacre	F/O T. M. Telford
F/O J. C. Wells	F/S J. J. Mather	P/O D. B. Coltman	Sgt W. H. Curness
Sgt C. Chadwick	Sgt J. D. Smith	F/S J. Smith	F/S R. H. A. Shirley
F/S D. H. B. Womar	F/O J. Allinson	W/O D. R. Tulloch	F/S J. J. New
F/O C. G. Whitaker	Sgt A. R. Hall	Sgt J. Rayton	Sgt R. Cederbraun
Sgt E. H. Barry			

ND 735 *Missing*	ND 811	ND 821	ND 895
P/O W. Still	F/L J. H. Nicholls	F/L J. Billing	F/L C. R. Snell
P/O E. Deveson	F/S A. Whitehead	F/S J. M. Campbell	F/L J. Lintott
W/O J. Holmwood	F/S W. D. Ogilvie	F/L E. E. Osler	F/L N. J. Smith
Sgt J. L. Tillam	F/S J. Gardner	P/O J. E. Moriarty	W/O W. Parker
F/S A. A. Stansbridge	F/O R. Easson	W/O R. D. Curtiss	F/S J. Grieve
Sgt C. Talby	W/O K. A. Jolley	P/O J. B. Finlay	F/S C. J. Green
Sgt W. J. Sander	Sgt S. A. C. Smith	F/S J. Smith	F/S N. Hamment
			F/S L. T. Harman

ND 898	ND 335	ND 450	ND 877
F/O L. Henson	W/C J. B. Voyce	F/O C. Lyon	F/S D. J. Farrant
F/O G. Parsons	F/O S. D. Smart	Sgt L. A. Chappell	Sgt J. Bannan
F/S E. J. D. Bill	F/O H. E. Brewster	F/S H. G. Howes	F/O T. F. Wilson
F/S N. Cohen	P/O G. M. Suttie	F/S E. V. Aspin	W/O R. T. Lord
F/S N. A. Sharpe	F/S C. W. Newman	F/S R. Lawley	Sgt R. H. Malthouse
F/O T. Woods	F/S P. Thompson	Sgt J. C. Guthrie	Sgt J. W. Nixon
F/S W. J. Whitbread	F/O R. H. Wright	W/O J. L. Atkinson	F/S A. I. G. Hunter

No 139 Sqdn — Mosquitos, 12 detailed, 10 attacked.

ML 909	DZ 521	DZ 601	KB 161
F/O E. A. F. Jackman	W/O H. A. Fawcett	F/L P. W. W. Nock	F/L G. W. Salter
F/O J. S. Button	Sgt L. J. Hadley	F/O A. A. Green	W/O A. C. Pearson

KB 329	LR 475	ML 924	DZ 478
S/L W. J. Rees	F/O W. A. Whitworth	F/O J. R. Cassells	F/O J. Page
F/L A. S. Grant	F/O D. W. Griffiths	F/O P. L. V. Cross	F/O S. Ainsworth

DK 324	DZ 421		
F/L N. P. Kerr	F/O C. S. Richards		
F/O J. G. Alcock	F/L A. M. Beach		

627 Sqdn — Oakington, Mosquitos: 6 attacked.

DZ 477	DZ 484	DZ 418	DZ 462
S/L E. F. Nelles	F/O R. W. Griffiths	F/O B. Boothright	F/L D. W. Peck
F/O A. E. Richards	F/O M. D. Gribbin	F/S J. Upton	F/L R. F. Davies

DZ 482	DK 353		
F/O A. Hindshaw	F/L H. Steere		
F/O J. F. Daly	F/O K. W. Gale		

692 Sqdn — Graveley, Mosquito: 1 detailed, attacked Berlin.

ML 935
F/O Goodwin
F/L H. B. Hay

Appendix C

Letter from the Mayor of Les Mesnuls to Flight Lieutenant R. B. Leigh, 1 Feb 1945

Sir:

I have just received your letter asking information about the death of Flight Lieutenant W. M. Conlon.

The 8th of June an imposing bomber squadron soared above the village. It returned at 2.30 a.m. in the night. Several bombers were attacked by German planes above the village. The plane of Lieutenant Conlon was attacked above the east end of the village of Les Mesnuls. I believe the crew were surprised by this attack as the airmen had no time to reply, and the plane crashed in the forest about two miles outside the village. About thirty-three hours later, knowing that the Germans had not buried the members of the crew, I went to the scene of the crash and I found a German sentry there. I asked him 'Who will bury the British airmen?' and he answered. 'You, if you please.' Two hours later I returned with several young men. We found a great quantity of wreckage and I believe there were six men in the crew.

If this information is any consolation and can soothe the great sorrow of Lt Conlon's mother, I can say that he had no time to realise what had happened when his plane crashed and he was killed without any pain. We placed the remains of the crew on two biers and carried them to the Chapel of our Church where they were set up by the young men of the village.

On the following Sunday we held a funeral service. We gave to this ceremony all solemnity that was possible for we must honour our Allies and at the same time our true feelings are displayed to the Germans.

More than six hundred people were assembled around the biers, which were blessed by the village Catholic priest. The grave as you will see by the photographs was completely covered with flowers. Since that day the grave is kept in good order by the inhabitants of the village. On the 11th of November during a ceremony for all the Allied soldiers who died for liberty, full military honours were given by a Canadian detachment, an American one and also the local F.F.I. group.

I still have a few things, a ring, two cigarette cases. If any day you will take leave for Paris, I cordially invite you to call here and see me. I shall take you to the churchyard and to the place where the plane crashed. Perhaps you will find something which belongs to your cousin.

I remain at your disposal for all information you may require of me. I pray you to write to Mrs Conlon and tell her I will answer all questions she will put to me. She can write directly for I understand a little English. Will you write her that the grave shall always be kept in good order, for the French people does not forget the men who fought with them and for them.

Les Mesnuls, our village, is between Versailles and Rambouillet, 25 miles West of Paris on the National road 191.

I am,
Sincerely yours,
(Signed) Rene Rousselle

Bibliography

Bennett, AVM D. C. T. *Pathfinder*, F. Muller Ltd, 1958

Bowyer, M. J. F. *2 Group R.A.F., A Complete History 1936-1945*, Faber & Faber, 1974

Dean, Sir Maurice *The Royal Air Force and Two World Wars*, Cassell, 1978

Gibson, Guy *Enemy Coast Ahead*, Michael Joseph, 1946

Harris, Sir Arthur, Marshal of the R.A.F. *The Bomber Offensive*, Collins, 1974

Jones, R. V. *Most Secret War*, Hamilton, 1978

Price, A. *Battle over the Reich*, Ian Allan Ltd, 1973

Saunders, H. St George *Royal Air Force, 1939-45*, vol. III, HMSO, 1954

Smith, M. *British Air Strategy Between the Wars*, Oxford, 1984

Speer, A. *Inside the Third Reich*, Weidenfield & Nicolson, 1970

Verrier, A. *The Bomber Offensive*, Batsford, 1968

Webster, Sir Charles and Frankland, Noble *The Strategic Air Offensive Against Germany 1939-1945*, vols. III and IV, HMSO, 1961

Index